FOREWORD

By Sacheverell Sitwell

THE opportunity of composing a Foreword to the life and work of the goldsmith and jeweller Peter Carl Fabergé is an invitation to enquire behind the text and illustrations into the depth and texture of nationality, as expressed in works of art. Why, and how is it, that so simple an object as a cigarette case can speak to us with a Russian accent, and be as strong of flavour as a phrase out of a Russian song? The cigarette case can be in 'red', or 'green', or 'yellow' gold; it does not matter. The finished object, as you handle it, is as 'Russian' as any character in Russian history. What is our own accent? What is the English signature upon a work of art? Or in simple things of daily life? When the musician Janáček, a neglected genius, who knew little or no English, came to London and stayed in an hotel in Russell Square, he tried to write down in musical notation in his notebook the strident cries of the page boys as they walked through the hall and called out the names of guests who were wanted on the telephone. This seemed to him typical of London; but then, Janáček was a composer who tried to approximate the musical and spoken phrase.

Accent, or if you prefer it, the personal landscape and background of the artist's life, can be expressed equally well in a few square inches of paint upon board, or canvas, or painted wall. Any person who has spent a few months of his childhood in Florence gets to know, and love, the paintings of Fra Angelico. They come to 'mean' Florence, to spell Florence in the memory, even more than the paintings of Botticelli, partly because Botticelli has to be seen in the Uffizi, amid all the paraphernalia of a picture gallery, the lifts, the turnstiles and ticket collectors, the coat and hat attendants and the postcard stalls, whereas Fra Angelico is to be admired in his own convent of San Marco, which does not seem to have changed much since it was a monastery. There are few textures in the world so beautiful as a square inch or two of a painting by Fra Angelico. It does really look as though it has been painted with a feather from an angel's wing. And it is not long before we begin to associate it in our minds with the air and skies of Florence, with the flowers of the street sellers, and with the very stones. But the Florentine churches are built, not of stone, but coloured marble; Giotto's Tower, San Miniato, Santa Maria Novella, are all of coloured marbles, and in the end we feel that Fra Angelico painted his pictures with the pollen or dust of these marbles after a dawn or sunset shower upon an April day.

The texture, the handling of other painters, is just as strong in accent and in what it tells us of their lives. For an instance, we choose a few square inches of a fresco by Tiepolo. It is not necessary to take the 'grand' scenes in his History of Antony and Cleopatra (in the Palazzo Labia, at Venice). The subordinate scenes are enough, which are like painted wings. They are like 'flaps' or side-wings in the theatre; and, in fact, fulfil that purpose exactly, for they support the main action, which is in a pair of acts or scenes, the disembarkation and the banquet.

v

There is one of the side scenes which consists only of a cook or scullion in a white cap holding a fiasco of red wine and standing near to some silver plates and dishes which are piled up on a buffet. An extreme æsthetic pleasure and satisfaction is to be had from the very grain or scumbling of the fresco, painted a little bit at a time, as frescos have to be, while the plaster is damp, and conveying, or so it seemed to me at a time when I went almost daily to admire the technique and handling, a sensation as though you had surprised Tiepolo in the act of laying down his brush for a moment and, perhaps, snatching something to eat and a drink of wine in the midst of his labours. Not only that, but there is the sea air of Venice in the very touch of his brush upon the plaster; you know that Tiepolo was a Venetian, that no one but a Venetian could have done this painting, that the white sails and rigging in another of the side scenes are the white sails and rigging of the trabaccoli (Venetian sailing boats) or the topi and bragozzi of Chioggia (the fishing town at the far end of the lagoon), that the gangway near to where Antony and Cleopatra are disembarking, hand in hand, could only have been painted by someone born to the gangplank and the landing stage. The fresco, it could almost be said, is in the soft Venetian dialect, substituting 'z's for 's's, and as much a part of Venice as the gondolas upon the Grand Canal.

It would be easy, by the same token, to discuss the French texture of one of Watteau's paintings, still more, perhaps, the texture of his red chalk drawings. These, too, could be by no one but a Frenchman. It is in the very grain of them; they are as French as an aria by Bellini is Italian. We can describe this by saying 'how' it is, by putting the effect it has upon us into words, but it is not so easy when it comes to answering the question 'why'. The reasons are more intangible than the processes. You can see those working, but you cannot tell what sets them into motion. It is not enough to say that Alabiev's *Nightingale* is a Russian song because it follows and imitates the intonations of the Russian words. For, as a matter of obvious fact, the song is more Russian than the trite words. It is the music of the song that is famous, not the poem. The music is Russian, perhaps, in its inflections; but it is much more so than that, and in a manner which it is difficult, almost impossible, to explain. An identical truth, or secret, is to be tasted in every phrase of Tchaikovsky. It is as Russian as a Russian cigarette.

But the whole history of the arts in Russia under the Tsars is a spectacle, a panorama of these mysteries. Who could there be more Russian than Catherine the Great, who was a German princess, and not Russian at all? Who is there who even remotely resembles her in Germany history? She is as Russian as Peter the Great. Now the foreign artists, craftsmen, architects, who came to work in Russia, seem to have been affected immediately by this atmosphere. The same thing, we say in parenthesis, is to be found in Spain, at the other end of Europe. Who more Spanish than El Greco, the Cretan; than Gil de Siloe, Juan Güas, sculptors, architects, who were Dutch or German; than Bizet or Debussy when they wrote Spanish music? More extraordinary still, neither composer had ever been to Spain! Spain, like Russia, is at a different perspective from the rest of Europe. There is a slightly derisive word for this, 'Espagnolade', under which many of Greco's paintings would be grouped, with Debussy's *Iberia*, and Bizet's *Carmen*.

PETER CARL
FABERGÉ

Goldsmith and Jeweller to the Russian Imperial Court

His Life and Work
by

HENRY CHARLES BAINBRIDGE

With a foreword by Sacheverell Sitwell

SPRING BOOKS

London · New York · Sydney · Toronto

This edition published 1966 by
The Hamlyn Publishing Group Ltd
London · New York · Sydney · Toronto
Astronaut House, Feltham, Middlesex, England

Sixth Impression 1974

Printed in Hong Kong by
Leefung-Asco Printers Limited

ISBN 0 600 01307 3

PETER CARL
FABERGÉ

His Life and Work

BUDDHA
In jadeite. Eyes, cabochon rubies and rose-diamonds; earrings, rose-diamonds; tongue, ruby. Belt in translucent white enamel, studded with cabochon rubies and rose-diamonds. The head, tongue and hands are balanced so delicately that the slightest touch sets them in motion.
Height: $5\frac{3}{8}$ inches. Width: $4\frac{3}{4}$ inches.
(*Privately owned.*)

Even Fabergé himself—a Huguenot by descent and therefore a Protestant—when he left Russia for a holiday abroad, always crossed himself and said 'Thank God' —the inference being that he was freed from this *genius loci* of such native force. But the very Spaniards, it could be argued in many instances, are guilty of the 'Espagnolade' themselves; while, certainly, in Russia, it was the Russians who carried the Russian characterization, dramatization, to its furthest points. Mussorgsky, we may like to remember, began by playing songs by Bellini and Donizetti in fashionable drawing-rooms; he ended, as we see him in the terrifying, drunken portrait by Repin, by writing *Boris Godunov* and *Khovanchtchina*. Yet, this is the curious fact, nothing in those operas is more Russian than a phrase or two from Tchaikovsky's *Sleeping Beauty*, which that composer intended to be in the style of Lully or Couperin, and to take the form of a spectacle at the court of Louis Quatorze. This masterpiece of Tchaikovsky is the exact contemporary to the era of Fabergé, which may be said to have begun with the reign of the giant Tsar Alexander III in 1881, and to have continued through what we call the Edwardian period until the Russian Revolution of 1917. It comprises, therefore, the reigns of two Tsars, Alexander III (1881-1894) and Nicholas II (1894-1917). This can be said with certainty, that there were no better craftsmen in the applied arts at work in any country during this period than those assembled in the workshops of Fabergé. Within their limits they were the best craftsmen of their time.

It is rare, indeed, for an enterprise of this scope and nature to be fully described by someone who worked with it and knew its secrets. More often this happens after all personal contact has been lost. This present book is, therefore, an invaluable recipe to show how such things are done. Incidentally, it is a very happy picture of a vanished epoch, and contrasting it with our own disastrous era, of a period when the world seemed young. No art whatever, we would remind ourselves, has come out of Russia since the Revolution. And this is another point of interest, the fables of Tsarist extravagance are dissipated in a breath. Even the fabled Imperial Easter Eggs prove to have been no more expensive than a valuable fur coat. The emphasis is upon craftsmanship more than precious stones. Here are no accounts of diamond and emerald tiaras, pearl necklaces, and so forth, but a multiplicity of objects ranging from caskets and bonbonnières to cigarette cases in Karelian birchwood, costing no more than the equivalent of a few pounds. Even the white hollywood boxes in which jewellery and pieces of fantasy were sent out were the objects of unremitting care, and the names of their makers, both Finns, are here recorded. Indeed, the majority of Fabergé's craftsmen were Finns or Swedish-Finns, and this fact must be taken into consideration in thinking of their handiwork. Fabergé was a firm of goldsmiths and jewellers working in Russia, and not, too exactly and definitely, a Russian firm.

Readers of this book will find that such things become simple in the telling. And I suppose it would be a simplification of the same order if we could enter into the premises of one of the Parisian goldsmiths of the eighteenth century, and discover that the gold and enamel snuff-boxes, which were among the wonders of that age, came from a shop no bigger than a village post-office and employing two men and a boy. I think that to many persons the photographs of Fabergé's premises in St. Petersburg will not be the least interesting illustrations in the book. Hence came forth the Imperial Easter Eggs, baubles that were little known or mentioned at the time, but they have become one of the symbols of their age. There is in them more than a hint of the court of the Byzantine Emperors, and this, not of design, but, as it were, by coincidence and force of circumstance. Looking at them, it is impossible not to be reminded of Stravinsky's *L'Oiseau du Feu*, that most beautiful and most 'Russian' of his ballets, written before the Russian Revolution, at a time when the Tsar was still giving one of the Eggs, at Easter, to the Tsarina, and another to the Dowager Empress (sister of Queen Alexandra). But, factually, the legend of The Firebird goes wrong in the telling, precipitating the most appalling miseries in human history. These extraordinary objects of craftsmanship and fantasy have to be looked at across this chasm and precipice of the intervening years, and it is almost painful to behold them. Too often, the 'surprise' is a set of miniatures of that murdered family. Certain of the Easter Eggs, one in pink enamel, with sprays of lily-of-the-valley; another, golden Egg; or another Easter Egg in rock-crystal; and one in lime green enamel, with their 'surprises', a jewelled peacock, a model of the Russian Imperial coronation coach, are worthy of Cuvillié's Amalienburg and of the fairy-tale splendours of Peterhof and Tsarskoe Selo, which is to say that, dating from within our lifetime, they are not excelled by the most finished and delicate workmanship of the Eighteenth Century.

Fabergé's sprays of flowers are beautiful in themselves and remarkable in that they raise the problem in æsthetics as to how, and why, a spray of *gypsophila*, of all plants, standing in a little jade jar, should be the complete expression of a particular period, even a decade, in time. The sprays of flowers are lifelike and naturalistic in style, though done under Chinese influence, yet they contrive to be entirely Russian. The figurines of Russian 'types' invite, and deserve, no such discussion. To my taste, they are the least successful creations of Fabergé's work-shops, though pleasurably reminiscent of Bilibine's coloured illustrations to Russian fairy stories. When obviously Russian, Fabergé or his craftsmen, in the end, are less Russian, after all. As against this, the birds, frogs, elephants, hippo-potami, and Sandringham animals, if taken not more seriously than was the intention, give a pleasure over and above their perfect workmanship.

But, the Imperial Easter Eggs apart, there are little boxes or bonbonnières in crystal and enamel, and in semi-precious stones, that will remain beautiful works of art, in miniature, for as long as the French snuff-boxes of the Wallace Collection are admired. Those can become, on long acquaintance, more satisfying than much of the French furniture, and even than some few of the paintings. And there is the elegance and diversity that this Russian goldsmith and his craftsmen could give to such a familiar object as the handle of a parasol. Last, and not least, there are the Fabergé cigarette cases, the nearest equivalent in our time to the snuff-boxes of the Eighteenth Century, in the different coloured golds from which the Fabergé craftsmen made such incomparable play, and with the Fabergé smooth hinges. Will objects of such craftsmanship ever be made again? Books, plays, films, music, there may be, and painting and sculpture; but it seems improbable that the world will see another great goldsmith; or, at least, until none of us is still living to contradict this judgment. The Fabergé workshops were the culmination of many centuries of inherited skill and experience, and the opportunity of a rich Imperial court to work for is not likely to come round again. When you touch or hold a Fabergé object, you are in contact with something, coming down to you, not only from the era of the Tsars, but of an ancestry far more ancient; for it is typical of all the Imperial courts there have ever been. Also, be the object what it may, it is Russian, and could be nothing else; though the unsolved mystery of why this is so remains the secret and signature of this last of the great goldsmiths, Peter Carl Fabergé, who died after the Russian Revolution, so lately as that, but whose roots go back five thousand years, and more, in time.

Looking into this splendid volume, the reader will taste a flavour of the recent past clinging to its pages. A past that is so near that many of us remember it, but so far off, now, that we can no longer reach it with our hands. I have recollections of it, myself, and can remember, as a child, many of the personalities of the Edwardian period. It was a time when the courts of Europe, that dead phrase, were still existing—and how many disasters have not overtaken us since they disappeared!

I think that Mr. Bainbridge, author and compiler of this book, has distilled much of the undisturbed wealth and happiness of the period into his pages. And as we read him, behind the top-hatted and frock-coated men of the world and their parasoled and jewelled ladies, we are transported to the fabulous Russia of legend. As a spectacle, it can have had no parallel, and I can remember before 1917 when Russia, where literature and the arts were concerned, was the land of the bright future: that prospect was wrecked, probably for ever, with the downfall of the Tsars. But how overwhelming was the impression of what came out of Russia!

One of the memorable experiences of my own life as an artist was when I was taken by my brother to hear Chaliapin sing in *Khovanchtchina*, during long-leave from Eton in the summer of 1914. Never, never shall I forget the brass instruments and the blaring of the orchestra. It was the sort of experience of childhood, described by Berlioz in his memoirs, that affects one all one's life. And, upon the night following, I heard *L'Oiseau du Feu*. That was the taste of Russia in two evenings, and having once tasted it, one never forgets it. This strong flavour of Russia is present in the pages that follow and not only in the illustrations. It is the St. Petersburg that is gone for ever—Versailles and Byzantium mingled, and the Babylon of the snows. The phantom sledges pass and repass; the snow glitters. Mr. Bainbridge in his book recaptures that for us; a past that is remote from us as the music of the immortal *Casse-Noisette*, and we must be grateful to him for that, and for the loving care with which he has prepared this work upon his hero, Fabergé. He spent his youth working for him, and has devoted the latter part of his life in bringing him to life again.

S. S.

LONDON

AUTHOR'S PREFACE

IN the history of the goldsmith's art there is no more remarkable a figure than Peter Carl Fabergé. There is something strangely inevitable about him. His personality and art remain to be reckoned with whether we will or no.

Look around to-day wherever fine work of the goldsmith is displayed and you will almost invariably find the notice 'By Fabergé'. Nothing can tell more eloquently of the man and his work than the compelling attention which his creations still evoke.

Fortunate in everything he undertook during his amazingly active life, Fabergé was doubly so in that he lived and worked in the time of the great art patrons of the end of the Nineteenth Century and the beginning of the Twentieth, a period which culminated in the Edwardian Era (an era not peculiar to England —but one the influence of which overspread the world). It was then that he reached a pinnacle of fame which even the masters of the Renaissance might have envied. Proclaimed by Kings, with Ambassadors as his heralds, Fabergé, through the medium of his art, made his influence felt in almost every corner of the globe.

It would seem enough that this Craftsman should have so impressed himself upon his age, but fortune again stepped in and what was tragedy unheard of for the Romanoffs, for him became the wheel which turned to yet more fame. In the Palaces of the Tsar many of the Imperial Easter Eggs were found, marvels of craftsmanship and ingenuity, and a large number of other objects.

For the second time the name of Fabergé became one to conjure with, and this time almost a household one. Soon everything which was found on the writing-tables of the Tsar and the Tsarina, the Grand Dukes and the aristocracy of Russia, whether the work of England, France, Russia, Italy or Germany, came to be attributed to him. In the markets of Europe pieces appeared which were no more Fabergé's than Cellini's.

The Russian Exhibition in London of 1935 only fanned the flame of his reputation. Fantastic stories were then spread about, such as 'Fabergé had made Catherine's Imperial Crown', 'the Sceptre as well as the Orb and the whole of the Crown Jewels of Russia, were the work of his hands'. 'Where was the ruby cup which he had fashioned for Cleopatra?'

It was thus that the fairy-tale of Fabergé was turned into a farce. But this is not all. Side by side with this adulation runs criticism which takes various forms. 'Fabergé was a Frenchman', some say, and therefore everything that he produced is French. 'There is nothing Russian about any of his work.' Some look askance at Fabergé's articles. 'They are not the work of the master', they say, 'but of his workmen.' Some indeed assert that 'Fabergé was nothing more than a *fournisseur* of pretty playthings', 'miracles of dainty expensiveness', for the imperialists of

Europe; that 'he and Art are miles apart', and when he did happen to create a work of art it was in effect nothing more than a *tour de force*.

All this needs to be put in a true perspective. And more. The ever-increasing circle of those interested in the art and craft of Carl Fabergé, sensing perhaps that the truth about him might easily outweigh in interest all the fiction they had heard concerning him, have long awaited the publication of an authentic monograph on his life and work. In the hope that I might in some measure counterbalance the extravagant and erroneous ideas which had been spread concerning this man, I contributed a number of articles from time to time to such periodicals as *The Connoisseur*, *Country Life*, and *Everybody's Weekly*. With the same purpose in view I toured America in 1937-38.

Perhaps, however, my book *Twice Seven*, published in 1933 and now out of print, may also be regarded as a fruitful source of information.* But who, when searching for information on the subject, would be likely to look for it in a work bearing such a title? The primary aim of that book was to kindle public understanding of the overwhelming might of Russia. It was written under stress of impending world disaster, out of which appeared to me only one road: the union of England, Russia and America. The book was successful, but only in so far as it drew attention, at the invitation of the critics, to the 'queerness' of the author rather than to what he was writing about, for to use the craftsmanship of the Tsarist goldsmith to develop the idea of the military might of Soviet Russia was to the critics of the time a thing unheard of.

But it is one thing to write autobiographically, to talk, and to publish short articles and quite another to launch out into a serious full-length portrait of a man and his total achievements. I may be wrong in what I conceive to be the *raison d'être* of such a work, but rightly or wrongly I have never thought of myself as adequately equipped for such an undertaking.

For one thing, I lived very close to Fabergé while I was associated with him. In the sunlit years of the Edwardian Era it fell to my lot personally to represent him. It was my luck to walk with him on the banks of the Neva and in the forest at Levaschova, to work with him behind the counter in St. Petersburg, to eat and drink with him and, perhaps most enlightening of all, to attend a funeral with him.

Pestered all day long for 'something new', keyed to a high pitch of expectancy, for he might have to receive anyone from anywhere at any time, pressed continually by his artists and workmasters for an opinion on this or that, he lived at a tension which must at times have been almost unbearable. And like many men highly sensible and sensitive, he was more reserved than any man I ever knew. An escape, an outlet of some sort must have been to him something to be greatly desired. Thus it was that when I came upon the scene he took hold of me. It must have been because I was something new to him, something unconnected with his daily irritating round, that I became the repository of his thoughts. Some of the finest things he ever uttered, the best key to his character, as chance would

---

* I wish to record my indebtedness to Messrs. George Routledge & Sons Ltd., the publishers of *Twice Seven*, for permission to draw upon this book.

have it, he said to me; sometimes in two words, sometimes in no words at all, but by a shrug of the shoulders or an extension of his arms and hands.

To record and pass on the amazing tolerance of the man, his elemental simplicity, in a manner which would make it reasonably certain that a reader could gauge his extraordinary nature, calls for a literary technique and skill which I am far from possessing.

Another thing. I have not come to the closing years of my life without knowing that there are things which are absolute and which must be accepted in their entirety. You cannot nibble at them here and there just as the fancy takes you and expect to come out unscathed. The main thing is that this knowledge tends to make me assertive and categorical in my statements to others, and such a habit I have always felt can be most irritating.

But there is still more. Russia. Any record of Fabergé which does not treat very largely of that vast continent would be no record at all. But to write about Russia to-day is to take a dive into a vast confusion and one so confounding that one may never rise to the surface again. Once again, so many of my friends fail to understand the real Russia. They veer from pole to pole completely lost, without sense of proportion or limitation. Fourteen years ago they told me Russia was good for nothing ; to-day they tell me she is in possession of the elixir which is to change all things base, and everywhere, into solid gold.

I have asked myself many times, was I likely to succeed to-day after my previous attempt in 1933. And if I should fail in this, that is in putting forward a conclusive argument to show what it is that Russia really stands for, then I should fail equally to convince the reading public what it is which so attracts them to the works of Fabergé.

It is in this way I have reviewed from time to time my association with the Craftsman and the course I should take to ensure that his achievements should not suffer by the manner in which they might be presented. So convinced did I become in the course of this review that my material would gain by filtration through another mind I spent much time in searching for a biographer.

But in this quest something invariably occurred which robbed me of success and which inevitably drove me back upon myself. In the end I had to conclude I must either do the job myself or Carl Fabergé must go unrecorded. As this was an eventuality which I could not permit myself to entertain, even for a moment, I decided to take the plunge.

It may be argued that this is no time for such a book and that we are concerned to-day with something much more vital than mere art. But the whole art of Fabergé sprang from, and was cradled in, his humanity. In the true spirit of the Renaissance he was intensely human. The joy of life, the delight in living, loveliness and harmony, were not only things to enjoy as they went fleeting by, they were there to grasp and be made permanent. 'Live and let live' were words forever on his lips. The most unbusinesslike of men and his methods the most topsy-turvy, judged by ordinary standards, yet Fabergé was one of the most

xiii

successful. He saw life with the inverted gaze of the artist; for him there was no haze and mist, but colour in everything, and that clearly defined. For him the ideal was 'practical politics' and 'practical politics' was the abstract.

Actually the life-story of Fabergé has much to tell this our barren and forlorn age, and if I am to judge from the way so many people have so generously come forward to help me since I undertook this record, it is waiting eagerly to know what he has to say.

PUBLISHER'S NOTE TO 1966 EDITION

Mr. Bainbridge's book was originally published by B. T. Batsford Ltd. in 1949 in a limited edition and dedicated to the late Queen Mary. The present edition differs only in that the illustrations have been slightly rearranged with suitable adjustments to the text and index.

Despite changed circumstances during the intervening years, Mr. Bainbridge's text has been left as it was originally written, apart from one passage where recent events have rendered the argument meaningless in its former context. Credits to some of the captions to the plates have been amended where changes of ownership have been easily verified, but no exhaustive attempt has been made to trace the present whereabouts of all the Fabergé objects illustrated in the book.

Mr. Bainbridge's original preface concluded with a detailed list of acknowledgments to all the individuals and organisations who provided him with assistance and advice with the illustrations and text. It has not been considered necessary to reproduce this rather lengthy list in the present book.

CONTENTS

LIST OF PLATES

xvii

LIST OF PLATES

CHAPTER I

THE FAMILY AND HOUSE OF FABERGÉ

WHAT is known of the early history of the family of Fabergé is scanty indeed. It amounts to little more than that they were Huguenots and that their original home was in Picardy, Northern France. But that is enough. If the knowledge is slight, the glory is great, for there is no name under heaven which, to my mind, conjures up a more arresting picture of what is fine and stable, just and right.

The first definite news of the family comes in 1685, that fateful year for France when Louis XIV, at the instigation of the Roman Catholic clergy, signed the Revocation of the Edict of Nantes and in so doing tore out of the body politic of France her very vitals by depriving his Protestant subjects of all religious and civic liberty, and subjecting them to the most refined and cruel torture of body and mind which it was possible for an advanced civilization to devise. So profound was the hatred engendered against these most unfortunate and distressed of people that all the frontiers and ports were closed in order to prevent the escape of a single person. Nevertheless, some half-million, we are told, contrived to find refuge in Switzerland, the Netherlands, Germany, England and other countries.

As the torment increased so the hunted prey surged towards the frontiers only to be met by the gravest question of all—how to cross to sanctuary. 'It is an ill wind', we say, and soon 'So much per head' occurred to someone as the appropriate answer. It was thus that a system of guides came into being. Men there were, as there always are, who, protected by their allegiance to the accepted religion of the moment, were ready to risk all penalties and eager to enrich themselves at the expense of those who for the moment were sorely misplaced. And so colonies of guides sprang up here and there, and one of the busiest was at Bohain in Picardy.

Now whether the family of Fabergé made use of this means of escape or not is unknown, but escape they did, and so began their wanderings of 1,200 miles through various parts of Northern Europe, which occupied no less than a century and a half before terminating at St. Petersburg, where in the year 1842, Gustav, the father of Carl Fabergé, eventually settled. How they kept going during this long period, how they occupied themselves, what trade or craft they followed, where they buried their dead, are not known. But three things are certain.

Their first recorded stopping place was Schwedt-on-Oder, near Stettin. Here they changed their name to Fabrier, for the same reason as before leaving France they had changed it to Fabri or Favri to escape persecution.

When next we hear of them they are in the Baltic Provinces of Russia where Peter, the grandfather of Carl Fabergé, became a Russian subject, and here the family reverted to their original name of Fabergé. In Pernau, in what is now known as Estonia, a son was born to Peter Fabergé, Gustav by name.

Gustav, who married a certain Charlotte Jungstedt of Swedish or Danish origin, eventually arrived at St. Petersburg, where he was apprenticed to the jewellers Spiegel, and in 1842 opened a goldsmith's and jeweller's shop in a basement flat in Morskaya Bolshaya Street. Thus was founded the House of Fabergé which was to become renowned throughout the world.

Within four years, that is on May 30th, 1846, a son was born to Gustav and Charlotte Fabergé, who was baptized in the Protestant Church in St. Petersburg and given the name of Peter Carl, to be known in general as Carl Fabergé and in Russia as Carl Gustavovitch Fabergé. He it is who is the subject of this record, and it matters little whether we speak of the House of Fabergé, or the man, for they are one and the same.

We may stop the narrative here for a moment to take note of this migration of the Fabergés to Russia. By far and away it is the most significant event in their history. Why did they not, like so many of the Huguenots, go to Switzerland, the Netherlands or England, and what induced them particularly to plod through Germany to settle themselves finally in St. Petersburg? For safety, is of course the answer, for it was only on arrival in Russia that they felt far enough away from persecution to revert to their original surname.

But safety was only the star which guided them to their destination. What they found there was salvation and of such unstrained quality* as could not be found elsewhere in the world; a salvation which can so bless the mind of man that he is for ever changed, so long, yes, so long . . . it is worth repeating . . . as he remains within the bounds of his sanctuary.

I refer, of course, to the Spirit of Russia, that magic *Genius Loci*, which is capable of inspiring a man to the seventh heaven of achievement, and equally, if he mis-uses it, of breaking his neck. Gorki says this:

'I see the Russian people as exceptionally, fantastically gifted, original. Even fools in Russia are foolish in an original way, in a peculiar manner, and as to loafers—these are positively geniuses. I am sure that by their fancifulness, by the unexpectedness of their twists, by the significant form, so to speak, of their thoughts and feelings, the Russian people are the most grateful material for an artist.'

The magic which is able to induce this originality was found at the end of their trek of twelve hundred miles by the Fabergés, and it was this spirit which so possessed and gripped the fine nature of the man whose life-work we are recording, as it had possessed that of many before him, which enabled him, Russian of the Russians as he became, to give to the world a supreme example of what Russia really stands for.

All this might have come to naught if his ancestors had taken the wrong turning and come to England instead. But this is not to belittle the spirit of this fair land; the two countries approach things from fundamentally different standpoints. Russia begins as in a fairy-tale and ends with fact, England begins with fact and ends as in a fairy-tale.

---

* *Cf.* Shakespeare's unstrained quality of mercy (*Merchant of Venice*).

But to return to our narrative. Gustav Fabergé carried on business in his small basement shop until 1860, when he retired to Dresden, leaving his affairs in the hands of a manager, by name Zaiontchkovsky. During this time the business grew, but there were no indications to foreshadow the significant part it was to play in the next fifty-eight years.

With the coming of Carl, great things took place. Of his early life little is known beyond the fact that he was educated in Paris and doubtless was there apprenticed to the goldsmith's craft. What is certain is that he worked in the family business for some years with Zaiontchkovsky as manager, and in 1870, at the age of twenty-four, was able to undertake the control of the House. The original basement shop was closed and a new one opened on the ground floor on the opposite side of the street. In 1890 this was doubled in size, but within eight years the growing demand for Fabergé wares necessitated a further change to still larger premises. In 1898, therefore, a building was purchased in the same street (now called Morskaya), at No. 24, and this was reconstructed to meet all the growing activities of the now renowned House.

Twenty-eight years at the head of a business, the nature of which made it even then one of the most delicate and exclusive, gave to Carl Fabergé all the experience he required to lay out the building to the best advantage.

He worked not only for elbow-room, but for mind-room, soul-room and not least of all, selling-room, for selling something is one of the joys and primal instincts of human nature. And so in the new building we find a library; unique certainly in a business establishment, containing almost every known work on the goldsmith's and lapidary's craft; larger studios, larger offices, and a larger shop, but the chief innovation was the bringing together of the principal workshops under the same roof as all the other activities of the firm. At this time some 700 craftsmen were working for Fabergé, but there was a wonderful single-mindedness among them, evinced in the consistent style and finish of the objects. This was made possible only by the close proximity of the workshops to the Head of the House whose controlling influence became manifest in every article throughout every stage of its making.

The new building, which also contained the Fabergé living apartments fronting on to the street, was finished in 1900 and occupied by the firm that year. I give exterior and interior illustrations in Plates 2 and 3.

Such was the establishment which all those who visited Russia during the next eighteen years were to know so well, for it was here the House of Fabergé rose to a fame unprecedented in the annals of the goldsmith's art.

On the outside there was no display of any kind to lure the passer-by within, nothing was shown in the windows, and on one side of the main entrance, on the left of the picture, was seen only the name FABERGÉ in Latin characters and on the other the word in Russian. It was in winter that I usually went to Petersburg, and many times I stood fascinated on the pavement just outside that main entrance, before moving inside, to watch the ceremony of admission; a little comedy, in which the door-keeper was the chief actor.

3

By this time perhaps it will be no surprise to the reader when I say that, as the world went by at the time of which I write, in Paris there was the glitter, but in Petersburg the gold, with London cold and remote as far as I was concerned. In those days there were no crude or awkward corners in St. Petersburg (or is it Petrograd by now); everything went with a swing, all things flowed, as it were, one into the other, to make of the whole city's life one unending sweep of dignity and poise. And if you wished to see this state of affairs at the very pinnacle, you went to Fabergé's at 24 Morskaya, where, on the very doorstep, you were introduced to manners in which the very elements appeared to take part.

Every arrival was reason enough for a state occasion. Sleighs noiselessly deposited their loads. By some quickened footstep, half-waltz, half-slide, the door-keeper raced the customer to reach the inner door, and always succeeded in getting there first. It was the prelude to what was to take place inside.

Of the interior, one can only say there was nothing much of style about it, there was no scheme of decoration sufficient to distract from the purpose for which the room had been planned, namely to sell the wares of Fabergé. Imagine a straight line from the clock down the centre of the room, allot the portion on the right of this, as you look at the picture, to articles of jewellery and that on the left to articles of fantasy and you have the room divided for its work.

The next thing to note is the door immediately under the clock. Open it, go through, turn at once to the right and in a few strides you will find yourself immediately behind the partition, in front of which in the picture at the right-hand corner sits the cashier. Here behind the partition at his desk sits the Head of the House, preparing sketch designs or sorting out his stones.

And now for the crowning feature, the counter. One sees from the picture (Plate 3) how formidable it looks, as if to say 'So far but not one step further'.

The rattle at the door has been heard and up jumps Carl Gustavovitch and takes a peep from behind the partition, to see who is coming in. He inclines his head and takes the proffered hand across the counter. One or two words of greeting, a joke maybe; the customer gives some indication what he wants—a flower, perhaps. . . . The Craftsman turns about (he is standing just to the left of the clock as you look at it), slides opened a mirrored door, thinks a moment and takes out two white holly-wood boxes.

These he places on the counter with the catch towards the customer. He opens one and waits a moment. He opens the other and waits again. There is no need for any story except that of the mind which conceived the objects and the hands which made them, and these are written on and in the objects themselves. When surprise—which is the *alpha* and *omega* of everything that is 'Fabergé'—has been overcome, so far as is possible with the flowers nested in their boxes, and the customer has noted the fixed prices on the tickets, the Craftsman lifts from out of its box the flower which appears to attract the customer. He holds it poised on the tips of his fingers and just far enough from his body to gain the full effect of exhibition, and his hand becomes the fulcrum for display, first to the right and slowly back again.

By this time, if you had been privileged to watch this display of salesmanship as I have watched it many a time, you would have been in no way surprised if the customer had suddenly exclaimed: 'Mr. Fabergé, if you do that any more you will persuade me to give you 500 roubles more than you're asking.' This, of course, never did happen, but what did, was the immediate sale of the object.

Perhaps this may strike a reader as making far too much of a small matter, but it fully deserves the delight I take in describing it, for it has in it the *multum in parvo* of everything connected with Carl Fabergé and his work. For one thing, his wares took such toil to think out and produce and not to transfer this fact to the mind of the customer, by great delicacy of action and reserve in display, would have been to kill his business at the very outset.

So much for the building at 24 Morskaya, except to say that none of the figures in the interior illustration (Plate 3) is a member of the family of Fabergé; that at the top right-hand corner is the cashier; the old gentlemen in the centre are two old pensioners of the firm; of the two immediately behind the counter on the left, one is an 'artellchik' whose business it was with others to polish the floor; and the one standing on the steps behind the two last is Paul Blomerius, a man of many languages who dealt with the foreign correspondence. And just one other thing; the steps on which Blomerius stands, and which were the writer's vantage ground as he surveyed the ever-moving scene, lead, as do those on the extreme left of the picture, to the offices and studios, and to the workshops on higher floors.

Thus much for the 'bricks and mortar'. And now for the soul, that from which sprang the spirit which gave the House its direction.

For a quarter of a century and more, many questions have been put to me. Have you found any fresh sources of information about the Fabergé family and especially of their early history? Have you an old Fabergé bill-head? Have you any letters written by the Craftsman? What about his mother; have you been able to find out anything about her character and way of living? Why not put up workshops in England and make some more Fabergé things?

Now the remarkable thing about all the questions addressed to me is this, that never once has there been any direct reference to Russia. The way of thinking with these questioners has been such as to make their minds a complete blank as to what might be the real state of affairs. Fabergé was a Frenchman, they have told me, with a French name, therefore everything to do with him, everything that he made, naturally must be French. With this established in their minds, then it was only necessary to find out all the remote, queer, subsidiary things, to fit them into their places and so make the biography complete.

My business is clear, and that is to create an entirely new outlook on Fabergé.

For this purpose the source of my material is Carl Fabergé himself, his younger brother Agathon (not Agathon his second son, of postage stamp fame), the Emperor Alexander III, and Russia. Concerning Carl and Agathon Fabergé

5

I have no qualms whatever. I know exactly where I have them and I will bring them in in their allotted places.

But Alexander III and Russia—and especially the latter! As a subject for enquiry and discussion, Russia has become more tyrannical than religion itself: she is the red rag which sets everyone aflame either one way or the other. Before I am done I may very well find myself torn limb from limb by the disputants, and Russia herself slipping away scot-free in the mêlée.

What I have to say about her is neither new nor revolutionary; it has been said before, but so clearly that it has been lost sight of. Charles Cameron, the Scotsman and architect, has said it in all the work he did for Catherine the Great; Falconet, the Frenchman, has said it in his statue to Peter the Great on the Neva; and Tressini in his spire in the fortress of Peter and Paul. Quarenghi, Rastrelli and Leblond have all said it in their different inimitable ways. And Elizabeth Petrovna, that Russian of the Russians, and Catherine the Great, the German, magnificently, in that life of hers, which transcends all in meaning, if Russia has any meaning at all; and Peter the Great above all when like a hurricane he swept all Russia to the northern seas, to look out, to go in search and *come back again*. And Sacheverell Sitwell has written about it in words which are unmistakable.

But there you are, we prefer to wrangle rather than read. Russia is paramount to my argument, and if in the forgetfulness of my friends I am allowed to re-kindle their attention so much the better for me. I can proceed as some inspired prophet and better still in no wilderness of mine own but supported by a host.

Now unless each of these witnesses lived a magnificent lie, unless the whole history of Russia from Rurik, 1,085 years ago, when she laid hands on the first of them, down to the present time, is nothing but a huge 'melancholy joke', one thing stands out crystal clear and this is that in Russia there has always been, is and always will be, one spirit which envelops all and one to which the whole gamut of Russian life is harnessed, from art to economics and regardless of régime. It is the spirit of self-appreciation, it permeates through and through to the very marrow of her bones. Partake of it too greedily and it will intoxicate all sense out of you.

For a tempestuous Russian the only thing to do if he would keep his balance is to fall back on Russian music, for in this he can work out his salvation in an ecstasy of richness enough to save his soul alive without bringing into purview the whole inhabited globe. But let him take a few words of almost any Russian writer from out of their context—a temptation not peculiar to him, but one which can have more dire consequences for him than most—and he can be caught up in a fire which can consume him. Here are such words:

'A really great people can never accept a secondary part in the history of Humanity, nor even of the first, but will have the first part. A nation which loses this belief ceases to be a nation. But there is only one truth, and therefore

6

only a single one out of the nations can have the true God, only one nation is "godbearing", that is the Russian people. . . .'*

Dostoievsky: Shatov in *The Possessed.*

But in this record we are not concerned with the cataclysmic possibilities of the actions of the few but with the growth of a business which had the good fortune to be founded in a continent covering one-sixth of the total land surface of the earth, with all its vastness, fruitfulness, potentiality, and power not distant from the the soul but pressing hard and immediately upon it, a continent which is an undivided, concentrated whole, not cut up by any oceans, and inhabited by a people who justly see, nay, who have been given no choice but to see in all this something for legitimate pride.

Self-appreciation leads to self-expression and this needs craftsmen to carry it into effect.

Thus from the very outset the House of Fabergé was in clover, and knee-deep. Placed as it was, and ruled as it was, it could not do otherwise than prosper to a pinnacle. And it was not craftsmanship alone, not even craftsmanship with some meaning of richness for its own sake, but craftsmanship with personal appeal to the beholder, as though there were written in it the history of his country or the record of his own life, which so fully satisfied the yearning of Russians and created a bond between the House and its customers that amounted almost to affection, a state of affairs not possible in what may be called more practically minded countries.

Symbolism touched everything, and on its wings the House could only be carried from one successful achievement to another. Every object was a symbol or an emblem, and not only ikons and Easter eggs, which occur to one as the most obvious illustrations, but animals and flowers. Everything had something inherent in it which made it something far more than a mere fabrication of gold, enamels and rare stones.

Whether under the sway of symbolism, art as art can flourish, a matter which has occupied many minds, is something upon which I am not competent to give an opinion, but I am sure Carl Fabergé did not concern himself with abstruse questions of this kind. He was far too much occupied in supplying a human need, and this in Russia ran to proportions which were literally enormous.

If a goldsmith was fortunate enough to find himself in Russia by reason of her influence upon his creative faculty, he was doubly so in being able to follow his craft in a land in which events do not come to pass simply to pass away, but to be moulded into something concrete to be grasped and felt. Jubilees and anniversaries of family life, of institutions, societies, regiments, victories, business houses and all the 'what have.you' of a nation occupying one-sixth of the earth's

*As I read over the proof of what I have written I fear that to many self-depreciating, easy-going Englishmen this quotation may read like nonsense, and as nothing more than the raving of one of the many drunken characters in Russian fiction. To those who are of this way of thinking I suggest they consult *Russian Horizon* (an anthology, compiled by Dr. Gangulee, formerly Professor of Calcutta University, and published in 1943), from which my quotation (out of some hundreds of others) is taken.

dry land, took on a significance quite beyond the ken of the arid West. And if this was true of the more lowly elements, what of the rulers, Emirs and Khans of the twenty-one provinces with their separate seventy-eight governments all to be welcomed on their arrival in St. Petersburg and speeded on their way with suitable gifts of cups and bratini, table clocks and writing sets, in Siberian stones, gold, silver and enamel! What of the visiting foreign potentates all to be provided for by way of large presentation pieces! What of the special embassies to foreign lands and the gifts they took with them, like the massive silver rice pan, one metre in diameter and 30 centimetres deep, standing on four big eagle's claws sent to the Negus Menelik of Abyssinia! What of the old aristocratic families of Russia and all their requirements? Illustrated in Plate 4 is a musical box in pale pink translucent enamel playing the regimental tune known as the 'White Lady'; presented to the Prince and Princess (Zénaïde) Youssoupoff on the 25th anniversary of their marriage.[1] It was for this lady, one of the most charming of Tsarist times, that Fabergé, on one occasion, designed a most original ball-dress. What of the ballerinas, those queens of graceful movement and self-expression, themselves consummate emblems in flesh and blood, whose art gave them rank but little below that of the Imperial Family—Ksheshinskaia and her Fabergé collection; Preobrajenskaia; Pavlova; Lopokova; and Karsavina and her mascot brooch, a wonderful Siberian amethyst, the finest of a set presented to Count Zuboff by Catherine the Great and set with a surround of single brilliants by Fabergé, illustrated in Plate 6; and Balletta of another art, but what matter, and her Fabergé smoky rock crystal goblet of surpassing beauty, illustrated in Plate 7, and perhaps the most beautiful thing Fabergé ever made; and Cavalieri, of still another art, and her Fabergé gold cup for *Traviata*.

All this, to say nothing of the Tsars Alexander III and Nicholas II, who were the *State;* and here one must stop for a breather, for what they gave and received by Fabergé was legion. If you multiply every piece illustrated in this book by 1,000, you will begin to get some idea what it meant to a craftsman to be in Russia and ruled over by the Tsars. To enumerate is impossible, but for quality take a look at the cigarette-box illustrated in Plate 17, given by Nicholas II to General Trepoff and now in the collection of Queen Mary, and the nephrite casket presented by the Tsar Nicholas II to Sidney, 14th Earl of Pembroke and Montgomery in 1896, and illustrated in Plate 8.[2] And then the Empresses Marie and Alexandra Feodorovna (and again for quality look at the *carnet* illustrated in Plate 9, given by the last Empress to Nicholas II and now in the collection of Dr. James Hasson—the chiselling of the gold is superb), and the Grand Dukes, some two score of them, I should say, when Alexander came to the throne, with their wives and families; their birthdays, christenings and weddings (and no Grand Duke considered himself adequately equipped for marriage without a *surtout-de-table* by Fabergé), all had to be provided for, not forgetting their equally innumerable relatives and friends abroad (and they were related to nearly all the royal families of Europe), again all to be provided for.

[1] Also note Plate 5 of Youssoupoff Easter Egg.
[2] Now in the collection of Sir Harold Wernher, Bt.

And the Coronation of the Tsar Nicholas II, and all the Fabergé brooches, pendants, sleeve links, cigarette cases and innumerable interesting objects, all emblems of the Crown; and the plates in gold, silver and silver gilt, many lavishly adorned with enamel and Siberian stones, on which every town in Russia sent to the Tsar their offerings of bread and salt, and of which an 'enormous' number was made by Fabergé.

And the Tercentenary of Romanoff rule in 1913, when again there were brooches and pendants of diamonds, stones of colour and pearls for all the Grand Duchesses and the ladies of the Court. And again a number of important Fabergé objects presented to the Tsar, one of the most interesting being what has now become known as 'The Bankers Box' illustrated in Plate 10, and now in the possession of Mr. B. L. Kilgour, Jnr., of Cincinnati. The box is of nephrite (Siberian jade) bordered with gold, and inside there is a gold plate engraved in Russian:—

1613—1913
To His Imperial Majesty to be used
at his Serene discretion for purposes of charity,
dutifully presented by the banks of St. Petersburg
and Moscow.

Inside the box, when it was presented to the Tsar, was a cheque for a million roubles!

Oh yes, the House of Fabergé was in clover, and knee-deep. It is true to say that at no time in history has a goldsmith become more identified with the life and aspirations of his native land; and when I say this I am not unmindful what other Russian jewellers and goldsmiths have done; for instance, Bolin, who made most of the jewellery for the wedding of the Grand Duchess Xenia, sister of the Tsar; and Hahn, who made the crown for the last Empress Alexandra Feodorovna; and Ovtchinnikoff, Morozoff, Khlebnikoff and Lorié.

One thing I regret is that I am not able to illustrate more national and civic presentation pieces given to and by the Tsar, Russian statesmen, generals, societies, companies and so on. There must be some left in Russia even if many have been destroyed. I have no information. In these days of 'cultural relations' this is a pity.

I am, however, able to illustrate, in Plate 18, one of the many objects presented to the Empress Alexandra Feodorovna and now in the possession of Messrs. Wartski—a gold basket containing lilies of the valley. On the bottom of the basket is an inscription in Russian of which the following is a translation:

To Her Imperial Majesty, Tsarina Alexandra Feodorovna, from the iron-works management and dealers in the Siberian iron section of the Nijegorodski Fair in the year 1896.

From all that has been said it will come as no surprise that the fame of the House of Fabergé, widely established as it was by all the gifts which the Romanoffs sent abroad, and by those brought away by travellers, soon spread to every other land as the *fournisseur par excellence* of objects as tokens given as pledges or expressions of feeling or intent, commodities indeed most useful, nay absolutely necessary, in a world in which one and the same spoken word can be made to mean either 'yes' or 'no' according to the twist or stress you give it.

But it was not in everyday tokens only that those abroad were eager for the help of Fabergé. As in Russia they soon called in his assistance in matters of great significance, national and private. As examples of the former I cannot do better than cite those made to the order of King Rama VI of Siam, consisting of an *Image of Buddha*, in nephrite (which arrived in Bangkok in 1914), kept in the Temple of the Emerald Buddha and throughout the reign of King Rama VI used in various official ceremonies; a *Bowl* in nephrite, supported by three Brahmin mythological figures in gold, one being that of the Garuda, half-man and half-bird, the vehicle or bearer of the god Rama, one of the incarnations of the god Vishnu. This bowl is now kept in the Royal Palace and was used as a container of Sacred Water at the birthday celebrations of King Rama VI; a *Shallow Bowl* in nephrite with handles of gold and pink enamel, supported on a pedestal of nephrite decorated with gold, pink enamel and diamonds. This bowl, also used in the birthday celebrations of King Rama VI and similarly in the early part of the reign of King Prajadhipok, is now kept in the Royal Palace; a pair of *Candle-sticks*, in the same materials and in the same style, Louis XVI, as the shallow bowl, and used on the same occasions and now preserved in the same place; and lastly another *Image of Buddha*, in nephrite, now housed in the National Museum. These objects with the exception of the candle sticks and one of the Buddhas are illustrated in Plates 11 and 12.

These pieces are representative of the larger works of Fabergé; unfortunately I am unable to give exact dimensions. The Siamese Government when most courteously sending me the illustrations did not give these particulars. Eugène Fabergé in reference to one of the Buddhas calls it a 'great Buddha', but in describing the shallow bowl he gives 45 centimetres, that is 1½ feet, as its approximate diameter. As all the objects are on the same scale I calculate that the Buddhas stand some 1½ to 2 feet high and the deep bowl including the supports some 1½ feet high and the bowl itself some 1¼ feet in diameter at its largest dimension.

All these works were not made without much travelling to and fro between Petersburg, London and Bangkok. They deserve the prominent place I give them not only on account of their own merit but because out of the expeditions entailed, over a period of some nine years from 1906, grew the further expeditions to the East, to the Mandarins of China and the Maharajahs of India.

In Plate 6 we have an illustration of a richly worked little cigarette case in translucent enamel on gold in the collection of Queen Mary, and presented, if I mistake not, to Her Majesty by the Maharajah of Bikanir, that Prince of India who was not only the archetype of an English gentleman but who spoke the English language in a way that was a lesson to all English men and women, and to all those of the Dominions and Colonies, who listened to him.

The invitation to visit Siam came from King Chulalongkorn and was conveyed to Fabergé in a letter from Prince Chakrabong in 1904. This Siamese Prince was educated in St. Petersburg, being a pupil of the Corps des Pages, and at one time was colonel of a Russian regiment of hussars. He spoke Russian fluently and was married, I believe, to a Russian lady. It was to him that Fabergé was primarily indebted for the interest taken in his wares in Siam and this ran to big figures. As I recall them they often made the efforts in Paris and London look small by comparison.

Fabergé was especially fortunate in going to Siam just at the time when there was a call not only for objects of fantasy but for much jewellery and not only for the Royal House but for the Siamese aristocracy. A craftsman of the type of Fabergé was lucky too in being called to a country which dedicated each year to a different animal. One of the years in question was under the sign of the pig and for this Fabergé made a large number of medals on which this animal was represented in enamel.

So much for examples of objects of national significance which Fabergé made for foreign countries. As an example of those objects of private significance I cannot do better than cite the ikon of the Madonna and Child which Fabergé made for the late Duchess of Norfolk. I give particulars of this with illustration in Chapter V, page 84.

So much for symbolism. But it is of little use standing in the market place with an empty stall; you have to work and fill it with goods and with those which are wanted.

Thus we come to the second stone in the spiritual edifice, Carl Fabergé himself and his younger brother, Agathon. The record of the House from the beginning is a wonderful concatenation; the consequences follow one another as though ordained. 'All things work together for good' is the decree of Heaven and if we come a cropper we have only our foolishness to blame when we get out of touch. 'A man never goes so far as when he does not know where he is going', said Oliver Cromwell.

Now just how far Carl Fabergé and his brother knew they were going I am not able to say, but of one thing I am sure: when they brought about a vital change in their business they had not the slightest idea how far they were in on a good thing or how near to the goal to which that change was eventually to bring them. Whether that change was due to a far-seeing prescience or simply to a blind following of the demands and feelings of the time, I am also not able to say, but knowing Carl Fabergé as I do I should say the latter. He kept his mind and hands immediately to the thing to be done, without any 'high-falutin' planning for a future prosperity in the skies.

At what date Agathon joined the family business I do not know. No doubt he had much the same experience in it as his brother, except that in 1895 he died, five years before the House moved into 24 Morskaya Street. Thus he did not live to enjoy those last eighteen years while his joint work with his brother was reaping such a phenomenal success.

Concerning the nature of Carl I have no need of secondhand information; his hyper-sensibility, his irony, his sarcasm and loving kindness were fully displayed every day when I saw him on my yearly visits to St. Petersburg. With his brother Agathon it is different; I never met him and can only rely on the information given to me by Carl's sons, Eugène and Agathon. From their accounts it is certain that Agathon was equally sensitive, if not more so, but he was a man of one purpose only, devoted entirely to designing, and in this, if there was anything to choose between the brothers, he was the greater artist.

But Agathon without Carl would have been lost. Carl was of a more versatile nature—nothing came amiss to him, and if his brother went one way, he would go every way. In another chapter I have made an attempt to give a picture of Carl; here I need only say he was the most complex and yet the simplest of men. It all depends on your individual outlook. If visible things are your fundamentals then his nature was of the most complex, if invisible then the simplest.

With this introduction, let us turn eagerly to the joint work of these young brothers when Carl took control in 1870. They were established with a sound business in their hands, but with no special significance attached to it. Jewellery and goldsmithery were then heavy and clumsy in Russia and the first thing to do was to lift both to a higher and more elegant level of craftsmanship. This in itself was a fine achievement and one which had far-reaching influence on the work of all the other jewellers and goldsmiths in Russia. But in the process of lifting something else happened. In some way goldsmithery was raised to a higher level than jewellery. Little by little, impersonal objects of fantasy (knick-knacks, if you prefer), such as cigarette cases, boxes, animals, flowers, Easter eggs, frames and clocks in gold, silver, enamel and beautiful stones, especially those of Siberia, nephrite, rhodonite, aventurine-quartz, chalcedony and agate, took precedence over objects for personal adornment in diamonds and precious stones. It is to the everlasting credit of the two Craftsmen that having taken the initial step, they followed their artistic instinct and sense of decency with more and more success, until in the end they found their business interests completely reversed, and instead of jewellery taking first place, articles of fantasy became the chief productions of the House.

Search as you may for the reason for the fame of Fabergé, you have it in that one fact, clear and unmistakable. From a business point of view the initial departure from jewellery to fantasy was complete lunacy. What the position is to-day I do not know, but, at the time of which I speak, jewellery was the breath of the nostrils, the bread and very much the butter of every goldsmith and jeweller.

And there for the time being, we may leave the two gentle Craftsmen.

There is here an important thing to be said, and one which vitally concerns another. The effect upon any reader must be climacteric, unless this record is to be in vain. I must interrupt myself, marshal my materials and stand still for a moment for the sake of self-clarification. And as I stand, let me say that I have given this record much thought over many years. For a long time I tried to work it out in the form of some *Belle Lettre*, written very academically and picturesquely and in the third person, most objectively, as though I had never seen Fabergé in my life and instead of 'I', referring always to myself as 'the writer'. Well, the plan did not work out at all. It was all very proper, but that was as far as it went.

And then one morning it came: 'Nothing counts like personal experience.' Those were the words. Where they came from heaven knows, but they put me

PLATE 1

MEDALLION PORTRAIT OF PETER CARL FABERGE
Modelled for this work by Alfred Pocock.

PLATE 2

EXTERIOR OF THE HEAD ESTABLISHMENT OF FABERGÉ IN ST. PETERSBURG.

PLATE 3

INTERIOR OF THE HEAD ESTABLISHMENT OF FABERGÉ IN ST. PETERSBURG.

PLATE 4

MUSICAL BOX. In pale translucent pink enamel on gold
with surrounds in opaque
white enamel flowers and
green enamel leaves.

Presented to Prince and
Princess Youssoupoff on
the 25th anniversary of
their marriage. Actual size.
(*Privately owned in America.*)

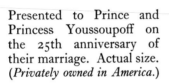

Thumb-piece in gold and
rose-diamonds with num-
ber 25 in Roman characters
also in rose-diamonds. The
six panels (of which three
are here shown) represent
six palaces of the Youssoupoff family, in warm sepia
enamel.

PLATE 5

EASTER EGG
In the form of a clock, commemorating the Silver Wedding of Prince Felix and
Princess Zénaidë Youssoupoff. In translucent pink and opaque white enamels,
gold and diamonds. Three miniatures are of Prince Felix and his sons. Approxi-
mate height: 9⅝ inches.
(*Privately owned in America.*)

PLATE 6

KARSAVINA'S MASCOT BROOCH. Siberian amethyst of superb colour set with diamonds. Length overall: $1\frac{11}{16}$ inches. Width: $1\frac{7}{16}$ inches.
(*In the possession of Madame Tamara Karsavina.*)

CIGARETTE CASE. In translucent yellow enamel on gold, bordered in translucent green and opaque white enamels and rose-diamonds. Each corner, emerald and diamonds. Centre, double-headed eagle in gold, surrounded by rose-diamonds.
(*From Queen Mary's Collection.*)

PLATE 7

GOBLET
In smoky rock crystal on gold base. Presented to Madame Elisabeth Balletta, formerly of the Imperial Michel Theatre. Overall height: 8¾ inches. Height of goblet: 6¼ inches. Top of goblet: 4¾ inches × 3⅓ inches. Photograph and information supplied by Mr. Eugène Fabergé.
(By courtesy of À La Vieille Russie.)

PLATE 8

CASKET
In nephrite, ornamented in polished red gold and in green gold. Double-headed
eagle in mat yellow gold with orb, sceptre and parts of crown polished. Height:
8⅜ inches.
(Collection of Sir Harold Wernher, Bt.)

PLATE 9

CARD CASE
In green morocco leather, bordered with
finely chiselled gold. Miniature of Empress
Alexandra Feodorovna by Zehngraf.
Height: 4 inches.
(*From Queen Mary's Collection.*)

Reverse of case showing 'Alix' in chiselled
gold. Presented by the Empress to the Tsar
Nicholas II.
(*Collection of Dr. James Hasson.*)

PLATE 10

THE BANKERS' BOX
In nephrite, with the monogram of the Tsar Nicholas II, Imperial Crown, catch and borders in gold. Length: 6 inches. Width: $5\frac{3}{16}$ inches. Depth: $1\frac{7}{16}$ inches.
(Collection of Mr. Bayard L. Kilgour, Jr.)

PLATE 11

IMAGE OF BUDDHA. In nephrite.
(*From H.M. The King of Siam's
Collection.*)

NEPHRITE BOWL. On sup-
porting Brahmin mytho-
logical gold figures.
(*From H.M. The King of
Siam's Collection.*)

PLATE 12

SHALLOW BOWL
In nephrite with supporting arms in gold, pink enamel and diamonds, on a
pedestal in nephrite ornamented with gold, pink enamel and diamonds.
(*From H.M. The King of Siam's Collection.*)

PLATE 13

TANKARD
Old Russian Style. Chiselled silver (oxydé). Height: $11\frac{1}{2}$ inches.
Selling price (1908) 600 roubles.
(*Original Fabergé photograph.*)

PLATE 14

ENDOVA

Old Russian Style. Chiselled silver (oxydé). Height: 7¾ inches. Diameter: 13 inches.
Length: 1 foot 5½ inches. Selling price (1908) 700 roubles.
(*Original Fabergé photograph.*)

PLATE 15

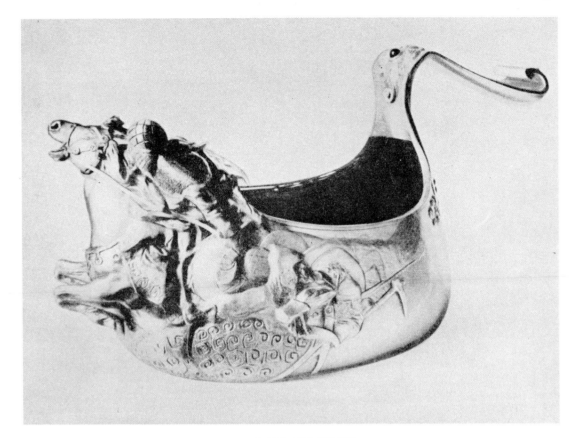

RACING TROPHY
Old Russian Style, silver, oxydé. Total approximate length: 1 foot 8 inches.
(*Original Fabergé photograph.*)

PLATE 16

CLOCK
Old Russian Style. Rhodonite. Mountings in chased silver, set with emeralds
and sapphires. Height: 11½ inches.
(*By courtesy of Hammer Galleries.*)

on the right track. When I came to think of it I knew I must never allow myself as a biographer to depreciate, or be frightened of personal experience, for it is the bed rock on which all records are built up. Whether the subject be some remote figure of antiquity or a contemporary makes no difference, it is from some word, written or spoken, of something once heard or seen that the rolling ball of history starts on its course for good or ill. The beginning is therefore everything, and the man (or woman) who gives the ball its first push becomes at once of equal importance with the man or woman he records. His sympathies or antipathies can make or mar the record of another's life. Colour blindness is not the only disability which can affect his vision. It is not only fair to the reader, therefore, but is in the interests of truth, that the writer should not bind himself too tightly to that fetish, objectivity, but should here and there in his narrative let himself go, giving some indication of what he thinks and feels about this and that.

When all this had got packed into my rather slow-going head, I suddenly realized I was on quite another plane to that of the great writer. I was *personal experience* and nothing more, it was my sole equipment. I realized that the beginning and end of the record of the House of Fabergé was in my hands and mine only, for good or ill, and that an immense responsibility was mine. And not only as regards events.

Events are always approaching a climax; and constantly at greater speed. And when the climax comes, poor unseeing creatures that we are, we have no idea that it has actually arrived. Thus we are always living at least a hundred years behind the times, and in our blindness we seek to bring about something which has already taken place.

This is to be the real story of Fabergé, so we release ourselves once more and come to the third stone in the spiritual edifice of the House. We allude to the Tsar Alexander III to whom history has been unfair from the moment on that fateful day in March, 1881, after the assassination of his soft-hearted, gentle father the emancipator, when with his wife on his arm, he stepped out of the Winter Palace the very personification of courage, determined at all costs to stamp out anarchy in Russia.

Nature cast this Emperor in a rough and out-size mould. A man of Herculean strength, gigantic, forthright, forceful and unyielding, with a stentorian voice and an extreme roughness of manner, a hatred of resounding phrases and melodrama, an utter contempt for the over-elegant, and complete freedom from all illusions, a hatred of all things German, but above all a passion for everything Russian, and so strong that it gave the impression that in order to be thoroughly Russian he thought he must take on something of the nature of the bear. . . . Such was Alexander III. When you add to this that he was a disciplinarian of the first degree, it is easy to understand how it was he struck something like terror into all those surrounding him. Queen Victoria said of him ' . . . a sovereign whom she does not look upon *as a gentleman*'.*

Yet it was this huge ruffian, as Europe pleased to think of him, who could bend

* *Henry Ponsonby*, by Lord Ponsonby, page 172.

a solid silver rouble with his vice-like thumb, who on one occasion picked up a silver fork, twisted it into a knot and threw it across the dinner table in the direction of the Austrian Ambassador, saying: 'That is what I am going to do to your two or three army corps', and who on October 17th, 1888, when his train had been derailed by revolutionaries, held up the roof of the dining-car on his Herculean shoulders and so saved his children and relatives. . . . I say it was this huge ruffian, by an act of superb patronage, one of those deeds of *noblesse oblige* which only royal princes have it in them to do, who fulfilled his mission so splendidly in the interest of art and craftsmanship.

I do not know that Alexander II ever had any dealings with the House of Fabergé, but there is every evidence that the other members of the Imperial Family had, and especially the Tsarevitch, for when the latter came to the throne as Alexander III, one of the first things he did was to appoint the House of Fabergé as goldsmiths and jewellers to the Court.

This was no mere framed acknowledgment that His Imperial Majesty had purchased a few things from the House and with that it must be satisfied as best it could; rather was it an undertaking on the part of the Emperor to protect and encourage the Craftsman, whom he so much admired; not by vague promises of good things to come, but by a clearly defined commission, an act of truly Imperial patronage, whereby the Craftsman was to make one outstanding object every year, with *carte blanche* as to subject and price, above and apart from any other commissions for the Emperor upon which the Craftsman might be engaged at the time.

I refer, of course, to the Imperial Easter eggs which the Emperor caused to be made as gifts to the Empress, and it is well to note that this goodwill of Alexander III was taken over by his son, Nicholas II, by whom the commission was expanded to two eggs each year, one for the new Empress and one for the Dowager Empress, his mother.

What importance this goodwill had for the House of Fabergé can be assessed by the fact that it continued without a break for some thirty-five years, right up to the end of the Tsarist régime, during which time some fifty-four to fifty-seven eggs in all were made. But there was far more to it than this. The promise of the continuous call upon his services must have given to the Craftsman a great sense of security and assured success and this without any doubt was the source of that superb confidence which eventually brought such magnificent rewards.

But these Imperial Easter eggs were not only symbolic, as we shall see in the chapter devoted to them, they were symptomatic; a vivid indication which way the wind was blowing in the Imperial mind.

'Which way the wind was blowing in the Imperial mind.' It is well to repeat these words. If there is confusion in the western world about Russia herself, and of this there is no doubt, there is equal confusion about the Romanoffs, and those chiefly responsible for this state of affairs are those at present in authority in Russia. Ruling a country possessed of the most fertile *Genius Loci* in the world, a spirit capable of making Russia the first paradise on earth, they throw away her birthright in a vain attempt to make a paradise of the whole world after their own pattern. Like many more, they suffer from that soul destroying disease 'The love for all mankind', or maybe a lust for power, but whichever it is they are equally dangerous.

Whatever may be that of other lands, Russia's way to glory lies at home, and very much there, with one-sixth of the earth's dry land in which to develop herself. Every page of her history has it written thus. The way of expansion, whether by land, interest or infiltration, is the way to her doom.

'Which way the wind was blowing in the Imperial mind.' Well, of course, it was not blowing at all because in Tsarist Russia there was no mind at all, as so many of my friends tell me. For them the Soviet, as some arcadic Omniarch, lit up and suspended in the firmament, attached neither to earth nor heaven, and sustained miraculously from nowhere, over-shadows all. Omniscient, omnipotent.

Mention Tsarist Russia to some and from a myriad facets of Crown Jewels comes a blinding flash. For them the Koh-i-nor and the Stars-of-Africa are but pebbles on the beach to be washed up from time to time in the cause of a State occasion or innocent enjoyment and when these are over to be rolled back again into the sea of our really serious undertakings. 'We can take it', they say, 'to our self-satisfaction and souls' refreshment'. All of which is splendid, all to the good and cause for much rejoicing.

But when these same people focus their attention on the Crown jewels of another land which very likely they have never seen and about which they know very little and especially if that land happens to be Russia, and of course Tsarist Russia, then they lose all sense of proportion. The Orloff and the Shah are not stones, let alone pebbles, but rocks which with others of their kind, formed, layer by layer, the stratified structure of a régime, the whole of whose economy was based on diamonds, rubies, emeralds and pearls.

But there are still others. They have been carried away by a new way of writing history and in consequence are completely lost. The Tsarist régime went out in such a blaze of fanaticism there is no wonder at all that any achievements of the later Romanoffs were swept away with it into oblivion. So convenient to some was this oblivion it at once became 'blessed' and ever since it has been as though Nicholas II and Alexander III never existed and thirty-six years of Russian history have been torn from the records.

Here was a new way of writing history. If Nicholas II and Alexander III, then why not Alexander II, Nicholas I and Alexander I? In fact why not tear up the whole record, it was so easy, and begin with St. Alexander Nevsky, take in Ivan the Terrible, give Peter the Great a bit of a running, slash through the intervening period, and so straight away to the U.S.S.R.

Now when history is written in this way there is little wonder that many people do not know where they are. It becomes quite a question with them which century they live in, and so as regards Tsarist Russia we find many to-day still dining with master-mariner Jenkinson off golden platter with Ivan the Terrible, in Moscow, in the Sixteenth Century.

This is something of the confusion amidst which I write, and it is a confusion which has to be met and cleared up before there can be any right understanding

15

of the full meaning of the achievement of the House of Fabergé. And it is to personal experience, unadulterated and unashamed, that I must go.

When I was in the vortex of the Edwardian Era, and it was during that time of abundance that Fabergé came into his own, I found myself amidst a whirl of Kings and Queens, Millionaires and Maharajahs. Fabergé objects were then passing through my fingers as fast as shoals of glistening herrings pass through the sea, and all I had to do was to look immaculate and say nothing. That there might be some underlying meaning in all this activity never entered one's mind. It was only some sixteen years after that things began to move and in such a way that I was bound to 'sit up', as we say, and 'take notice'.

Pamela de Bayou, a lady who crossed my path by the merest chance and one to whom I am as greatly indebted as Benvenuto Cellini was to Madonna Porzia, demanded that I should tell her about Fabergé. This was the beginning, and in a state of much mental excitement, and sometimes, I am afraid, of aberration, I did what I could for her in my book *Twice Seven* in 1933. In 1934, Edward Wenham, the then Editor of *The Connoisseur*, became interested, and he commissioned articles on the subject of Fabergé's Imperial Easter Eggs. In 1935 came the Russian Exhibition, at Madame Koch de Gooreynd's house in Belgrave Square, and this brought more enquiries.

Then, in February 1937, Queen Mary honoured me by receiving me at Marlborough House to discuss her Fabergé collection. And this moment cannot pass without an expression of my humble duty and gratitude. Not only has Her Majesty gone out of her way at all times to give me access to her collection, but the particular manner in which she has presented each object to me for examination, has given me so much encouragement that without it I should never have undertaken this record. It has been my good fortune to be surrounded by the delightful things of life, and as I write I am inspired by the thought that whereas one Queen of England, Alexandra, did so much by her patronage to support the House of Fabergé, another Queen of England, Mary, has so graciously set the coping stone on its record by permitting this work to be dedicated to her.

In 1937 also, came a call from the U.S.A. when Dr. Armand Hammer invited me to go there and talk to the American public. And for his support I now tender to him grateful thanks.

Lastly, it was about the same time, after much fumbling at the Victoria and Albert Museum Library, that by pure chance I found Baron A. E. Foelkersam's *Inventaire de l'Argenterie*, published in 1907, two volumes devoted to the table silver, etc., in the possession of the Tsar Nicholas II. Not only did I find catalogued many pieces by Fabergé, and especially the table service made by him in 1896 in Louis XVI style, but a short history of the House of Fabergé with special mention of the five workmasters, Kollin, Perchin, Wigström, Rappoport and Holmström.

But what gave me most delight was this sentence of Foelkersam's: 'This firm (Fabergé) is the best and most celebrated in the world.'

By this time I was fully awake to the extent of my responsibility. A great man had lived who had enriched his generation in such a way that the time in which he flourished might, without any undue estimate of his worth, very well be called 'The Age of Fabergé'. Now he had passed away and I found myself the sole repository of all that concerned him. Without a doubt something now was up to me, but I wanted light and whither to look. I began to climb laboriously, step by step, only to fall back again many times into the slough of despond.

And then one morning light came, as it always does if you seek long enough: 'Alexander did not commission Fabergé to make him a set of tiaras but a set of Easter eggs.'

I worked on this idea for weeks, repeating 'Not tiaras but Easter eggs', and with every repetition my focus cleared till at last a scheme of things became apparent, but on far too high a plane for me to dare to set it down on paper without support. But no support was forthcoming.

By the middle of the summer of 1937 I was well on the way to completing preparations for my visit to America when out of the blue the looked-for support came. It is always 'out of the blue' if you wait long enough. 'Yechidar!' it said, and there at the other end of the telephone was Agathon Fabergé, the second son of Carl, making use of our usual salutation of long ago in St. Petersburg. He had just arrived in this country. I told him to come along and take up his abode with me in Hampstead for the period of his stay in this country.

Nobody could have been more welcome at the time, for even if I had felt sure of myself, here was the one man who could make the feeling a certainty. It was a piece of astonishing good fortune. You know, there are times when all the hope of the world concentrates in one man. Cabinets may sit, Big Fours and Sixes and Sevens may wrangle for months and crowds cry themselves hoarse for a hearing, but in the end it depends on one man, and sometimes a quite insignificant fellow, like Victor Hugo's shepherd. His word or action decides the destiny of the world for generations. This provides the spice of life, and every man should hold himself ready, for he never knows when the call may come.

Not only had Agathon Fabergé an intimate knowledge of the work of his father's House, but before the debacle of 1917 everything concerning the Regalia and Crown jewels of Russia was concentrated in him. Acting on behalf of his father, he it was who periodically examined them, and saw to their maintenance. Nobody knew the history of them in greater detail and nobody brought to them a more consummate knowledge of precious stones. If these jewels finally went into the hands of the Soviet Government in what certainly may be called mint condition, first it has to thank the Tsars of Russia and then Agathon Fabergé for the care he gave to them.

Every evening for two months, up to my departure, we sat and talked AND TALKED. Of the idiosyncrasies of his father and stories about him; memories of his home at Levaschova on the Finnish border where I had spent so many happy days with him and his family; his imprisonments by the Bolsheviks, for he was imprisoned twice; his valuation of the Regalia and Crown Jewels; his final escape in January 1928 from Russia with his family in sleighs over the frozen Gulf of Finland, with the guns of Kronstadt firing before and behind them—these and other things crowded the hours and, of course, my estimate of the work of his father.

It was this estimate of mine upon which I wanted to be assured more than anything else, so I said to him one night: 'Tell me, Mr. Fabergé, am I right? Was it craftsmanship?' He looked at me for a while, nodded his head, shut his eyes and as in a dream, and very deliberately, said this:

'Yes. Not the works of nature, but the works of man. It was one of those ever-recurring ages of craftsmanship, perhaps the last and greatest of all, but we never talked about it, did we? We were all of us too busy working it out. It is only on looking back that one sees the astonishing scope of it. You are right. Certainly in our line, that of the goldsmith, I would claim that no age has done more. The Age of Fabergé! Yes, you are right.'

And so, my very patient and gentle reader, if you still bear with me, at last I have to tell you that I rose to the occasion, no longer confounded but emboldened. When the time came, as come I felt it must, I would put down the words as they had been given to me to say. Now is that time, just ten years afterwards. And here they are.

All the time I had been feverishly engaged in selling Fabergé wares in all quarters of the globe, without knowing it I had been adding my little to what Colonel Walter Elliot calls 'one of the enormous creative moments', those periods of time which come and go in the history of the world, when men intoxicated and elated by a common 'conscious artistic' effort, and happy in working to some glad end, set up standards for the guidance of mankind, whether their achievements be in 'the building of Cathedrals' or 'the marching after Alamein'.

Every object of fantasy made by Fabergé was a creative moment, his total output was 'one of the enormous creative moments'. It was epochal. An epoch is a point in the course of history when something happens which checks the behaviour of the period which immediately precedes it.

All standards are criteria of excellence and all excellence is by way of restraint. All progress of any worth is by the same way and all art of consequence is an exhibition of this solid fact. The way to paradise does not consist in growing new antlers but in the drawing in of horns.

Carl and Agathon Fabergé drew in their horns when they made their now historic departure from objects of jewellery to objects of fantasy. Alexander III drew in his horns when he commissioned Fabergé to make him a set of Easter eggs and not tiaras. Alexander had travelled a long way from 'the barbaric splendour' of his predecessors and from Catherine the Great, who, immediately on taking possession of the throne in 1762, commissioned her French jeweller Posier, to make her a new crown which was to be 'the finest jewel in all the world', and which she was in much need of to hypnotize all Russia into the belief that she was indeed the rightful Empress.

These three men virtually killed the diamond and all the other precious stones; not as objects of brilliance and beauty in their own right, but as those symbols of power and riches and magic which endowed the possessors of them with heaven-sent qualities, setting them, as they imagined, high above their fellows and specially ordained.

In other words, these three men pointed the eternal way, that only by the work of his own hands can man fully realize himself, that to obsess himself with those things in which he has had no hand in the making is to induce a state of creeping sickness leading finally to ruin.

This achievement of Alexander III and the House of Fabergé had immediate and far-reaching consequences. So great was its effect that it brought into being what may very well be called 'The Fabergé Charter', regulating the conduct and behaviour of a large part of the cultured world, unwritten, yes, but all the more formidable on that account.

From henceforth it was assumed that to offer any gift in which the value of the workmanship was exceeded by that of the materials employed, that is to say any article which had blatantly written across it 'I have cost a lot of money' was taboo. To this rule there was one exception only, when the recipient was a near relative or very dear friend.

This high principle, of course, had been laid down and acted upon before, for example in the time of Louis XV and Madame de Pompadour when all those master craftsmen, Jean George, Ducrollay, Sageret, Dubos, Delafons, Thierry, Fillassier and many others, carried it so scrupulously into effect, but never before had it been sent forth as an implied edict on such a scale, and never before had the carrying out been so completely vested in one man.

The Age of Fabergé, so magnificently inaugurated by the Tsar Alexander III, and of which his brother-in-law, King Edward VII, was an outstanding figure, was not as so many would have us believe, a time of licentious extravagance without end. With abundance at hand enough to destroy completely the whole moral fibre of those who played their part in it, there existed an unwritten law of restraint never before recognised on such a scale, and certainly never brought so completely into effect.

Make no mistake, it is not the things which are blazoned from the house-tops; not the things in newspapers or which are broadcast which really matter, but those things which are taking place apart, and often far ahead of common knowledge and which are 'off the record'. Sometimes they seem of little significance at the time of their happening because they take place under our very noses and we can neither see nor hear them. Often they are happening in the most paradoxical cir-cumstances, and at the most unexpected times.

And now to return to our narrative and to the exhibitions. The House of Fabergé first exhibited its wares at the Pan-Russian Exhibition in Moscow in 1882. Here the Craftsman received the gold medal and achieved his first great public success. Again at the Fine Art Exhibition in Nürnberg in 1885 he was awarded the gold medal for his exhibits of reproductions of the old Greek orna-ments 400 B.C. found at Kertsh in the Crimea, the originals of which were housed in the Hermitage Museum of the Winter Palace. These reproductions were made at the suggestion of the art-connoisseur, Count Stroganoff, and by permission of

19

the Tsar. In 1896 came the Pan-Russian Exhibition at Nijny-Novgorod, and once more Fabergé was awarded the gold medal.

At the Northern Exhibition held in Stockholm in 1897, Fabergé exhibited *hors concours*, his son Eugène being a member of the jury. In 1900 came the 'Exposition Internationale Universelle' in Paris. Here again he exhibited *hors concours*, being himself a member of the jury. This was the outstanding public event in the history of the House of Fabergé, for it was here in the land of the French masters of the Eighteenth Century that the Russian Craftsman revealed his full stature as the master goldsmith-craftsman of his age, and perhaps of any age. Graciously assisted by the Empress Alexandra Feodorovna and the Dowager Empress Marie Feodorovna, who loaned their Fabergé Easter eggs for the occasion, the Craftsman put on exhibition a display of objects which literally caused a furore, he himself being the object of a remarkable demonstration of homage on the part of the goldsmiths of France and other countries to which I will refer in another chapter. To mark the occasion, Carl Fabergé was decorated with the Knight's Cross of the Légion d'Honneur, his son Eugène was made an Officer of the Academy and the principal assistants received gold and silver medals. This exhibition did more than any other event to spread the fame of the Craftsman all over the world.

There remain two things. Some mention must be made of the chief assistants associated with the Head Establishment in St. Petersburg and a short notice given to the Branches of the firm and those in control of them. A special chapter is devoted to the workmasters, artists and sculptors.

To begin with St. Petersburg, the first to claim attention is *Peter Hiskias Pendin*. He was a Finn, born in St. Michel, Finland, and chief assistant to Gustav Fabergé, the founder of the firm. A man of great character and witty, not only was he much in favour with the customers but as a first-class jeweller and goldsmith, was of much practical assistance to his chief. He remained in the business until 1882, when he died. Having served the firm from the beginning for forty years; having seen it through its initial stages until its name became one of high renown and giving the same invaluable service to Carl Fabergé as to his father, he deserves to be cited as one of the pillars of the House of Fabergé and one to whom all admirers of Fabergé craftsmanship are indebted.

Working with Gustav Fabergé also in the beginning were two Petersburg Germans, *Gunst* and *Eckhardt*.

Next comes *Zaiontchkovsky*. No particulars are available about him except the one given by Baron Foelkersam in his *Inventaire de l'Argenterie*, that when Gustav Fabergé retired in 1860 he was left as manager until Carl Fabergé took over control in 1870.

Two more who should be mentioned are *Wilhelm Goetz* of German extraction, born in St. Petersburg, and *Emil Melanchtovitch*, a cousin of Carl Fabergé and a native of the Baltic. Both had over thirty years' service to their credit, and both I remember well. Goetz was chief salesman and Melanchtovitch general factotum.

And another, *Paul Blomerius*, who was of Swedish extraction, born in Moscow. A man of many languages, he was foreign correspondent and much else besides.

All things considered, he was the live wire of the House of Fabergé in its later years, especially in its foreign undertakings, and the success of the firm abroad was in large measure due to his energy. As outward movement of any kind was anathema to his chief, Blomerius was often very unpleasantly placed. Time and again Fabergé said to me, 'Why Siam?' 'Why India?' 'Why China, and all the rest of it? Haven't we more than enough to do at home?' And never was there truer son of Russia than this great Craftsman.

I am under an eternal debt to Blomerius for the care with which he turned (or translated) my English into Russian during my yearly visits, but he taught me one important lesson, that any man whose business it is to make decisions of an international character should never burden himself with any language but his own.

Blomerius was an outstanding example of the 'internationally' minded. When he spoke French he was a Frenchman, when he spoke German he was a German, when Russian a Russian, when English an Englishman, and when he woke up in the morning he was Dutch. It was on one of the last occasions that he came to me and said: 'You know that what we decided last night was quite wrong'.

Lastly there are *Eugène* and *Agathon Fabergé*, the eldest and second sons of Carl. Of Agathon we have already spoken, and there will be more to say about him in Chapter III. Eugène devoted himself almost entirely to designing, thus following in the tradition of his uncle Agathon. Quiet and unassuming, he worked behind the partition in the shop, in collaboration with his father, on initial ideas. The quality of his work can be assessed from the fact that at the Pushkin Exhibition arranged by Serge Lifar in Paris in 1937, his portrait of the poet was adjudged the best existing likeness of him. In the absence of his father it was to him and to his brother Agathon that all ideas, projects and designs, emanating from the studios, for new objects, were submitted, and it was they who made the final examination of finished new objects before they were put out on display.

Since the Revolution, from January 1921, Eugène has lived in Paris, where in association with his brother, Alexander, Andrea Marchetti, an Italian born in Moscow and formerly associated with the Moscow Branch of Fabergé, and Giulio Guerrieri, formerly of the jewellery firm of Th. Lorié in Moscow, under the name of Fabergé et Cie, he has carried on business as a jeweller and goldsmith, acting as agent for the sale of Fabergé objects, and undertaking the repairing of them even to re-enamelling, with which he has had success. In making this mention of Eugène and Alexander Fabergé and their present harbourage in France one cannot but be impressed by the fact that some families are but the sport of time, she flings them out, roots them and then uproots them just as the fancy takes her, whereas others she leaves alone for a thousand years.

And now for the Branches of the House. That in Moscow, established in 1887, was the most important. Here were the large silver workshops of the firm, making silver objects of every description, including table silver, *surtouts-de-table*, and so on. There were large workshops, too, for the making of jewellery and objects of fantasy. When opening this branch, Fabergé took into partnership *Allan Bowe*, an Englishman born in South Africa, who was assisted by his brothers *Arthur* and *Charles*. Bowe may have had something to do with the branches at Odessa and Kieff, but he had no interest in the St. Petersburg Establishment, which Fabergé reserved to his own control entirely.

The partnership between Fabergé and Allan Bowe was dissolved in 1906 and *Otto Jarke*, a German from Moscow, was appointed manager. When he left the firm, *Andrea Marchetti*, a specialist in silver work and precious stones, became manager. Later, and up to 1918, when the firm was broken up by the Bolsheviks, *Alexander Fabergé*, the third son of Carl, was manager. His speciality, like that of his brother Eugène, was designing.

I have no information when the Odessa Branch was founded. Its first managers were *Allan Gibson*, a Moscow Englishman, and *Ivan Antony*, a native of the Baltic. After them came *George Piggott*, another Moscow Englishman, and after him *George Kral*, a Czech born in Russia. After the death of Kral, *Zinovieff*, a Russian, became the last manager.

The Branch at Kieff was founded in 1905, but only existed for five years until 1910, when it was closed down in order to concentrate the whole of the South Russian business of the firm in the older established branch in Odessa. For the period of its existence the management was in the hands of *Vladimir Drugoff*.

Lastly, London. This representation began in a very small way when in 1903 Allan Bowe sent his brother Arthur from Moscow with a selection of wares mostly drawn from the Moscow Branch, and the first business done was from Berners Hotel. Later a Branch of the Moscow business was opened at Portman House, Duke Street, Grosvenor Square, under the management of *Arthur Bowe*,* and afterwards removed to 32 Old Burlington Street. In 1906, after the dissolution of partnership with Allan Bowe, Carl Fabergé opened a Branch of his St. Petersburg House at 48 Dover Street, Piccadilly, under the joint management of *Nicholas Fabergé*, his fourth son, and *H. C. Bainbridge*, the present biographer, and later, after the death of King Edward VII, removed it to 173 New Bond Street, where it carried on business until shortly after the beginning of the First Great War.

It must be said that Carl Fabergé himself took no interest whatever in the sale of Fabergé wares in London until he opened a Branch entirely under his sole control. For the first time he became personally represented abroad, and the Branch, under instructions from St. Petersburg, became the outpost from which all Fabergé interests were carried forward throughout the world; to the Siamese Court in Bangkok, to the Maharajahs of India, to China, Rome, Paris, Cannes and so on. Those in charge of the expeditions were Alexander Fabergé, Nicholas Fabergé, Norman Wall, an Englishman, and R. W. Bainbridge, another Englishman, the brother of the present writer. But long before Fabergé wares were sold in London, the Romanoffs were in the habit of sending them to their relatives and

* As so many of my friends have asked me how I came to be associated with Fabergé, perhaps I should make a personal intrusion to say that while recovering from lead poisoning (contracted when working out the Bischof white lead process for Dr. Ludwig Mond) at Bushey Heath in 1904, I met a girl, Violet Powell by name. She sent me to her uncle, Arthur Bowe, and it was in consequence of this chance introduction that I became associated with the House of Fabergé.

friends. Queen Victoria herself must have received many, and choosing a gift for this Great Little Lady was no easy matter.

There was yet another source of introduction beyond the Romanoffs, and that was the City of London. Here, as in everything else, London was to the fore. Ever since 'certain grave and wise citizens of London' in the middle of the Sixteenth Century subscribing twenty-five pounds apiece to a total of six thousand pounds, fitted out three ships, the *Buona Esperanza*, the *Edward Bonaventure* and the *Buona Confidenza* to search for and discover a north-eastern passage to new and unknown countries, the merchants and bankers of the City of London have always cultivated a thirst for distant enterprise and it has been their endeavour 'to prove that commerce is the fulfilment of the command of the great and Almighty God who hath given unto mankind such an heart and desire that every man desireth to join friendship with other, to love and to be loved; also to give and receive mutual benefits'.*

It was in search of this same 'love' and 'to give and receive' these same mutual benefits that at the end of the Nineteenth Century and the beginning of the Twentieth, certain merchants and bankers of the City engaged themselves with much business in Russia. The second Lord Revelstoke was one of the foremost; Robert Younger, K.C., who became Lord Blanesburgh (this time it was 'the Law'), was another; William Koch de Gooreynd of Panmure Gordon was another; John Blessig, Sir Vincent Caillard, a Mr. Armstrong of the big engineering firm of Bruce Peebles & Co., Ltd., and many more. They travelled to and fro and on their return brought back with them gifts for their English friends which they had chosen at Fabergé's in Petersburg and Moscow.

The final downfall of the House of Fabergé in 1918, after being established in Russia for seventy-six years, when the Bolsheviks nationalised the firm by closing it down and confiscating as many precious stones and wares as they could put their hands upon, is a story of grief, of a brave but broken heart, and is best left for description in the next chapter which I have devoted to 'Fabergé, the Man'.

---

* *First forty years of Intercourse between England and Russia,* 1553-1593, by George Tolstoy. Published in St. Petersburg, 1875.

CHAPTER II

PETER CARL FABERGÉ, THE MAN

IN a recent review of Mr. Herbert Weinstock's book, *Tchaikovski*, Mr. Ernest Newman says this: 'The theory that life sometimes imitates art finds a good deal of support in Tchaikovski's story. . . . Tchaikovski apparently plunged into that senseless marriage because the man in him was unconsciously taking his cue from the artist. . . . At a later date, when engaged on his Manfred Symphony, he told a friend that "under the influence of the gloomy Manfred" he had been "nervous and full of spleen all summer long".'

But art by no means holds the monopoly of the ability to incite peculiarity in a man. Every trade shares it, and not at special moments of stress only, but continuously, shaping in men characteristics which distinguish them from their fellows. Every occupation has its particular mood, gloomy, cheerful, harassing, delightful, pompous, murderous, loving, humble, and so on.

The Church, the Stage, Medicine, the Law, the Turf, all have their peculiar personalities well known to everyone of us.

But if I were asked what trade or craft which under a certain condition was most likely to produce the most peculiar man of all, the man who has something in him particularly his own, I should say it was that of the goldsmith and jeweller. No calling so subjects a man to discipline, so binds him down to detail and attention to small things, or offers so limited an area for the display of his activities. Indeed, he works in miniature, with a magnifying glass to his eye, and he sees small things magnified.

But if the man so employed is not just a mere man, but one possessed of a most sensitive nature, then it is that you encounter most certainly, a being apart.

Such a man was Carl Fabergé. If you would know him you must always think of him with a magnifying glass to his eye and an amplifier to his ear, whether at work or play, seeing and hearing things which the average man rarely sees and never hears. Acutely conscious of the rudiments and mainsprings of life, he took things as they were presented to him, one by one. Each individual man and thing counted, but the sum of them not at all.

You get a pretty good picture of Fabergé when I say that what the ordinary man does he avoided doing. Writing letters; talking unnecessarily; attaching importance to legal documents, and to corporations of men banded together for the protection of some special interest; studying banking accounts and sales sheets; talking politics; and so on—if men thought of these things as important, well, let them go on thinking in that way, it was not for him to interfere; but as for himself, it was as though he said: 'In these things I see nothing but complications, so let me go my own way and do not interfere with me'.

Fabergé possessed many faculties which contributed to his success, but the chief undoubtedly was his sense of humour. The ready recognition of the ridiculous

PLATE 17

(*Top*) CIGARETTE CASE. In translucent steel blue enamel on gold, bordered in white-opal enamel, rose-diamonds and 10 larger diamonds. Miniature of Nicholas II surrounded by rose-diamonds. Measurements: $3\frac{3}{4}$ in. × $2\frac{1}{2}$ in. × $1\frac{3}{16}$ in. Given by Tsar Nicholas II to General Trepoff.
(*From Queen Mary's Collection.*)

(*Below*) CIGARETTE CASE. In translucent pale yellow enamel on gold, bordered in translucent green, red, white-opal and opaque white enamels. Miniature of Peter-the-Great's statue, by Zuieff, dated 1913, bordered in translucent red and opaque white enamels. Diamond thumb-piece. Measurements: $3\frac{5}{8}$ in. × $\frac{9}{16}$ in.
(*From Queen Mary's Collection.*)

PLATE 18

BASKET OF LILIES OF THE VALLEY
Flowers in pearls and rose-diamonds: leaves in nephrite: stalks in gold. Basket and moss in gold. Measurements: $8\frac{1}{2}$ in. $\times$ $7\frac{1}{2}$ in. $\times$ $5\frac{7}{8}$ in.
(*By courtesy of Messrs. Wartski.*)

PLATE 19

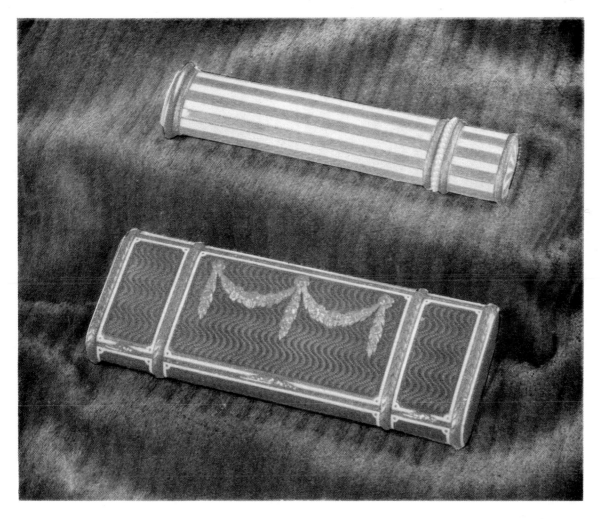

(*Top*) SEALING WAX HOLDER. In translucent green and white enamels, mounted with gold leaf
borders and pearls. Length: $4\frac{1}{4}$ inches.
(*Below*) NÉCESSAIRE. In enamel on silver, bordered in opaque white enamel, garland in different
coloured golds and rose-diamonds. Rose-diamond thumb-pieces. Length: $4\frac{7}{16}$ inches.
(*Both objects in the Collection of Lady Zia Wernher.*)

PLATE 20

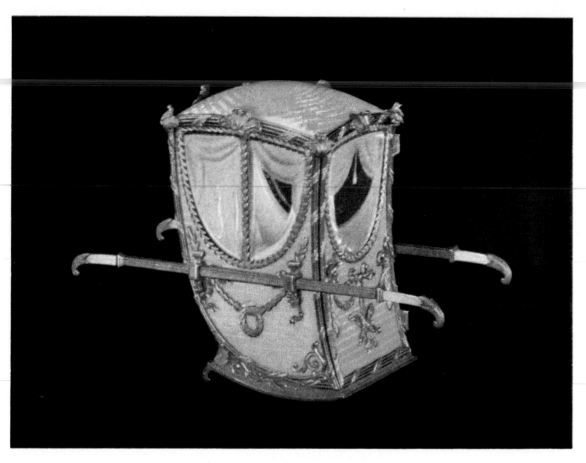

SEDAN CHAIR (WORKING MODEL)

In pink translucent enamel on gold. Mountings in red and green gold. Windows in rock crystal, engraved. Inside furnishings in mother-of-pearl and poles in red and green gold, with ends in mother-of-pearl. Measurements: 3 in. × 2 in. × $1\frac{5}{8}$ in. Length of poles: $4\frac{7}{16}$ inches.

(By courtesy of Messrs. Wartski.)

gave him that sense of proportion which carried him so triumphantly through all his trials and irritations and he had many. But not only did he enjoy the humour of a situation, he had the knack of communicating it to others, and more often than not without a smile. Here are the bare facts of one such communication.

There was nothing of the gun or 'tally-ho' about Carl Fabergé. To imagine him behind the butts with a couple of loaders at his side is preposterous and it is equally ridiculous to think of him shooting over dogs. Nevertheless, strange to say, he once went bear shooting. As told by Fabergé it was a wonderful story, but one can only say it concerned a sort of chicken-house on wheels, with a round opening for a gun and a door which could be securely fastened. This was moved up to the vicinity of the bear and into it jumped the sportsman, who was to shoot the bear, a small pig and The Last of the Great Craftsmen. The sportsman having secured the door then kicked the pig and the bear approached attracted by the squeals. As the punishment increased so the bear came nearer and nearer and the pig relieved itself continuously and voluminously in a corner. Russians always leave their stories on an imaginary note, and so I leave this one.

One can approach Fabergé in another way. We all have moments which stand out for ever memorable, when all the hurly-burly of things seems to stand still and we are in unison with our surroundings. Such moments stretch out towards something indefinable when the perfect moment seems just on the point of happening. It is as though, for just a twinkling, we catch the beginnings of some haunting melody, but which owing to our frailty we are unable to develop. We stand, it may be, on some high moorland on a hot August afternoon and listen to the bees buzzing in the heather and as we listen we hear the distant sounds of the valley below, the sounds muted and the valley half-hidden from us in a haze of shimmering sunlight.

For most of us these moments serve but to punctuate our life, for Fabergé, if I know anything at all about him, they merged continuously one into another. There was about him that which Zangwill has expressed as 'simply being', but in his case an intense 'being', or I would rather say, 'wholly being'. There was a completeness in his way of living in which scrupulous behaviour towards his fellowmen was for him just as necessary to the attainment of his end as his artistic endeavours. I often thought of him as going through life touching wood for fear the spell might break. It was as though he was fully conscious of the flood of good things which carried him on and that he must do nothing which might cast him high and dry on the bank. There was an element of sane uncertainty about him, that it was just as well not to be too cocksure of anything. In nothing was he over-serious. And this was not born of irresolution, but of an understanding that in a world of 'infinite difference' there were many forces at work.

He always lived therefore very much to the point, confining himself to the business of the moment. The whole man was sharpened and there was no waste about his actions or his speech. When he worked, he worked; when he ate, he ate; and when he talked, if one word would do instead of two, he used it, and if a gesture were better still, he limited himself to that. But in everything he did and said he left something over for the next adventure. Well do I remember at a dinner party, feeling out of the conversation, I rashly took a plunge and addressing him, said: 'I see Lord Swaythling is dead'. 'And who may Lord Swaythling be?' he asked. 'A banker', I replied. And then came the devastating question: 'And what can I do with a dead banker?'

About his dress Fabergé was punctilious in his own particular way, that is, he rarely if ever wore black but favoured well-cut tweeds with the coat of tails, the whole finished off with just a slight show of clean linen. There was an air of the country gentleman about him, at times he reminded one of an immaculate gamekeeper with large pockets.

I never heard Fabergé say one word about an after life, but from all his words and actions there was only one thing to be inferred: that whatever immortality there was laid up for him arose out of his mortality. I never heard him speak ill of anyone and could only conclude that he kept good things constantly before him and of the bad he never gave a thought.

Taking him all in all, Fabergé came as near to a complete understanding of human nature as it is possible for a man to come, with one word only inscribed on his banner, and that word—tolerance. There is no doubt whatever that this consideration for the worth of others was the foundation of his success. It was the means whereby he radiated his artistic greatness among the 700 craftsmen and staff working with him. In no other way could thousands of objects have been made with the same feeling and finish running through each one of them.

It is curious, that we find no limit to evil. We never say something is 'too bad to be true', and our interest never flags in any recitation of it, but we can soon get too much of a good thing. For some reason we think it not quite nice to be thoroughly good. It is too near perhaps to what we suppose to be divine for us to allow untarnished goodness to poor human nature. More than anything else, I think, it was the knowledge that sooner or later I would come to the question of the goodness of Fabergé which made me so chary to undertake this record of him. I felt I would never be able to put his 'goodness' before a reader in such a way that it would be readily understood what it really amounted to. I would be put down as a hero worshipper and the Craftsman as precious.

But I am in the thick of it now and must make some attempt. If we are to find some explanation for the goodness of Fabergé, and his success is reason enough for trying, we must go once again to his sense of humour, his sense of the ridiculous. Shortly put, I would say this, when anything presented itself to be done, he never thought of it as 'bad' or 'good', as generally defined, but as silly and stupid or not silly and not stupid. And with that said I must leave readers to their own meditations.

The fact that Fabergé was so different from the ordinary run of men was no stumbling block to me. It was the more reason for fitting myself into his scheme of things as soon as possible. The men into whose company I had been fortunate enough to be drawn, and their achievements, had always been fantastic. Coming to Fabergé straight from four years' close association with Corvo (Frederick William Rolfe), when he was writing *The Chronicles of the House of Borgia* and *Hadrian VII*, was only like passing from one stepping-stone to another. To pass

26

from the fantasy of using brilliant words to one of no words at all was only to further one's education. Fantasy was more than ever in the air, and the fact that Fabergé had made such an enormous success made it all the more commendable.

But please do not think I had a monopoly of the fairy tale; it was common knowledge in the studios, offices and workshops. More than this, each man felt himself to be part and parcel of it. 'Have you heard the latest about Carl Gustavovitch?' was an everyday question, and then someone would give his latest experience. I well remember recounting to him some particularly dirty business, only to get the reply: 'But men must live!'

He bore cheerfully with those who would draw him into conversation with inane remarks, but they served to sharpen his wit, and it was part of the entertainment in St. Petersburg to listen to him. 'My dear Fabergé', said King Ferdinand, 'if you were in Bulgaria I would make you my minister', and the reply, 'No, no, your Majesty, not politics, I beg of you; but minister of the goldsmith's art, why yes, Sire, if you will it'.

That is Fabergé in St. Petersburg, the easy, comfortable Fabergé, master of the ready word, at home with potentates and princes from whatever quarter of the globe they came. There in his native city you saw him at his best, for he was of the very essence of that 'Tiara of Towers' where everything moved with an easy dignity and courtesy and manners were at their peak. But take him out of his locality, not on holiday but on business bent, and you get quite a different Fabergé. Take him to London on such a mission and a sudden change takes place. Out of his native air he would wilt.

So to London. But before we transport him let us take a look at this outpost of the House of Fabergé in the West.

When the craftsman was at the height of his fame, that is in the time of King Edward VII, when his card was a passport of admission to all palaces and embassies, wherever they might be, he personally was quite unknown in the largest city of the world. There was nothing extraordinary in this, for you, readers, will have noticed that the best of everything has a way of secluding itself. It avoids publicity and prefers to make itself known to a few rather than to the many. The best has always to be sought for, and paradoxically enough this desire for secrecy is shared by every living soul. It is innate in every man and woman. There is nothing which takes such a hold on us as being the depository of something unknown to the many and then doling it out in small quantities to the few.

It was therefore as it should be that Fabergé should be out of the way in London. At the height of King Edward's reign his establishment was to be found on the first floor of 48 Dover Street, Piccadilly. On either side of the main entrance was written FABERGE in small letters, but no indication anywhere to show the sort of thing which was to be seen upstairs.

When I first took these rooms for Fabergé I made every arrangement for the easy and ceremonious reception of those calling. When a visitor arrived he was supposed to walk into the lift, the commissionaire was supposed to touch a button ringing a bell in the rooms above, and upstairs we were supposed to jump to attention and throw open the door and usher in the caller with all ceremony.

But it never worked like that. In those days Kings and Queens and Royal Princes, I found out afterwards, rarely used lifts outside their palaces, but walked upstairs and knocked on the door with their knuckles. It used to be exciting. Was it the postman or the Shah of Persia? It became so exciting and appeared to be so in keeping with my royal visitors' expectations that I never made any alteration in our procedure. So everyone kept on knocking on the door.

To call these rooms 'showrooms' or 'galleries' would not be fair to them; they were far too modest for such glorification. A 'backwater' is a better term, for it was here, quite unknown to the passing crowd in Piccadilly, that Kings put aside their crowns, that ambassadors, maharajahs and magnates of all kinds, gay lords, grave lords, law-lords, and the lords of the Daily Press, together with the throng of Edwardian Society, cast off their chains of office, and leaving the main-stream of their activities for a while, spent a cool and refreshing half-hour.

And Queens, too, and of course I should have put them first, one Queen in particular, Alexandra of England; since it was for her that Fabergé made his modest gesture. The rooms were hers, so that she might come and go at her pleasure and see what Fabergé was doing at the time. One late afternoon in particular I remember when she brought with her the King and Queen of Norway, the King of Greece, the King of Denmark, if I remember rightly, Princess Victoria and Miss Charlotte Knollys. It is always the little things which stick in one's memory. 'May we open the drawers?' the Queen asked.

And Queen Mary and King George V, when they were Princess and Prince of Wales, often came too. The Prince sometimes came alone at eleven o'clock in the morning, accompanied by Viscount Crichton. And again it is the little thing that one remembers. On one occasion, picking up a pair of opera glasses, quite small and only fit for ladies, the Prince said 'Do they work?' He put them to his eyes, focussed a notice in a tavern opposite and read, 'Your beer will be dearer'. 'Look, Crichton', he said, 'you can see quite well'. And Viscount Crichton: 'Yes, Sir, quite'.

And to 'Mrs. Leopold's' (Rothschild) 'May I come in?' I always felt inclined to reply, 'Yes, Madam, please do, and burgle the lot'.

So the days went by, especially in the 'Season'. It was good to be in London then on a sunny June morning, and better still to be oneself. Nobody can ever have had such a delightful job, so easy, so fortunate. To be the keeper of the cave into which cigarette cases, fluted and ribbed in all manner of shades of gold, in mint condition, and by the dozen, and every kind of thing to delight the fancy and the eye, made by the greatest craftsman of his day and dropped daily as it were from heaven; to be the arbiter as to who should have this and who that; to deal with those who with *grâce d'état* always gave one the impression that you and not they were 'top dog'; to read in the newspapers that such and such interesting people had arrived in London and to know that before they left they were bound to come your way without the slightest effort on your part; to control a business which had nothing to do with the seamy, black side of life, the ills, suspicions, sorrows and dark depths of human nature, but to be constantly in the light of bright and happy doings, was to live in a 'Fabergé in Wonderland' of one's own.

Not that the Aftermaths, those who had passed through the Valley and had come out smiling, did not sometimes come one's way. They did. Two in particular, I remember.

About six o'clock in the evening of the second day of December 1910, I was just shutting up the shop when a youth, accompanied by the Marquis de Soveral, came in. He was deathly pale, but not unnerved. It was impossible to mistake his bearing. I had never seen anything like it, and perhaps never will again. 'Manners are the happy way of doing things.' He was so easy and moved as no other youth had moved before. I felt inclined to say to him: 'Sire, walk in, please, just once again'. He was just of age, his name was Manoel, he had been a King but was a King no longer.

Take one other flash, which may be called 'The Last of the Fairy Tales'.

An old Lady of nearly ninety dressed in black, stands at the door. She supports herself with a stick and her lady-in-waiting is in very close attendance. She is the Empress Eugénie, the Tragic Empress, as she has been called.

She has come to buy a box, she says, yet no sooner is she seated than she asks how many assistants I have and may she see them? When they line up in front of her she wishes to know just what each of them intends to do with his life, whence he has come, and why he is doing his present job. And then she picks out two and out comes the question 'How is it you are not in the Navy? Strong healthy boys like you. Why, there is only one place for you'. And then we listen to the panegyric. She should have toured the country to awaken the wobblers. As she hammers out her points I watch her fingers. She wears black gloves and not one of her fingers comes to the end of them, so that when she presses the table, five loose black tabs protrude from the end of each hand.

If she likes the Navy, I like the tabs. They seem like the records of her life all turned over, finished with and flattened out. Like her glories, they belong to the past. Never again will twelve Emperors and Kings, six ruling Princes, six Heirs-Apparent and one Viceroy ride out to do her homage and kiss those fingers. No longer is she Eugénie at the Saluting Point, the Empress of the 'Eau de Nil', 'the blending of the green and grey, the silver sheen of the Nile by moonlight'. No longer is she Queen Regent of France, setting all the world aflame with her beauty, making every whim a fashion and every step a dance.

She has come merely to buy a box. And then she puts her left hand on the table. Empress of Splendour, she is Empress of Sorrow, too. 'Sédan! Vive la République!' 'Flight and Itelezi'. A barren land, a torrid sun; wind and rain and fever. Prostrate in prayer at the fatal spot and Zulus dancing around her.

'Mais, voyez-vous', she said at the summit of her glory, 'it is not easy always to find questions to ask', and again, 'I told you I died in 1870'; and once again, 'I am just an old fluttering bat, nothing more, but like the butterflies I have always to be in the sunshine'.

I choose the last Empress of the French for this flash partly because she drank to the dregs the bitterest draught that perhaps has ever been offered to the lips of a woman, and took it with the smile she never lost, and partly because the caval-cade, as it passed in and out of 48 Dover Street, is seen in epitome in her, for she had run the whole gamut of life, up and down. And she was of such great age. But this is not to say that the place was dedicated to her, for as I have said before, it was to the then Queen of England, Alexandra, that Fabergé made his modest gesture, and it was for the purpose of satisfying himself that it had been made fitting to receive her that he made his memorable visit to London on January 29th, 1908. A visit fraught with bewilderment.

Queen Alexandra had said to me sometime before: 'If Mr. Fabergé ever comes to London you must bring him to see me'. After lunch on the day of his arrival seemed to be the right time to speak to him. This was the conversation which followed:

Fabergé. 'The Queen wants to see me. What for?'

Myself. 'Well, you know what an admirer she is of all your things. She wants to see you, that's all.'

Fabergé. 'Nonsense! Besides, she will have forgotten all about it by now and won't want to be troubled.'

Myself. 'But really, Mr. Fabergé, she did give me that message. If she should hear you have been in London and have not informed her, it will be very awkward to explain.'

Fabergé. 'But I am *en voyage* and I have no clothes. Look at me, I cannot go like this! There is my son Nicholas and yourself.'

Myself. 'Yes, I know, but we are not you. Come, do let me write to Miss Knollys to tell her you are here, or I could telephone straight away.'

It was no use. We walked back to Dover Street. He asked when the next train left for Paris and within half-an-hour was gone.

There was no question here of disrespect for his Royal Patroness, around whom for him everything in England revolved and on whose account he had just made the journey from St. Petersburg. Fabergé was out of his locality, that was all, a locality so strong in its influence on his super-sensitive nature that when he was left without its support he was drained of that superb and easy confidence natural to him at home in Russia.

But his whole attitude was that he had a certain job in hand and when that was finished there was no more to do. Shakespeare has him perfectly:

> 'We come not to offend
> But with good will. To show our simple skill
> That is the true beginning of our end'.

I must admit that even after over a year's experience of Fabergé this was an outcome which I had not expected, and yet when the disappointment had gone and I thought it over, it was all in tune with the man. The only way was never to expect the normal, but to construct a topsy-turvy world in which everything was not as it was but as we all would have it, as in our dreams, and then to put him and oneself into it, and make up one's mind to enjoy it thoroughly.

Just over a year previously I had had my first experience of Fabergé and that was topsy-turvy enough to satisfy the most exacting taste. It is not part of this record to go into all the details of how I came to be associated with him. Suffice it to say that the story began on the moors of Teesdale, when I was ten years old, with an intense desire to go to Russia, and when there was not the slightest likelihood that I would ever get there, and ended when I walked into 24 Morskaya, St. Petersburg, in October 1906, at the age of thirty-two, without my having made the slightest effort to get there.

My dream had come true. As I look back on the story it is not the intensity of the original desire which astonishes one so much to-day, but the fact that the thought came into one's head at all. Every writer, or at any rate those who have had a struggle, and who has not, knows what I am driving at. He or she comes to a dead end and waits, maybe until next morning when 'something comes into their heads'. Is it from a fount within them or from outside? That is the question. All others sink into insignificance beside it.

In one's own case perhaps it was a picture or a story which suggested the thought. Or perhaps the best that is in the world is drawn to the child rather than to those of mature age and for very obvious reasons. But however we may surmise, the hard fact remains it is the strong man in man who always nearly destroys the world and the babe in him who saves it. And when that is exhausted by sheer starvation, the Fates step in and take a hand.

Mankind can never make the complaint that it is dealt with other than faithfully.

I for my part can only say I have been treated in a most generous fashion. The fairy-tale which had landed me so successfully in St. Petersburg developed into reality the moment I arrived there, and in a quite astonishing manner.

While attempting to take the measure of the great Craftsman I must tell you, reader, that up to the time of meeting him I had no knowledge whatever of diamonds and emeralds and of goldsmithery in general, and that I was completely ignorant of the ways of Kings and Queens except from history books. Being a coalminer and research chemist there was nothing about me to suggest that I might be of use to one of the most exclusive businesses in the world. I walked into 24 Morskaya, therefore, feeling very much like the proverbial lamb.

But the Craftsman had his troubles, too, as I learned afterwards. He was then at the very zenith of his fame and his affairs had outgrown by leaps and bounds the area in which he would have confined them had he had his way. To cover the world was no part of his attitude towards his work, he would rather have limited it to the area he could himself control. So, owing to circumstances, he was bound to appoint a representative. But it was much more than this, he had to find someone to whom he could transmit his personality, his way of thinking and acting; someone who, for the sake of the art of Fabergé, would obliterate himself, his interests and his name, if success were to be the outcome. Now this was taking place every hour of the day among his staff and workmen; it was an automatic process and he was unconscious of its working. But when it came to making a conscious effort in this direction it was another matter, and to a man of Fabergé's

31

sensitive nature it was an ordeal. For such a man to hand over to another his name and his honour (nothing mattered to him more than this), at his time of life must have been torture.

Now if the Craftsman had been the ordinary bargaining, questioning, accumulating business man, I should have stood no chance with him whatever, but he was not. He accepted the human material which came his way and made the best of it. Certainly, I had been recommended to him and he had sent me his telegram to come to Russia, but it would have been the same if I had just walked in and offered myself.

So, reader, you must content yourself with the fact that two personalities, one age 60 and the other 32, met and there was no more ado. He put on his hat and coat and out we went. And so began a preparation for a very serious business undertaking which perhaps has no parallel for fantasy. For six weeks we went here, there and everywhere. The sole idea, as far as I could make out, was that I should gain some knowledge of Russia. We walked along the Neva Embankment and gazed at the spire of Peter and Paul disappearing like a pin-point in the sky; we took a droshky up the Nevski Prospect to the Monastery of St. Alexander Nevsky; we spent much time at the Hermitage Museum and among the treasures he pointed out were miniature reproductions of the Imperial Crown, Sceptre and Orb, the work of his house, and doubly interesting because they were the only objects in the Museum given a place there during the lifetime of the craftsman concerned; he pointed out the painted signs over and about the shop windows; we examined the ikons at the Kazan Cathedral, went to St. Isaac's, stood before Peter the Great's monument, roamed the forest at Levaschova on Sunday mornings, picked up skeleton leaves, watched *riabchicks* in the trees and in the evenings the setting sun through the firs and silver birches—we did all of these things and many more, eating of the best Petersburg had to offer and drinking fine wines, exchanging very little in the way of conversation, with never one word of business said except when I grasped a bonbonnière like a piece of coal, which made him shiver.

So it went on until the day of my departure. I went in to say good-bye to him and he put on his hat and coat and drove with me to the station, something, I was afterwards told, he had never been known to have done before. Up and down the platform we walked and never a word. And then just as the train was on the move he pulled down my head and whispered. Two words he said, 'Be noble', and quickly turned away as though ashamed of such an outburst.

My education was finished, and thus I came to represent one of the most sensitive, gentle and understanding of men whom it has been my lot to know.

I have said that Fabergé was never over-serious, I think that was his best quality. He took life with a ripple, and now and again with a splash which could be a little disconcerting. There was no stench of stagnant water about him. We have had him at work, let us look at him at play.

St. Petersburg in its golden days was noteworthy for many things but in nothing was it happier than in practical joking, and if out of a joke you could stage a pageant so much the better, even if, as it sometimes did, it cost quite a lot of money. Fabergé had a friend called Koenig who had a factory of some sort. Having installed a lot of new machinery and plant, Koenig invited his friends, Fabergé among them, to inspect the installation. On arrival Fabergé noticed a large copper boiler lying on a heap of waste material. 'Surely you are not going to throw that away, it would fetch a lot of money', he said to Koenig. On leaving, Fabergé again drew his friend's attention to the boiler: 'Mind you do something about it', he said in a joking manner. Some days afterwards if you had been in the Nevski Prospect you would have seen a large lorry drawn by four horses all gaily caparisoned and holding up the traffic. On the lorry was the boiler garnished with laurel leaves and flowers on the way to the Craftsman as a gift.

Carl Fabergé had another friend called John who lived at Saratov on the Volga. One summer his friend visited him in Petersburg. Said Carl: 'John, for twenty years you have sent me caviare at Christmas but there are other things in Russia, camels for example'. Later in the year a gaily dressed Kalmuck arrived in St. Petersburg bearing a letter which read: 'My Dear Carl, you asked me for a camel. I have sent you one'. And sure enough, standing in the street was the camel, as odd a sight as if it had been in Bond Street or Fifth Avenue.

And then there is the story of how Fabergé viewed the coronation procession of the last Tsar. He unearthed a four-wheeler which turned out to be past its prime. During the course of the journey, the bottom fell out, but its occupant continued on foot, still inside the cab.

There you have something of the humour of the man. Like a body with catalytic properties, his mere presence re-acted on others, bringing an assembly of people up to the bubble when it otherwise might have gone very flat. He never lost an opportunity to keep things going in light-hearted fashion. Once at a dinner party, noticing that I was not getting on very hopefully with my German partner, he brought in a Hindustani dictionary and placing it between us said, 'Perhaps that will help you'. Again it was waste of a good thing to give you fine wines unless you prepared your palate. If he had an extra fine after-dinner wine to give you, he would kick you gently under the table to stop you drinking coffee, and if it was a fine port he had to offer he had a small salt cellar ready so that you might take a tiny pinch to clear your palate between each sip. Away from his work he relaxed all the time. Even at work you, reader, will have gathered he was never too tightly bound, always, as it were, waiting on something. It was this loose grip on everything which stood him in good stead at that tremendous moment of his life in September 1918 when, in a flash, all he possessed was taken from him. All cultured Russians are this way, they give up with the same grace that they enjoy, as hundreds of examples bear witness to this day.

Fabergé's finest possession was the House of Fabergé, and this stood for much more than the mere provision of a comfortable living for the family who owned it. Fabergé objects have attracted such widespread attention that the system under which they were produced has been largely overlooked. It is this system which was the chief glory of Fabergé. We shall hear more of it in the chapter on 'The Workmasters of Fabergé'. In the meantime there is this to be said, that when the Soviet Government dispossessed Fabergé they dispossessed seven hundred craftsmen of a means of working and living.

33

They prospered under a system which had gradually developed for seventy-six years. They lived, worked, ate and slept as it is man's desire to do these things. They wanted for nothing. The very thing which the Soviet was devised to inaugurate was already flourishing in Russia when the new régime came into being. Flourishing on a small scale, no doubt, but highly organised and intensive. A system under which every man was given full opportunity to express himself, and took it, for his own benefit and that of those working with him; simple to a degree but capable of unlimited expansion.

Yet it was this system which the Soviet ruthlessly, there is no other word, uprooted when it came to power. There was no sense in it as men understand sense. 'Nothing substantial can be done in a hurry', says Newman in his *Essays*. It was all part and parcel of the wholesale disintegration of established orders when men suddenly come to power, for the Sovereignty of God or the love of man, or so they persuade themselves, root up everything which has gone before, in the vain hope that they can forestall destiny by an entirely new order. It is a dangerous proceeding, as witness the case of France, which we only now begin to see.

I do not speak thus to carp. There is something due to me. I have paid my footing. For six years before the last great war, when the prestige of the Soviet was a heap of spent ashes, by printed word so far as my pen permitted, I extolled the Soviet, bringing my efforts to an end by an extensive tour of the United States of America in 1937-38. In epitome, I said, 'Here is a mighty nation, take heed'. But America, like England, took no heed. Will the Soviet have the sense to see their limitations in time? That is now the burden of what I have to say.

And so back to tragedy and September 1918. Reader, let all you know of bitterest grief take you by the hand. What counts now? A dead banker, an old copper boiler, a camel, a Hindustani dictionary, a bear, a squealing pig, a rotten cab bottom, a skeleton leaf, swirling snow, the setting sun between the firs and silver birches? Yes, and for everything. The broken heart had yet to come to him who had done so much to keep his fellow men on an even keel. I should have liked to have been able to give an hour to hour account of what happened on the fatal day when Fabergé gave up all and got away from Petrograd, or is it Leningrad by now, but I have no definite information. Hearsay there is. For instance I have heard that the Craftsman on being forced to leave his house of business and his home, only said this: 'Give me ten minutes to put on my hat and coat'. If these were his words then they would be in full accord with what was to be expected from him. But as I say, I do not know this as a fact. At any rate at this crucial moment there is no doubt that his sense of humour would come to his support. 'Humour is creative', I have read somewhere, and there are instances enough when men have bridged the abyss of insanity by their sense of the ridiculous.

But if I cannot point to the dramatic moment of Fabergé's departure, I can give some facts of general and particular interest of what was happening to the firm and its possessions just prior to the Revolution, at the beginning of it, and as time went on.

During the first great war, 1914-18, the workshops of the firm were gradually given over to the manufacture of small arms, and also parts for great projectiles in copper and aluminium, and medical supplies. The making of *objets d'art* got less and less and more austere as the war lasted. We shall see in the chapter devoted to the Imperial Easter Eggs how the egg delivered to the Empress Alexandra Feodorovna at Easter 1916 was severe indeed.

At the beginning of the Revolution Fabergé's shop was closed for a short while, but soon re-opened when sales continued. It is always interesting and comforting, too, I think, to note how the ordinary pursuits of ordinary men and women always persist however dreadful the upheaval which overtakes them. Men and women continue to marry, to have children and go about their ordinary business in face of all the difficulties they encounter.

Fabergé supported the Provisional Government, but it must have been under harassing restrictions, sometimes very stupid, as we shall see in the chapter on Imperial Easter Eggs. But however provocative the Provisional Government may have been, it was at least possible to parley with it, a state of affairs quite impossible when the Bolsheviks took control.

The philosophy of this record arises out of facts and where these are not within my own experience they have been drawn from first hand authoritative sources. In nothing have I been more careful than to find out the relations which existed between the firm of Fabergé and the Soviet Government. In particular I framed my questions, to those who were able to inform me at first hand, in such a way, and in the hope, that I might extract from the Soviet's behaviour to a small but nevertheless very significant portion of the teeming millions of Russia, and which had never violated by word or deed the high principle of a decent living for everybody, some indication of the benefits it was to bring to Russia and all mankind. Some sign that it was the intention of the Soviet to rule in the spirit of all good Russians, that is to say to give effect to those altruistic feelings, that sense of sharing everything which has always prevailed in Russia among aristocrat and peasant alike. (See *My Russian Memoirs*, Bernard Pares, 1931.)

But however I might twist the answers I received I have not been able to draw out of them one iota of hope that the Soviet means well by anyone or anything except that phantom IDEOLOGY. Over them all was written one word 'FORCE'. Time and again there was no opportunity given to twist at all, for that one word was the only one to appear and that in capital letters: 'NOTHING! ONLY FORCE!'— 'WITH THE GOVERNMENT OF THE BOLSHEVIKS IT WAS IMPOSSIBLE TO SPEAK!!!' —'The firm of Fabergé had existed nearly seventy-seven years and was then nationalized by the Bolsheviks, who then robbed it of what they could find on the premises'. Such have been the replies to my questions.

On the premises the Bolsheviks found the total stock of Fabergé less a very small portion which Eugène Fabergé managed to get away to Finland. Thus those responsible for the new régime became possessed of a rich mine of beautiful Fabergé objects for which they had not given the slightest compensation, and they lost little time in turning them into cash, using the same shop* for this purpose

*Mr. Emanuel Snowman, of Messrs. Wartski, can testify that the collection of Fabergé pieces, including some six Imperial Easter Eggs acquired by him in Russia and brought to London at various times from 1925 to 1939, was in fact purchased by him from the accredited Soviet agent at this very shop.

as that used by the Craftsman since 1900.* Whether by this time the Soviet has exhausted its stock of Fabergé objects or whether it now appreciates their value and is putting them away for a rainy day I do not know, but at any rate the Fabergé premises at 24 Morskaya are used by it to this day for the sale of *objets d'art*.

What I have said refers, of course, to the Head Establishment of Fabergé in St. Petersburg, but it applies equally to the Branch Establishments in Moscow and Odessa.

And that, reader, is as much as I can tell you. There is nothing in the account to lead one to imagine that the Craftsman's departure from his native city was for him a time of rejoicing. In mind and body he must have left it a stricken man.

And so, once again, back to tragedy and September 1918. In the dead of night, and why should we not think so for it was black enough, he left as a courier attached to a foreign Embassy. First to Riga; then when the Bolsheviks attacked this town he fled to Berlin. When revolution broke out there, he fled to Frankfort-on-Main, then to Homburg, and so to Wiesbaden, where in May 1920 he spent his seventy-fourth birthday surrounded by fifteen of his old Petersburg friends. It was here he began to say 'This is life no more'—words which he kept on repeating for the short time which remained to him. His heart was breaking now.

Shortly after his birthday he fell ill and Madame Fabergé, his wife, came from Lausanne and Eugène, his eldest son, from Stockholm to look after him. Madame Fabergé, too, had passed through tribulation. Leaving Petrograd secretly with Eugène in December 1918, first by rail, then by sledge for twenty kilometres, on foot by night through woods blocked with snow and carrying her bag, she came to Kexholm on Lake Ladoga, thence by rail to Terioki and on to Helsingfors. Here she parted company with Eugène and travelled via England to Lausanne.

When Carl Fabergé was well enough to be moved from Wiesbaden, with his wife and Eugène he journeyed to Lausanne where he arrived in June 1920. Here on Lake Geneva, rejuvenated with the splendid air, he began to feel a little more himself, even to taking excursions in the district to Ouchy, Nyon, Vevey, and Montreux with his grandson Peter.

But it was the last flicker of a fire which was fast burning out. He reviewed in retrospect the senseless uprooting of himself and all those with him. 'This is life no more', he kept on repeating. At the end of July he fell from weakness in his room and his friends put him to bed. Even now the indomitable spirit rallied; he interested himself in the news of the day and books were brought him from the library. On the morning of the 24th September, 1920, he died, having half-an-hour before smoked half a cigarette. His body was cremated at the Lausanne Crematorium.

Madame Fabergé died on the 27th January, 1925, at Cannes, and was buried in the Protestant Cemetery there.

In May 1930 Eugène brought the remains of his father from Lausanne and buried them in the grave with his mother, and following the wish of the Craftsman

* I have since learned that these same premises at 24 Morskaya were occupied by the Court jeweller, Ador, in the time of the Empress Elizabeth Petrovna.

he erected over them a tombstone of black Swedish porphyry with an inscription in golden letters. What that is I do not know, but it might well have been 'He was never over-serious'.

And now Carl Gustavovitch, the last word for yourself. Little did you and I dream as we went on our escapades that it would one day fail to my lot to make this record of you; but such is life. We are all destined to some deed and however we may put it aside it takes us by the hand at last and persuades us to the doing, sometimes it compels us. Do you remember that evening in St. Petersburg when we went for a walk after dinner? We came to cross-roads and you said 'I go to the right and you to the left'. What you meant I never knew, but when at last I found my way back to your study there you were, wrapping brown paper around your feet; you said they were so cold. I gave you my spats and you said 'They're for that, are they?'

Doe svidanya, Carl Gustavovitch.

CHAPTER III

THE ART AND CRAFT OF FABERGÉ

IN the execution of his work, Fabergé invoked the aid of many styles, and absorbed them all: the French of Louis XIV, Louis XV, Louis XVI, the Italian of the Renaissance, Old Russian and Greek. Some of his objects are in the 'art nouveau' manner, some are purely naturalistic, and some are caricatures; yet to-day all his work is embodied in a single style, recognized as 'Fabergé'. Whether the article is an animal in nephrite, a cigarette case in gold adorned in one of the French classic styles, some object in 'art nouveau', or a typically Russian figurine in a variety of stones, the same quality pervades them all, a quality so emphatic and distinctive that it admits of no error on the part of the seeing eye. I go further and say it is a quality which can be felt.*

Such is creation: and it stamps Carl Fabergé as the Master he was. What further is to be said is best stated in the words of his contemporaries. At the Paris Exhibition of 1900, where he exhibited his productions *hors concours* and received the award of the *Legion of Honour*, his work created a sensation. It was then that he was acclaimed by the goldsmiths of France: *Louis Quatorze; Louis Quinze; Louis Seize!* 'Where are they now?' they said, and themselves replied: 'In Petersburg, for we now call them "Fabergé".' England was equally happy in her recognition of him, for it was Mr. Leopold Davis, the art connoisseur, who proclaimed him 'The Last of the Great Craftsmen'.

Now I propose to take the verdict of the French goldsmiths as my text and to examine it in the hope that I may make clear in what this quality, which Fabergé managed to instil, as if by magic, into all his articles, consists, and why it is that it exerts such an attraction over all those who collect his objects. It is evident from the action of the Frenchmen that they did not mean that Fabergé had in some way appropriated their styles, and by some successful coup had made more objects and done more business than they themselves had done in France. The only meaning to be attached to what they said is that Fabergé, while still keeping their styles recognisable as such, had managed to do something to them which had enhanced their virtues.

This actually is what the craftsman did, and it is this 'something' which is his chief contribution to Art.

If to-day you ask someone well versed in Fabergiana (a dreadful word, but I use it because Fabergé matters have largely become a field of general interest and investigation) to tell you what this 'something' is, he will most likely say that it is something which his experience tells him is good, but which he cannot put into words, just as he knows very well the difference between a South African and a Brazilian diamond, but for the life of him cannot tell you in what it lies.

* The infinite variety of Fabergé's craftsmanship, both as regards objects and styles, will be seen in illustrations in Plates 13-48.

I propose to go further than this, and I hasten to add that though what I have to say is the result of my association with Fabergé, it is his contribution, not mine. He flowered in his works, not in speech. His mind was of that type which may be called centripetal, not centrifugal. As soon as a subject presented itself to him, it worked inwards to the root of the matter, not outward to the flower. He was no long-winded story-teller therefore, and learned to express himself concisely in the fewest of words, the meaning of which left no doubt whatever in the minds of his hearers.

In the first place I would say to any investigator that he must at once get off the material plane and on to one which is not material, as we understand this word, otherwise there will be no practical outcome to his enquiry and he will come to a dead end. To illustrate my meaning I return to the South African and Brazilian diamonds. Everyone will agree that whatever difficulty there may be in explaining in words the difference between these stones, one thing is certain: one is the product of South Africa and the other of Brazil. Further, to expect to find South African stones in Brazil and *vice versa* is to hope for the impossible. Still further, that the South African stone owes its specific qualities to certain physical conditions prevalent in South Africa and the Brazilian to the physical conditions prevailing in Brazil. But when you put forward the suggestion that the *genius loci* of any country can be just as potent as a creative force, and even more so, then it is that only the dreamer and the poet are fully with you. Having hit so many nails on the head long before the nails were there to hit, they know what you are talking about. To the many, you are living in the limbo of the lost in a fool's paradise.

And yet there is no need to travel far and wide in search of some demonstration of the power of locality. One has only to walk into a court of law, into the House of Commons, into a cathedral, go down a coal mine or, for a matter of that, walk into one's own home to be assured of the fact.

Writers on art to some extent acknowledge the existence of this power, but rarely do they emphasise it as a creative agent just as potent and concrete as rocks and soils.

And this brings me to Russia. By this time, you, reader, should have a very good idea which way we are going, so it will not come to you too suddenly when I say that the idiom of Russia is the idiom of Fabergé.

Nowhere in all the world is the 'spirit of place' more powerful than in this one-sixth of the total land surface of the earth. Here it is certainly no will-o'-the-wisp, for it takes you by the throat. Why it should be so potent, who can say? It may be due to its vast spaces, or to the snows, for there is no fertiliser like it. With four-fifths of Russia in Asia and one-fifth in Europe, here East and West actually do meet. As East meets West, so does the negative meet the positive; the alkaline, the acid; the heart, the will and the intellect, and all these cannot come together without some reaction taking place. May it not be that the 'spirit of place' partakes of some essence compounded of all these? Who can say? But to whatever the spirit of Russia is due, there is no gainsaying its potency and its magic.

And here, reader, it is well that you should take the next step in the company of another. No man has made a finer contribution to the understanding of Russia than Mr. Sacheverell Sitwell in his book, *Valse des Fleurs*. Here he describes a day in the St. Petersburg of 1868 in the time of Alexander II, and on page 53 he begins:

'It is to be remarked that the foreign shops have caught the spirit, or the *genius loci*. The Fidèle Bergère . . . has a lavish fantasy that it would not have in France. There is much display of the double-headed eagle. It appears, many times over, on the wrapping of every parcel; and there are inventions in the window that are pure Russian. It is thus with every Western art that has been transplanted to the Russian soil, from the cuisine à la Russe, so largely the work of Gouffet, chef-de-cuisine to Alexander II, to the buildings of Rastrelli, Charles Cameron, Quarenghi, or Thomas de Thomon. *In fact, the Russian style, like the style à l'espagnole, is largely a foreign creation. That is to say, after perhaps one generation of foreign inspiration, the Russians seized upon what had been discovered for them and carried it still further.'*

The italics are mine, for it is in these two sentences that you have it. First the sense to invite and accept direction, secondly the ability to transform that which is invited. And not *things* only, but first the men and the woman, for Catherine the Great is the outstanding example of what Russia is capable of doing to human beings. Born a German, she became more Russian than the Russians. As the first female figure of her time, History may well give her a still more exalted place. What the *genius loci* can do with Russians themselves has been well said by Gorki, already noted in Chapter I.

It was Peter the Great who first focussed the attention of the outside world on the inspiring force of locality in Russia. With him the first thing was to catch his man, then bring him to Russia, and once there the *genius loci* did the rest. Having transformed the man, he in turn transformed the thing.

We are here concerned with art, and it is well to waste no more time but fix our minds right away on the one thing which, so far, is the supreme example of Russia's magic. The Cathedral of St. Basil, in Moscow. It is the 'ALL in All', because it is in this 'complicated disorder' of bulbous domes and fantastic details supported by an abundance of gilding and colourings that Russia has not only set her riddle but at the same time answered it. The whole structure hypnotizes the beholder. The same applies to Falconet's statue of Peter the Great on the Neva, of which Diderot said in 1773: 'The first look arrests you . . . we give ourselves up to it . . . we examine nothing apart, we have not time to think. . . .'

But we are going too fast. We are not in the eighteenth century but in the fifteenth, or as near as may be. Nobody knows who built St. Basil's; possibly an Italian, like the Spaskoi Vorota, the 'Gate of the Redeemer', and the Uspenski Sobor, the Cathedral of the Assumption.

The intriguing thing about Russia is her *finesse*, and therefore, to the unperceiving minds of the western world she is, and always has been, a mystery. But no country has been so frank; by signs and symbols, ever since she started her borrowings from Byzantium, she has been at pains to put her writing on the wall. But she has asked for a little imagination from the beholder. Instead of putting her heart openly on the table, to change the metaphor, she has preferred that he should go in search of it. The best, therefore, that she has within her she has enshrined.

The magic building of St. Basil's is the archetype of thousands in Russia of a similar nature. It can lead you sadly astray, or be a shining light. If you allow yourself to be hypnotised by its outward Byzantine barbaric splendour then you will be lost, and among those who see in Russian art nothing but the Byzantine. If you are persuaded to look below the surface you will see that the outward form enshrines a great idea, the idiom of Russia, which is her own, and once having that firmly fixed in mind, you will come to see that this same idiom can take many forms. You will come out of darkness, that is, if you are of those who are groping about, into the light, and the art and craft of Fabergé will be as clear to you as the midday sun.

To bring about this happy ending let us go to Mr. Granville Fell. In the *Connoisseur* of March 1944, he says this:

'Why is it, we may wonder, that some shape or combination of shapes gives more satisfaction to the eye and mind than others? On their immediate impact, and without the least attempt at analysis, we accept without inquiry certain arrangements and dispositions which strike us as being in perfect harmony in all their parts and relations and of unchallengeable rightness.'

All this applies to St. Basil's exactly. In spite of its complicated disorder it strikes you as being unchallengeably right. That is the magic of it. And what is it which this rightness conveys to the seeing eye? Let Mr. Fell put the finishing touch, for he goes on to say:

'There is some all-embracing element which knits the entire work together and suggests strength, stability and completeness.'

And there you have it. I would only add that 'strength, stability and completeness' can be rounded off in one word, and that is *Substance*.

In St. Basil's is substance and it *is* substance, call it 'body', 'guts', an ability to tap the blood, to get down to the elements of what you will, which is the idiom of Russia; that which is her own, native to her, and is so strong that exotic art can, by some magic transformation, become as if indigenous. Before it can be fully grasped that the idiom of Russia is the idiom of Fabergé, there is just a step or two to take.

By some grim and grave misfortune men at large are rarely in the habit of looking below the surface, therefore all they have seen in St. Basil's and the host of buildings of a similar nature, has been an exhibition of barbaric gorgeousness, inflated grandiosity and pomp, all things truly Russian they have said.

Now these are things which ultimately lead to the disintegration of a nation and there is no doubt that by continually thinking of them the Chancelleries of Europe had become imbued with the idea that Russia sooner or later was bound to come to grief. Perhaps the wish was father to the thought. Be this as it may, from the time of Catherine I (the wife of Peter the Great and his successor on the throne) the habit grew up of belittling Russia and soon became a tradition—whatever the successes, whatever the defeats of this one-sixth of the total land surface of the earth, the one persistent outcry has been 'The Collapse of Russia is Imminent'.

Such hallucinations largely precluded the possibility of bridging the Tsarist and Soviet régimes and kept the same tradition alive, when wise men gave us of their wisdom between the two great wars. Then it was we had the illuminating headlines, 'The Wheat Gamble', 'The Oil Gamble', 'The Gamble of the Five Year Plan'. If Russia did not do away with herself, then nature would very obligingly do it for her, and so we had the headline: 'Nature's final blow to Bolshevist hopes.'

Now all this was the first consequence of a disease, which for a better name, I call 'Byzantinism', the main sympton of which was an obstinate belief that all things Russian ended in Moscow. Byzantium, Kieff, Novgorod, Moscow! All this was in the true apostolic succession, so it was said, and having once arrived in that city of bulbous domes, all Russia had come to a magnificent standstill, gorgeous and grandiose, but good for very little.

How sadly Petersburg, and by this time I should perhaps call it Petrograd, came to be forgotten! . . . Forgotten? No, for she became the Great Imperial Cocotte, the bastard of the capitals of Europe, the outcome of a great spirit gone wrong. To-day the belief is much the same, for we have been told that she has no reality whatever and is gone for evermore. It was this way of thinking which set all Western ideas awry between the two great wars and for years before. With the choice before it, between Petersburg and Moscow, between progress and decline, between good and evil, between life and death, the wisdom of the world, military, social, economic and artistic, chose Moscow. So was born the great miscalculation, the greatest perhaps which history will have to record.

But we must go back to 'substance'. Now that we have succeeded, or I hope so, in tracing this as far as Moscow, all that remains is to find it established in St. Petersburg and our job is finished. Fortunately there is no need for any special flights of imagination, or to put forward any personal experience, because Peter the Great, Elizabeth Petrovna and Catherine the Great have set the whole matter down into writing.

First, Peter. This colossus was in the habit of writing down exactly whither he was going for the guidance of those coming after him. At times he used paper, often stones, but best of all, bones. When in 1724 he removed the mortal remains of the Grand Duke Alexander Yaroslavitch, Prince of Novgorod, Grand Duke of Vladimir, St. Alexander Nevsky, from the Monastery of Vladimir where they had been at rest for four and a half centuries, brought them to St. Petersburg and entombed them in the Cathedral of the Trinity in the Monastery of St. Alexander Nevsky, built for this very purpose, he did the mightiest of all his deeds.*

By this one act purely Russian, he not only brought St. Alexander Nevsky

---

* For information on this as well as other matters concerning St. Petersburg consult *Palmyra of the North*, by Christopher Marsden.

but Rurik and Vladimir and Yaroslav, Dimitri of the Don, and all the rest, all that was of the best in old Russia, of Kieff, of Novgorod, of Moscow, and the whole mighty magic of Russia from the beginning, he brought all these things to life again and harnessed them to the new Russia, which was St. Petersburg. Henceforth, therefore, for Peter, Petersburg was everything: it was Russia in her stride. That was the message which, as though with some missile, he, the most colossal figure in Russian history, almost deified, discharged into the consciousness of posterity in the hope that it might awaken.

Elizabeth Petrovna, his irrepressible daughter and a Russian of the Russians, in order to put the seal upon the work of her gigantic father, did something equally significant. In 1752 she enshrined the relics of St. Alexander Nevsky in a silver sarcophagus weighing one and a half tons made from the then most precious metal, the first fruits of the mines of Kolyvan.*

And then came Catherine the Great. The Classic, the Universal, the Archetype of Russia's magic in flesh and blood. By a *coup de maître* only possible to genius, in bronze and granite she interpreted for futurity the intention and meaning of St. Basil's in a manner unmistakable.

In Falconet's monument to Peter the Great on the Neva, set up by this great Queen and accounted the greatest equestrian statue of modern times, the soul of Russia stands revealed in the simplest of realistic forms—the thing itself. Here Russia takes no chances. If you won't take her in one way, you are bound to in the other. There is no escape from a decision in her favour, unless of course you are stone-blind, which unfortunately the majority of us are. The monument is of set purpose made up of two parts; the statue proper and the pedestal. In the statue is all the display, the verve, the parade, the rapture and imagination, the magnetism and romance, in, by, and with which Russia will always delight to invest herself but which is merely her camouflage. But behind it all is Mr. Fell's 'unchallengeable rightness': 'Strength, stability and completeness.' The statue is in a highly realistic style, of which no nation has the monopoly and the whole is thoroughly de-Byzantinized.

If you won't take Russia this way, then you have to in the pedestal, for there in the one-piece granite rock, substance stares you in the face, stark and naked.

Here once and for all the *coup de grace* is given to the idea that any one specific artistic style has the monopoly of national expression. The 'unchallengeable rightness' of St. Basil's of Moscow is equally the 'unchallengeable rightness' of the modern pinnacles and buildings of St. Petersburg, the Cathedral of SS. Peter and Paul, the Admiralty, the Winter Palace, the Great Palace of Tsarkoe-Selo, the Colonnade of Cameron and all the rest.

The history of Falconet's statue is too well known to call for recapitulation here. No statue of any time has received more criticism or more praise, and no statue of any time was made with more expense of time and thought. The gist of the matter which concerns us is to be found in Diderot's pronouncement in a letter to Falconet, the sculptor, on December 6th, 1773.

* I believe it to be a fact that this sarcophagus, with the relics of the Saint, has now been removed, for safe keeping, to the Hermitage Museum of the Winter Palace, and that the man largely responsible for this was Professor Sergey Troinitzky, Director of the Hermitage Museum in Tsarist times.

'And I will never pronounce again upon any piece of sculpture if you have not erected a sublime monument. . . . Your horse is no more a copy of the finest horse existing than the Belvedere Apollo is the exact copy of the finest man. . . . That extended hand commands and protects exactly as it ought to do. . . . The first look arrests you . . . we give ourselves up to it . . . we examine nothing apart, we have not time to think. . . .'

The 'unchallengeable rightness' of the horse and rider was so explicit that Diderot was hypnotized. He saw 'nothing apart', and no doubt for him no more was necessary. But those of us who were fortunate enough to feast ourselves on this profound and mighty work, the joint production of Catherine and Falconet, were not possessed of Diderot's seeing eye. We gazed at the statue as in a dream until some unknown hand tapped us on the shoulder and said: 'What you see, my friend, is wonderful; but what you do *not* see is a miracle.' And the pointing hand directed our attention to the huge one-piece granite rock upon which the horse and rider stand. And then we listened to the story.

Bogged in the marshes of Finland, there it lay, an inert, gigantic mass of granite, weighing one thousand tons and measuring thirty-seven feet long by twenty-two high, as afterwards ascertained. It was the very thing. But how to fetch it? For Catherine, here was the supreme difficulty, which capped all others in the making of the monument.

The task was undertaken and completed with all the energy of this Queen. It took four hundred men nearly two years, from December 1768 to October 1770, to put the rock in motion, roll it up to the sea, load it on to an enormous raft, and finally deposit it on the banks of the Neva. At the time it was nicknamed 'The Rolling Mountain'. In August 1782, the Empress unveiled the monument. As she pulled the cord, she humbled herself; the only time, it is said, she made public obeisance.

And there, my friend the reader, you have it. Peter's monument is St. Basil's over again, but presented in modern form and stripped of everything Byzantine. In doubly plain language it is written there for all to read that where Russia strives she hides the strain; with her it is what you do *not* see which counts, and that in the huge one-piece granite rock, in 'the thing' itself, unadorned and stark in its simplicity, stand 'strength, stability, and completeness'.

The idiom of Russia is the idiom of Fabergé. Now we can say it, knowing exactly where we are and how we stand. Whether Carl Fabergé was a Russian, a Frenchman, an Italian or an Englishman, whatever style of ornamentation he employed, whether French, Italian, Greek or old Russian is not to the point. With Voronikhin, Zakharoff, Tressini, Rastrelli, Quarenghi, Leblond, Cameron, Gardner, Falconet and all the rest, to whatever Russian activity you go, Fabergé is in the great tradition and of the band of supreme artists whom Russia captured never to let go, and whom she so worked upon with her magic that everything they touched turned to solid gold or, in another word, 'substance'.

That is the 'something' which Fabergé instilled into the French classic styles, when he appropriated them, and which so completely captivated the French goldsmiths

PLATE 21

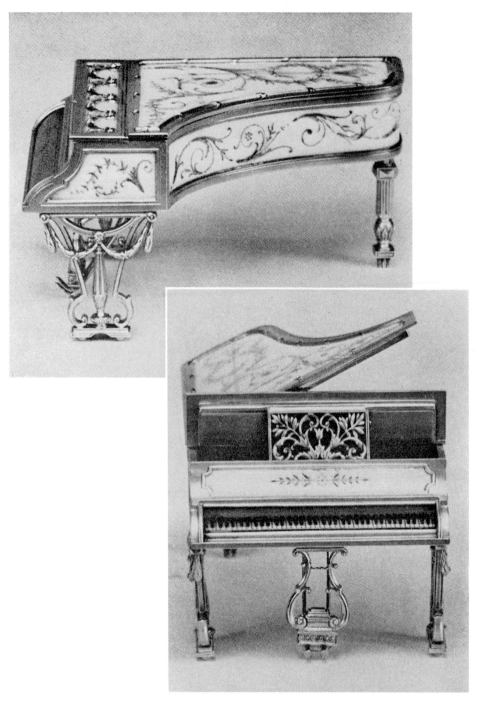

MINIATURE GRAND PIANO
Pale translucent enamel on gold. Actual size.
(*By courtesy of Messrs. Berry-Hill.*)

PLATE 22

TRAY. In nephrite, with handles in gold studded with rose-diamonds and inlaid with translucent red enamel. Total length: $17\frac{7}{16}$ inches. Diameter of tray: $10\frac{1}{2}$ inches.
(*Collection of Sir Harold Wernher, Bt.*)

TRAY. In nephrite, with handles in gold studded with rose-diamonds and inlaid with plaques of translucent red enamel. Length: $13\frac{5}{8}$ inches. Width: 5 inches. Depth: $1\frac{5}{8}$ inches.
(*By courtesy of A La Vieille Russie.*)

PLATE 23

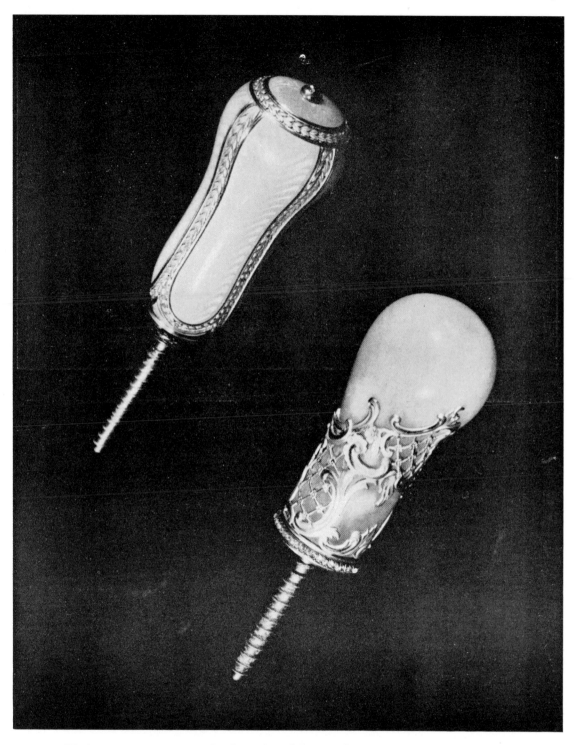

(*Top*) PARASOL HANDLE. In lavender-pink translucent enamel. It is typically
Fabergé and representative of a large part of the work of the House in style,
workmanship and enamel.
(*Below*) PARASOL HANDLE. In jadeite mounted in gold of rococo design admirably
adapted to the rounded contours of the stone. Of especial interest, the designer
being Agathon Fabergé, Carl Fabergé's brother.
(*By courtesy of A La Vieille Russie.*)

PLATE 24

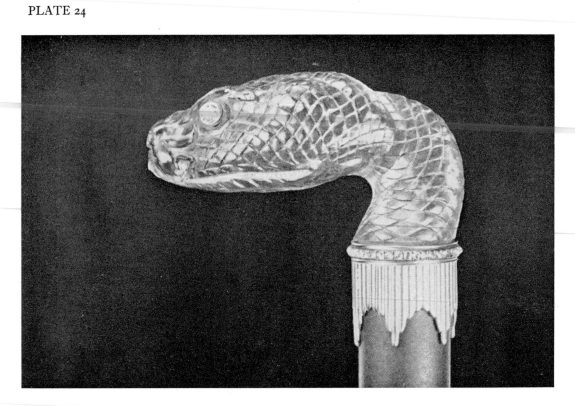

STICK HANDLE. In smoky rock crystal, gold and rose-diamonds; eyes of snake in diamonds.
Length: 3 in.
(*By courtesy of a Private Collector.*)

HIPPOPOTAMUS. In grey jasper with cabochon ruby eyes. Length: 4¼ inches.
(*By courtesy of Messrs. Wartski.*)

PLATE 25

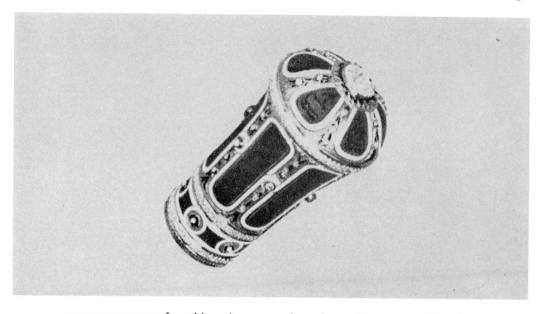

PARASOL HANDLE. In gold, various enamels, and rose-diamonds, and bearing the marking of Holmström. Length: 2⅝ inches.

When examining Queen Mary's Fabergé parasol handles at Marlborough House in March 1949 the writer drew her attention to the mint condition of the piece illustrated. Her Majesty's reaction was to go at once to her table and write out the following: 'Used on a parasol by the Duchess of Cornwall and York when the Duke opened the Federal Parliament in Melbourne, Victoria, Australia, in May 1901.' When the writer asked Her Majesty if she were not a little afraid to use such a fragile object on such an occasion Her Majesty replied: 'I kept my hand on it all the time.'

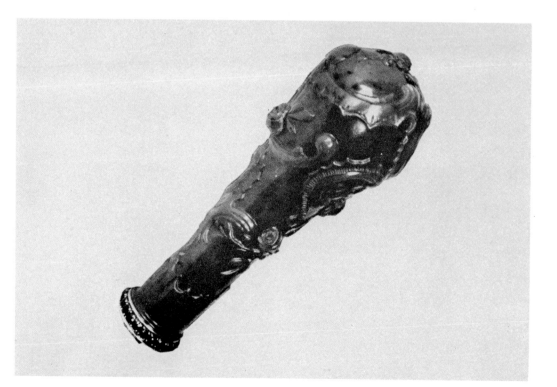

PARASOL HANDLE. In nephrite, carved and set with garnets. Length: 4⅛ inches
(*Both the above objects are from Queen's Mary's Collection.*)

PLATE 26

GOLD CHALICE. Interesting on account of the introduction of lapis-lazuli egg and because it bears same year and monogram surmounted by Imperial Crown as bridal fan given to the Grand Duchess Olga Alexandrovna, Plate 44. Height: $4\frac{1}{10}$ inches.
(By courtesy of Messrs. Tessiers.)

TAZZA. In Greek Style. Nephrite with mountings in gold, set with cabochon sapphires and rose-diamonds. Length: 8 inches. Height: $2\frac{7}{8}$ inches.
(Collection of Dr. James Hasson.)

PLATE 27

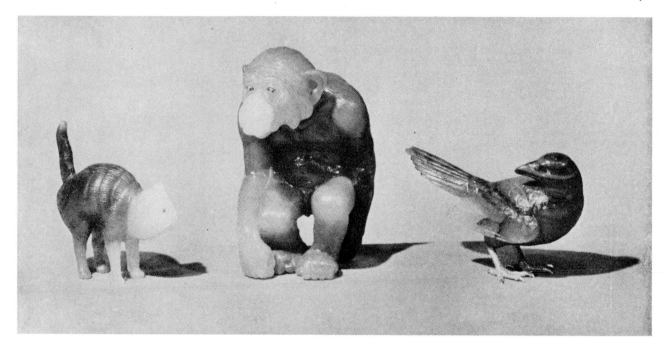

CAT. In light and dark grey agate. Eyes, sapphires.
CHIMPANZEE. In grey, black and reddish agate. Eyes, rose-diamonds.
JACKDAW. In grey and black striated agate. Eyes, rose-diamonds. Claws, gold 72.
(Cat and Chimpanzee in the Collection of Mr. H. T. de Vere Clifton, and Jackdaw by courtesy of Messrs. Spink & Son.)

CAUCASIAN IBEX. In cornelian. Eyes, rose-diamonds.
(Collection of Sir George Cooper, Bt.)

PLATE 28

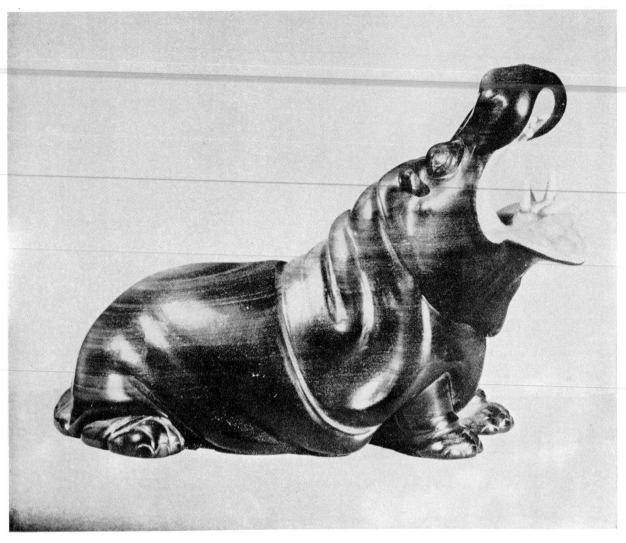

HIPPOPOTAMUS
In obsidian. Interior of mouth in rhodonite with ivory teeth. Eyes, emeralds.
Length: 8 inches (approximately.)
(*Collection of Mr. E. J. C. Vint.*)

PLATE 29

CHESTNUT LEAF ASHTRAY. In nephrite. Berries in mat green gold, one showing ruby. Leaf $5\frac{4}{10}$ inches across.
(*By courtesy of Messrs. Tessiers.*)

RHINOCEROS. In nephrite. Rose-diamond eyes. Length: $7\frac{1}{8}$ inches. Height: $2\frac{5}{8}$ inches.
(*By courtesy of Messrs. Wartski.*)

PLATE 30

SNUFF BOX. In form of a frog in translucent green jade (nephrite), mouth set with diamonds, eyes in cabochon rubies, surrounded with diamonds. The lid, on bottom, in gold.
(*By courtesy of Messrs. Wartski.*)

BOX. In translucent yellow enamel on gold, bordered with finely chiselled gold. Double-headed eagles in black enamel and diamonds. Initial of Nicholas II, surround and Imperial Crown all in diamonds, on a background of white opal enamel. Measurements: $3\frac{3}{16}$ inches square $\times \frac{15}{16}$ inches deep. A piece of outstanding craftsmanship.
(*Collection of Sir William Seeds, K.C.M.G.*)

PLATE 31

TRIPTYCH

In silver gilt decorated with enamel and set with cabochon rubies, emeralds, sapphires, tourmalines and a garnet. Central panel of Our Lady of Kazan, with the Holy Vernicle above. On the left is St. Alexandra and on right St. Nicholas. All panels framed in borders of translucent red enamel. Back of triptych engraved with monogram and crown of the Empress Alexandra Feodorovna, wife of Nicholas II. Beneath the monogram is the date November 14th, 1894, the day planned for the wedding of the Imperial couple, but which, owning to the death of Alexander III, actually took place later in the same year.
(*Collection of Mrs. F. W. Roebling.*)

PLATE 32

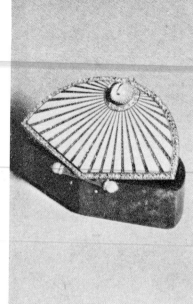

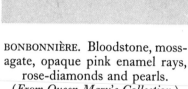

MINIATURE GOBLET. In rock crystal, stem and base in gold, dark blue and white opaque enamels, circled by gold leaf mount.
(*From Queen Mary's Collection.*)

BONBONNIÈRE. Bloodstone, moss-agate, opaque pink enamel rays, rose-diamonds and pearls.
(*From Queen Mary's Collection.*)

SMALL VASE. In aventurine quartz, mounted in gold, set with three moonstones.
(*From Queen Mary's Collection.*)

BONBONNIÈRE. In gold and enamels. Fortress of Peter and Paul, St. Petersburg, on lid in warm sepia enamel.
(*Original Fabergé photograph.*)

MINIATURE FRAME. In nephrite mounted with garland of flowers in different coloured golds and set with pearls and rose-diamonds.
(*Collection of Dr. James Hasson.*)

PLATE 33

BOX. In gold, pale pink enamel and diamonds. Monogram of Nicholas II in diamonds. Measurements: $3\frac{7}{8}$ in. $\times$ $1\frac{3}{4}$ in. $\times$ 1 in. The richness of this piece can only be appreciated by trying to visualize the pink colour of the enamel foundation.
(*By courtesy of Messrs. Berry-Hill.*)

MINIATURE COFFEE AND TEA SET. In opaque white enamel, mounted in gold. Actual size.
(*From Queen Mary's Collection.*)

PLATE 34

CLOCK. Translucent steel-blue and pink enamel panels, divided by lines of opaque white enamel of fine sharp finish. Outer leaf border, gold. Face encircled with pearls. Measures 4 inches across.
(*Collection of Lady Zia Wernher.*)

CLOCK. In translucent pink enamel mounted in gold. Four panels in translucent white enamel with moss-agate motifs in warm sepia enamel, framed with borders of opaque white enamel and green enamel leaves. Note the fine sharp finish of the whole of the work, especially that of the thin opaque white borders. Measurements: 4 inches square approximately.
(*Collection of Mrs. H. T. de Vere Clifton.*)

PLATE 35

FLOWERS AND GRASSES IN EGG-SHAPED BASKET
Flowers in blue, pink, white, yellow enamels on gold. Grasses in gold. Basket in white opal enamel on silver, trellised with rose-diamonds. Base in blue enamel, trellised with rose-diamonds. Handle in rose-diamonds. This is *not* an Imperial Easter Egg, and for whom it was made is not known.
(*From Queen Alexandra's Collection.*)

PLATE 36

TEA POT
Painted enamels various colours, on background of opaque white enamel on silver.
(*Collection of Mr. and Mrs. R. C. Barlow.*)

PLATE 37

EARS OF CORN AND SPRAY OF CORN-FLOWERS
The corn in mat gold, corn-flowers in translucent blue enamel, diamonds and
rose-diamonds. Vase, rock crystal. Height: 8¼ inches. No marks.
(*From H.M. Queen Elizabeth, the Queen Mother's Collection.*)

PLATE 38

GYPSOPHILA

Flowers in rose-diamonds and green enamel on gold. Stalks gold. Jar nephrite. Total height:
7 inches. So delicate is the workmanship the spray is always on the move. No marks.
(Formerly property of Queen Olga of Greece, now in Collection of Lady Zia Wernher.)

PLATE 39

POPPY. Leaves in nephrite. Flower, translucent red enamel on gold with rose-diamond centre; stalk, gold: the vase in rock crystal. No marks.
(*Privately owned.*)

FORGET-ME-NOT. Flowers, turquoise and rose-diamonds. Leaves, nephrite. Stalk, gold. Vase, rock crystal. No marks.
(*Privately owned.*)

PLATE 40

BOWL AND TRAY
In nephrite. Diameter of opening of bowl: 7$\frac{15}{16}$ inches. Diameter of bowl at
greatest circumference: 9$\frac{3}{4}$ inches. Diameter of tray: 13$\frac{3}{4}$ inches.
(*By courtesy of a Private Collector.*)

PLATE 41

MINIATURE TABLE. In nephrite,
mounted in gold.
(*From Queen Mary's Collection.*)

WRITING TABLE SET. Comprising clock, candlesticks and gum bottle in nephrite.
Mounted in red and green gold.
(*Privately owned.*)

PLATE 42

CLOCK. In rhodonite with gold dial. Height: $4\frac{1}{4}$ inches. Width at base: $2\frac{1}{16}$ inches. Depth of base: $1\frac{5}{8}$ inches. (*By courtesy of Messrs. Berry-Hill.*)

CLOCK. Purpurine. Face in white opal enamel on gold, bordered with gold and rose-diamonds. Measurements: $2\frac{3}{8}$ in. $\times$ $1\frac{3}{8}$ in. $\times$ $1\frac{1}{8}$ in. (*Collection of Major W. H. Daubney.*)

PLATE 43

EASTER EGG. In pale green translucent enamel on gold latticed with rose-diamonds. The rose blooms in opaque light and dark pink enamel, leaves in translucent green. Interior lined with satin with impression of an oval locket which, originally, it must have contained.

Height: $3\frac{1}{16}$ inches.

The Gallery record states 'Nicholas II'. It is not known whether this is an Imperial Easter Egg, but its beauty and workmanship justify this distinction.

SMALL URN WITH COVER. In Siberian green jade (nephrite). Gold mounts set with rubies and rose-diamonds; on cover, doves and Cupid's bow and arrow in gold and diamonds. Height: $3\frac{5}{8}$ inches.

(Both objects in the Walters Art Gallery, Baltimore U.S.A.)

PLATE 44

BRIDAL FAN

Presented to the Grand Duchess Olga Alexandrovna, July 27th, 1901, by the Tsar Nicholas II on the occasion of her marriage to Prince Peter of Oldenburg. Central painting by Solomko, shows Imperial couple receiving gifts of bread and salt after ancient custom. Below this is a view of the Oldenburg Palace in St. Petersburg. Guards are of gold, overlaid with translucent yellow enamel, surrounded by diamonds. One of these, adorned alternatively with monogram of Grand Duchess and double-headed eagle, in diamonds; the other with heart-shaped diamonds and year 1901 in diamonds.

(By courtesy of Hammer Galleries.)

PLATE 45

IMPERIAL WRITING TABLET

The cover consisting of a rectangular panel of translucent green jade (nephrite) mounted in a gold border (inset with pearls and festoons of flowers in platinum and vari-coloured gold, enriched with rubies). The cylindrical jade hinge contains a pencil mounted in gold and cabochon stone. Measurements: $6\frac{3}{4}$ in. × 4 in.

(*By courtesy of a Private Collector.*)

PLATE 46

COFFEE SET
In mat gold 72 (18 carat), relieved by polished parts. Length of tray about 9 inches.
(*Photograph by courtesy of Messrs. Wartski.*)

PLATE 47

KETTLE AND STAND
In silver, oxydé. Ornamentation encompassing kettle and stand typical of that
used by Fabergé on silver articles for table service.
(*Photograph by courtesy of Messrs. Wartski.*)

PLATE 48

CLOCK

In nephrite, mounted in red and green gold, translucent pink enamel and rose-diamonds.
Measurements: $4\frac{5}{8}$ inches diameter; $2\frac{3}{16}$ inches high.
(*By courtesy of Messrs. Spink & Son.*)

PLATE 49

IMPERIAL RUSSIAN EASTER EGG

In lapis-lazuli ornamented with chased gold, style Louis XV, surmounted by a table-top diamond, showing the initials of the Tsarina Alexandra Feodorovna, the Imperial Crown and the year 1912. The bottom is set with a large diamond. The 'surprise' inside the egg is a double-headed Imperial Russian Eagle profusely set, back and front, with diamonds, which frames a miniature of the Tsarevitch Alexey. Height: 4¾ inches.

(In the Lillian Thomas Pratt Collection of the Virginia Museum of Fine Arts, U.S.A.)

PLATE 50

IMPERIAL
RUSSIAN EASTER EGG
Made to commemorate the Bicentenary of the founding of the City of St. Petersburg in 1703. Executed in gold and in rococo design, the curves of which are set with diamonds and rubies. Bulrushes in green gold superbly chased, the spikyheads being set with square-cut rubies. On opening the egg the mechanism within raises a miniature model in gold, on a sapphire pedestal, of Peter-the-Great's Monument on the Neva. Height of egg: 6 inches (approximately).
(*By courtesy of Mr. Alexander S. Schaffer.*)

PLATE 51

REVERSE OF CAMEO

Contained in the egg illustrated in colour in Plate 55. It records, with the date 1914, the name of the five children of the Tsar, Nicholas II, in Russian characters in monochrome enamel. Surrounded by diamonds and pearls in green enamel cups surmounted by the Imperial crown in diamonds, this record is supported on a stand of gold, opaque white enamel, diamonds, pearls and green sapphires.

(From Queen Mary's Collection.)

PLATE 52

IMPERIAL RUSSIAN EASTER EGG
Showing the 'surprise' extended. In Plate 56 the egg is reproduced in colour.
(*By courtesy of Messrs. Wartski.*)

of 1900. But styles apart, it is substance which pervades, through and through every piece he ever made, and gives it that distinction we now call 'Fabergé'.

This substance of Fabergé has shape, and shape is a wizard. There can be no argument about it, for the Almighty himself has assured us of this fact. In the beginning it was shape and in the end it will be shape. In all aftermaths, shape comes to the rescue. At bottom the solution of all difficulties is to be found in her, for chaos is shapelessness, and shapelessness has no existence. Not for nothing does Keats say: 'O Attic shape!'

But, as Mr. Fell has so timely reminded us, shape is but the road which leads to our salvation. Behind shape is the idea. In a fast disintegrating world, or so it seems, when artists, so-called, prostitute their art in the worship of chaos and cacophony, it is well for mankind that there are simple men who still build and furnish mansions of harmony, of beauty and of joy for the preservation of our sanity.

In every little thing of Fabergé's, for they are mostly small in scale and to the unseeing eye but gewgaws, there is a gift. By subtle artistry he instilled a balm into all his work, and *through and through*, and substantially enough to dispel misery. At our first sight of every object, and perhaps more so at first touch, the music within us responds, ringing out in chords of merriment and melody.

This is Carl Fabergé's abounding contribution to art.

As I read over what I have written, it is obvious that I lay myself wide open to criticism, in that as such an out-and-out Russophile I have left nothing except a crumb or two for any other country; what I have said must be taken with a big pinch of the proverbial salt. In passing, therefore, let me say that if in Russia I came up against a mystery, I have found a still greater mystery—England; and by England I mean the land in which was conceived the spirit which pervades the United Kingdom and the British Empire.

Russia having written her idiom in letters of blood and given such evidence of her might, there is now a feeling abroad that she is bound to swallow everything and everybody in a world-sweeping universality peculiarly her own. Big brains and wise men are at it again in full flood. There is now no question of collapse. What nation is to be the first tasty morsel for the monster, and what next, is the question occupying so many minds. That is the ultimate of their prognostications.

Once again our teachers and mentors are not big enough to grasp the simple implications of the situation which confronts them. Once again it is special phases and special men which are the burden of their thoughts. Again they fail to base themselves on fundamentals.

A man in authority of any country is only great when he acts within the limits of the true spirit of his country, and a country rises or falls just as her rulers are great or small. To the torment of mankind, the fundamental has largely become the monopoly of the dreamer, and it is therefore at rare moments only when the man of action is at the same time the dreamer that a nation comes to full maturity.

What I have to say is categorical. But I have been categorical throughout except for a patch here and there, and I have had to turn on Rachmaninoff, and Tchaikowsky, to get down to these. The plain fact is that it was utterly impossible for anyone to be intimately associated with Dr. Ludwig Mond, the chemist, Frederick William Rolfe (Corvo), the writer, and Carl Fabergé, the goldsmith, all three of them pre-eminent in their special way and touching life at the three points of the triangle of the scheme of things—it was quite impossible for anyone to have this experience and come out unscathed. Out of this experience certain things emerged as absolute, such as 'Thou shalt love' and 'Thou shalt not kill'. To accept these was life, to go against them was certain death. There was no half-way house.

I had sense enough to know that, equipped as I was, it would be unwise for me to attempt any record of Fabergé because as a writer it would be expected of me that I should be persuasive, picturesque and discursive. I would have to state facts in such a way that my reader, if she or he happened to be of the half-way house variety, and who of us is not, would have an easy and agreeable way of escape.

Having no ability for this sort of thing and feeling sure that if I attempted it I would not only irritate myself but exasperate my reader, I tried to persuade Mr. A. J. A. Symons to undertake the record, I to supply atmosphere and material. To my sorrow Mr. Symons died. So it was that having made every effort to rid myself of a duty, which, judging from the encouragement my friends have given me, was evidently mine to do, I find myself with the duty still around my own neck. It has been, and is still, my endeavour neither to hurt the reader nor hang myself. Times have changed and this makes things easier. Formulæ of escape are now less the fashion, and frankness is the first item on the agenda.

Having thus relieved myself I can now proceed. The stronger the power of locality the tighter the grip it has upon those living within its sphere of operation. This needs no dressing-up, it is axiomatic, a truism. Equally to remove oneself from the sphere of operation, where the spirit of place is all powerful, is very much to feel the wind. Put a judge of the High Court down a coal mine and he counts for very little. He is, as we say, out of his element.

Apply all this to Russia and there can be no doubt about the situation which confronts all those living within her boundaries and the foreigner without. Possessed of a priceless heritage, a *genius loci* of amazing native force, she fulfils her destiny, gloriously, only by remaining within it. The further her boundaries are extended the weaker her spirit becomes.

With England it is different. Her genius is not local, but universal. Therefore, however distasteful this may be to some, she fulfils her destiny gloriously only by extending it to the four quarters of the globe. It is not for me to say *how* it is, but *why* it is, is plain to be seen. Over forty-three years ago Rolfe put it like this in *Hadrian VII*:

'The Pope (that is to say Rolfe himself) affirmed that the English Race naturally was fitted to give an example to humanity. In particular He categorically distinguished its solid worth, its dignified good sense, its deliberate tenacity, its imperturbable habit, its superb impassiveness in reverses, its stoical firmness under the most cruel deceptions, its unshaken determination to conquer under any circumstances. In general, He noted its faculties of self-restraint, of construction, of administration and . . . of altruism.'

46

In this there is not only style, but something far beyond. Comprehensive yet compact, exact in every detail, the character of England shines resplendent in every word of it. Forty-three years ago it went utterly unnoticed. In more recent years the spirit of it was unsensed by Nazi Germany, by some in America, and even by some in England herself.

To-day it is the hall-mark of England's destiny and inheritance, the charter by which she is not only privileged, but which constrains her to bestow upon others the blessings which have been bestowed so lavishly upon her.

The reason why the genius of England is universal calls for no further words from me. The writing is on the wall. Perhaps I should add this. When a sorely tried mother in the north of England admonishes her child she does not say: 'Conduct yourself like a good capitalist, or a good bolshevist, menshevist, fascist, communist, or socialist, or even a good bureaucrat, democrat, aristocrat, proletarian, or bourgeois, because the child would not have the remotest idea what she was driving at. She says: 'Behave, will yer!' And the child knows instinctively and at once what she means (Behabban—Anglo-Saxon, restrain: hold in check). There is nothing precious and of the 'Oh lovely soil of England' about this, it is a hard solid fact which the rest of the world seems quite incapable of understanding, short of positive and unequivocal demonstration.

How little thought those in authority give to such matters is well illustrated by some remarks of an honourable member of the House of Commons during the Yalta Conference debate. 'Isn't it about time we had a conference here?' asked this gentleman. 'There is a feeling in the country that there is too much going about savouring of the cap in hand . . . to other countries. We all know the old saying: "If the mountain won't come to Mohammed, Mohammed must go to the mountain." But there is no reason why Mohammed should go to a whole range of mountains.' (Laughter.)

Mr. Churchill knew his England too well to allow such remarks to cramp his style, and his is the style of England, personified as never before. There is, of course, every reason why Mohammed should always go to the mountain, and even to a whole range of mountains. He has no face to lose. That is the beauty of it.

One would have thought that by this time it was common knowledge that the Englishman when he goes abroad has learned to take the British Empire with him and his gear (Mulberry Harbour is the outstanding example). Having arrived at his base of operations, whatever or wherever they may be, he at once sets up his *genius loci*, seats himself amidst familiar scenery, feels himself supremely comfortable and ready for anything and anybody. Thus he supports his natural modesty as a citizen of an Empire, the size and glory of which he knows very little indeed.

With the Russian it is all the other way. No oceans separate him from his Empire. As it has grown, so it has pressed more and more immediately upon him until its vastness has enveloped him. Thus supported, as a consequence he has come to appreciate himself as something part and parcel with it, which he truly is. *At home* he is amidst familiar scenery, feels supremely comfortable and ready for anything and anybody, and filled to overflowing with hospitality.

47

But once let a Russian roam abroad on affairs and he is largely lost because it has not been given to him to take his gear and his Empire with him. Uneasy and out of his element he looks about for protection, is unhappy and uncomfortable, and in consequence behaves unnaturally.

There is little else to add except this. There are no two peoples who have a greater affinity for one another than those of England and Russia, and with the former I join the U.S.A. As opposites they are marshalled, one as positive, the other as negative; one acid, the other alkaline. They have it in them, as no other lands, intimately to combine in the formation of the new compound which all mankind awaits.

Unless I have been too long-winded in these passing remarks, the reader will remember that we left Carl Fabergé with two things firmly established, first that he was of Russia, pure and simple, second, that his work was Russian.

Now we come to those people who are only interested in an object of art when it is the work of one man from beginning to end. For them, any object which is the result of the inspiration of one man and the handicraft of another is not a work of art. This matter will claim our full attention in the chapter on 'The Work-masters of Fabergé'. In the meantime we need only say that in a world of Wrens we should have so many houses that we should not know what to do with them, and in a world of Rembrandts no houses at all.

And so we pass to those who see in Fabergé nothing more than a *fournisseur* of pretty things for the imperialists of Europe, their complaint being that as such, he and Art are miles apart. Art has as many definitions as there are men to make them, for it concerns the dreams and activities of all men, of all nations, and at all times. It is clear, therefore, that before any measure can be taken of a man's transgressions you must know with what dreams and activities he is concerned.

Fabergé was a goldsmith, silversmith, and jeweller; and as such, practised one of the oldest trades in the world. Its history is of peculiar interest to all Englishmen. During the Renaissance goldsmithery was held in the highest respect in Italy as the mother of the fine arts. Almost all the great masters in the graphic and plastic arts subjected themselves to its discipline before embarking on their works of large proportions and dimensions.

In England, round about the Seventeenth Century, having facilities for the safe keeping of money, the goldsmiths prostituted their art by receiving money on deposit. They then conceived the idea of 'running-cashes' with their customers and initiated what has now become the Banking system of this country. These activities became very lucrative, so much so that John Evelyn, towards the end of the Seventeenth Century, says this:

'To this add the fraud of the Bankers and Goldsmiths who have gotten immense riches by extortion, keepe up their treasure in expectation of enhancing its value; Duncombe not long since a meane goldsmith having made a purchase of the late Duke of Buckingham's estate at neere £90,000 and reported to have neere as much in cash.'

In and about the end of the Seventeenth Century and the beginning of the Eighteenth came the great divide. A number of the goldsmiths, finding that the system of 'running-cashes' was much more profitable than the making of gold ornaments and vessels, left the fold. They gave up their energies entirely to dealing in money and their businesses became the private banking houses which founded that 'unrivalled reputation' of English banking which is represented by what we call 'The Big Five'. Thus the aristocracy of money was established on a solid and permanent footing and those associated with it rose to great social state.

Those of the goldsmiths who stuck to the fold continued to make gold ornaments and vessels. They retailed their handiwork over the counter and became known as 'retail traders' with all the obloquy attaching to the term, as seeing nothing wrong in supplying the individual needs of the community. By the end of the Nineteenth Century a better spirit prevailed when their status was raised in the social scale by prefixing them with the possessive pronoun, and they became '*my* goldsmith', '*my* jeweller', like '*my* doctor', '*my* lawyer', with a precedence just below that of the professions.

This was something to be thankful for, but unfortunately about this time the artist came along and announced that as the goldsmiths and jewellers were merely concerned with 'applied art' they were not artists at all but shopkeepers, pure and simple. It is a tribute to these goldsmiths that such a reproof neither deterred nor disheartened them. They continued as before with the making of their ornaments and vessels, and took money for them quite openly over the counter.

And then, about the beginning of the Twentieth Century something happened, and no goldsmith had more to do with this revelation than Carl Fabergé. It was discovered that goldsmiths and jewellers were in reality not goldsmiths and jewellers, but *spokesmen*. That is to say, when any member of the community has something very personal or private to say to someone else, whether it concerns his 'humble duty' to his Sovereign, love for those nearest and dearest to him, or great regard for some particular person, and is unable to find words adequate to the occasion, or he has come to the conclusion that the saying may be done more delicately by a third party, then he goes to the goldsmith and jeweller who says it for him. This is the art which primarily, the goldsmith and jeweller practises, and it is a great art for it is concerned with the dreams and desires of the heart.

As a purveyor of good will, the goldsmith is a man apart. Even in a small country town he must be a man of versatility if he is to succeed (and you find him often in quite outlying countrysides) for his wares have to say not what he thinks but exactly what his customers want to convey. Here is the rub, and just so far as he is successful in helping them to express themselves, just so far is he an artist. If he should persuade them to purchase Cellini's golden salt-cellar or the medallions of Clement VII and Alessandro de Medici (if he could get hold of them), when these are unsuitable for the *purpose desired*, then he is merely a shopkeeper.

This is the situation which confronts the goldsmith and jeweller when the area of his operations is limited.

But when the area is the world, and the time that of the great patrons of the end of the Nineteenth Century and the beginning of the Twentieth, when each object has to be made to meet some special taste and to say some special thing, and the donors and recipients are Emperors, Kings and Queens, Millionaires, Mandarins and Maharajahs, and all those notable in all walks of life whether of finance, medicine or the law, literature, the press, the stage, politics, industry, diplomacy or music, men and women of great taste and sometimes with a complete lack of it, some with and some without an abundance of money, and of both hemispheres, and above all, when unwritten laws have to be observed as to the sort of thing which can or cannot be given or received, and standards of decency maintained which forbid an undue outlay of money—then it can be truly said the goldsmith and jeweller has his work set.

It was just this situation which confronted Carl Fabergé. That he emerged at all from such a maze of conditions is something to be remarked. But he not only emerged, he came through triumphantly enough to rouse the wonder of Cellini, could he be brought to life again to see what had been accomplished.

For Fabergé, responding triumphantly to the pressing demands of his time, not only materialized in gold, enamel and rare stones, the delicacy, the love, aye, the madness of a glamorous age, when there was more time in which to be delicate, more time in which to love and more Kings to whom to bend the knee; but he has left for grim posterity a legacy of delight which is evidenced by the eagerness with which men now surround themselves with his handiwork.

This is Art, and there is no gainsaying the fact, for it is in accord with the great canon: 'Art for Man's sake.'

For the second time in this chronicle we have mentioned Benvenuto Cellini. No record of the Russian goldsmith would be complete without some further reference to the Italian giant. And the first thing to strike one is that Cellini wrote his own life story and Fabergé did not. Cellini says this: 'All men of whatsoever quality they be who have done anything of excellence, ought, if they be persons of truth and honesty, to describe their life with their own hand; but they ought not to attempt so fine an enterprise till they have passed the age of forty.'

Vain, vigorous, and self-assertive, with an over-weening sense of self-importance and filled to overflowing with the exuberance, the efflorescence and the glory of the Renaissance, it was the most natural thing in the world for Cellini to write his autobiography, the most revealing of all life stories.*

Not so Fabergé. If the proposal had been made to him that he should write his life story, he would have said that he was concerned with the doing of his work, not writing about it, and he would have embellished this information with some pretty caustic remarks. His nature being centripetal, he continually sought the core of inspiration from within himself from which to draw re-creation. This, together with his extreme reserve and hatred of the written word, made any expectation of a life story from him utterly hopeless.

It is a very moot question indeed whether an artist achieves much by writing of his works. In the end he stands or falls by the works themselves. Except for a few bibliophiles and suchlike, the world at large takes very little cognisance of the

* *Cf.* Life of Benvenuto Cellini, translated by John Addington Symonds.

written word. All the wisdom that can be known is already written down and yet men at large never realise it until a rousing smack on the face, delivered by an all-seeing and all-protecting stroke of fate, brings them to their senses. Then only is it that they say: 'Oh, that's it, is it?'

Certain it is that Cellini achieved very little if anything by writing his auto-biography. The man as he was is generally quite unknown to-day, for all the pains he took to reveal himself. Take only one aspect of him. To-day men think of him as a supreme example of the lone star in art. By this I mean that everything he did was not only the product of his own personal inspiration but of his own hands. No other person had anything whatever to do with his work except Cellini him-self, people are apt to think. Yet he goes to much pains in his autobiography to tell us that this was not the case.

Here are some quotations: 'I occupied an apartment far away from my workmen's room as well as from the shop.'... 'I chose one of my shop lads who was twelve years' old.'... 'all my business there (Rome) I left in the hands of my partner, Felice.'... 'I have in Rome a shop open with journeymen and a pretty business; as soon as I have got my pardon I will leave all the devotion of Rome to a pupil of mine there and will come back.'... 'sleeping in the same bed as an excellent workman, named Manno.'... 'During this while I had sent my devoted comrade, Felice, back to Rome, to look after my business there.'... 'pur-sued my journey to Rome, where I found my most faithful Felice, to whom I abandoned my old shop with all its furniture and appurtenances and opened another much larger and roomier, next to Sugherello the perfumer.'... 'and in the meanwhile began the bason and jug ordered by the Cardinal of Ferrara. I had a crowd of workmen and many large affairs on hand in gold and silver.'... 'I employed eight work-people and worked day and night together with them, for the sake of honour and gain.'

One gathers from this that a number of hands went to the making of Cellini's objects, that he was not solely dependent upon the commissions of those in high places, and that his work was open to public view and purchase at his shop 'next door to Sugherello the perfumer'.* There is nothing here of the precious aloofness of 'Art for Art's sake', but everything to support the fact that Cellini was a retail dealer attending to the needs of his customers and selling his wares over the public counter for gain. If he were carrying on business to-day he would be subjected, by those who ascribe to themselves superiority, as being concerned with more noble undertakings, to the same ban which denounces his fellow goldsmiths and jewellers of to-day as dealing only in 'applied art'.

The idea of the lone star shining in the firmament in solitary glory, unchal-lenged in any way by stars of lesser light, is one which has taken a great hold on those most intimately concerned with works of art; that is the collector and dealer.

---

* The same in Paris in 1540. His shop there, he says, 'began to make a grand show'. When Francis Ist paid him a visit 'All my people,' he says, 'were at work so that the king came upon us quite unexpectedly. As he entered the saloon, the first object he perceived was myself, with a large piece of plate in my hand, which I had not yet placed and which was to make the body of Jupiter (silver statue); another was employed on the head, another again on the legs, so that the shop resounded with the beating of hammers'.

Each reacts on the interests of the other in such a way that demand and supply can only be met by maintaining for all works of art or of virtu the idea that they are the work of one hand only. It has almost come to be understood that of a picture from a single hand, and one of equal merit painted by two men, the latter is considered to be the inferior of the two. When you add to this the veneration for the old, and the fact that a Tenth Century Byzantine ikon, for example, is regarded as one hundred times more valuable than a replica made in the Eighteenth Century, although the latter is superior in every way in craftsmanship and as a work of art, then you are riding for a fall, with beauty and harmony no longer in the running, hopelessly outdistanced by pounds, shillings and pence.

Fabergé has just been caught in time. One hundred years hence he would be fully established with a halo round his head as the lone star in the firmament of Nineteenth Century goldsmithery. As it is, we know that he inspired the work of seven hundred men, artists, workmasters, workmen and staff, men of all nationalities, who accomplished the miracle of producing thousands of objects, and whether great or small, all with the same quality of finish.

The most frequent question asked of me has been, 'Did Fabergé make everything with his own hand?' And it has been addressed to me in the hope, well to be sensed and seen, that he did.

When comparing the Genius of the Renaissance, who represented in himself more than any other man the exquisite sensibility to form, the swagger, the lawlessness and ruffianism of his age, who went from place to place killing a man here and a man there just as the fancy took him, and what was more, was forgiven and even his actions extolled by spiritual authority. . . . 'You do not understand', said Pope Paul III to his gentlemen who submitted that His Holiness would show too much clemency in pardoning Cellini for an outrageous murder committed in the streets of Rome, 'You do not understand the matter as well as I do. I must inform you that men like Benvenuto, unique in their profession, are not bound by the laws' . . . I say, when comparing the Genius of the Renaissance with the humanity loving, order loving and modest Russian Craftsman of the Nineteenth Century, four things of more than usual interest stand out.

First it was the case with both of them of *cherchez la femme*. Like most outstanding men, they each of them owed much to a woman. It was Josiah Wedgwood who went about among his artists and workpeople, exclaiming: 'Not too much caution! Not too much caution!' when he received the order from Catherine the Great for the Wedgwood dinner service. He always called the Empress his 'Great Patroness of the North.'

Cellini, in his autobiography, says this: 'Madonna Porzia now advised me to open a shop of my own (in Rome). This I did and I never stopped working for that excellent and gentle lady, who paid me exceedingly well, and by whose means perhaps it was that I became a figure in the world.'

Alexander III and Nicholas II were, of course, the chief patrons of the Russian goldsmith in Russia, but in Europe and the West the lady to whom he owed everything was Queen Alexandra. It was she who fostered his art in England for there was never any doubt among her relatives and friends what to give her on her birthday; it was 'Fabergé, Fabergé', every time. If the craftsman had been a man of words he would have called her his 'Great Patroness of the West'. The Queen was more demonstrative, for every time she received anything by Fabergé, she exclaimed: 'Oh, how lovely!'

Second, as regards their art. The chief difference between the two men is, I think, this: Cellini worked in the round and Fabergé chiefly in the flat. Although the former remained a goldsmith until he was forty years of age, it is in his work as a sculptor that you find the true measure of the man—in such masterpieces as his Perseus in bronze in Florence, and his Crucifix, with the figure of Christ in marble, in the church of S. Lorenzo in the Escorial.

It is this feeling for sculpture which you find continuously reappearing in his goldsmithery. All his objects are furnished with combinations of figures of children, animals, flowers, fruits and other fantastic imaginings in the round or in relief, and mostly charmingly enamelled with extensive use of opaque white. There is no piece by Cellini, or attributed to him, which does not give out a lively, luxuriously comfortable sense of well-being; they positively bulge with 'round-ness' and 'roundness' has a universal attraction.

This working in the round and in relief is a distinctive feature of all the best work of the Italian Renaissance, and this it is which makes it almost impossible to say whether any particular piece of his period is by Cellini unless supported by unimpeachable evidence. In the *Burlington Magazine*, Vol. VIII, Oct. 1905-March 1906, p. 37, the Reverend Herbert Thurston, S.J., draws attention to the 'holocaust of 1797' when Pius VI, 'at his wits end for resources, was compelled to fall back upon his plate and jewellery' to meet the demands of Napoleon under the treaty with the Holy See concluded at Tolentino. He says this: ' . . . of the works of art which found their way to the melting-pot . . . the most famous was probably the gold cope-clasp . . . which had been executed by Benvenuto Cellini for his patron Clement VII.' John Addington Symonds, in his introduction to his translation of Cellini's autobiography, says this: 'Artists who aspire to immortality should shun the precious metals.' It is very clear, as I have already said, that before any work of goldsmithery can be accepted as by Cellini, unimpeachable evidence of its genuineness is imperative.

Apropos of the work of Cellini, I am reminded of the many times when Mr. Leopold de Rothschild at Hamilton Place showed me his silver partridge and four little groups in enamel representing Spring, Summer, Autumn, Winter. 'Have you seen my silver partridge and Cellini's seasons?' was his invariable question. In my time it was not possible to tell a Rothschild anything he did not already know, whether it concerned horses or carts, orchids, enamels, foods, or wines, but to-day I often wonder about those 'Seasons'. Are they chronicled anywhere?

So much for Cellini, and now to pass to Fabergé.

As I have said, Fabergé's work is in the flat, but this must not be taken too literally; it serves only as a general distinction between his work and that of Cellini. So far as the general collector is concerned, the work of the Russian goldsmith *is* in the flat, in such objects as cigarette cases, boxes, frames, clocks and things bounded more or less by simple straight lines. Such like were made to be carried on the person and for convenient use on the writing-table, etc., and not intended as museum pieces. To have furnished these objects with cherubs and fantastic excrescences in the round would have been impracticable.

The same disadvantages attach to objects in *cloisonné, champlevé* and painted enamels; not only are they too heavy (those objects of Fabergé's in translucent enamel are heavy enough as it is) but they are very liable to catch in the clothing, etc. Objects in these enamels have always had a great vogue in Russia, in fact from earliest days and even up to the time of Fabergé, the *cloisonné, champlevé* and painted enamel methods were the ones chiefly employed; so much was this the case that they became known as 'Russian enamels'. But among cultured men and women in Russia, as well as the West, they have never had much attraction, the close proximity of so many colours being too bizarre and vulgar to appeal to people of taste. Nevertheless, for all I have said, now and again, Fabergé produced pieces following these methods which, on account of the admirable taste with which he chose the colourings, far excelled anything of the sort generally produced in Russia. In Plate 36 I give a picture of a tea-pot, part of a tea-set, which is one of the best examples by Fabergé, carried out in painted enamels.

But to return to the previous paragraph and to Fabergé's work in the flat. Roundness implies living and flatness is dead. It was Fabergé's business to make flatness live. Like all goldsmiths of all times he was subject to popular caprice and fashion, but living in a time when there was an urge among cultured men and women to surround themselves with things of elegance, it was natural that his craftsmanship should evoke universal admiration. Thus it was that Fabergé found himself loaded with demands for articles in common use. It was required of him, therefore, that he should make the practical attractive without being bulky and inconvenient. He accomplished this in various ways, by the use of stones like nephrite, chalcedony, aventurine-quartz, rhodonite, lapis-lazuli and by the use of gold of various colours. And there is another substance, the work of man, not nature, but none the worse for that, at any rate from the point of rarity, for its creator is dead and it can never be made again as his secret died with him. I refer to the vitreous substance called purpurine. It was the invention of a workman called Petouchoff of the Imperial Glass Factory in St. Petersburg. The material has much the nature of obsidian, is of that wonderful red colour named by the French *sang de bœuf*, and is very heavy, having gold in its composition.* Personally I call this the rarest of all the substances, natural and artificial, used by Fabergé. But in none of the various ways employed by the Craftsman to make the practical attractive, was he more successful than in the use he made of translucent enamels on a guilloché background of gold and silver.

He was, of course, making use of methods which had already been employed in days gone by. But these methods had largely declined, and it was his work to resuscitate this art and craft. Not only did Fabergé do this, but he carried the work much further, so far indeed that the large flat surface of translucent enamel became one of the main characteristics of his objects. And let it be noted

* As I go to press Captain Harold Spink has shown me a remarkable specimen of purpurine in the form of a plate, 8½ inches in diameter.

54

that the enamel was not just of any colour. It is here you get the greatest attraction. The enamelling workshops of Fabergé were research laboratories. Work went on continually to find new colours, and as in all research work, quite often it was by accident that the finest results were achieved, such, for instance, as raspberry red. Accident produced this but only in very limited quantity. As the composition was never fully known, the number of articles enamelled in this colour was small. Collectors should note this, as also colours like opalescent pink, 'love-bird' green and different shades of steel blue.

But Fabergé by no means limited himself to work in the flat. There is nothing extravagant in thinking of him as more versatile than Cellini. For one thing, the Russian goldsmith was more fortunate than the Italian, in that he was able to avail himself of all the developments which three centuries bring; therefore you find him producing a greater number of different sorts of things than the Italian and in more styles than one. Fabergé, too, worked in the round, and in more ways than one, his animals, each cut out of one piece of stone, his figurines, each one made up of many stones, his flowers in rock crystal pots in the making of which gold, enamel, precious and rare stones are employed, and such objects as large stone bowls, statuettes, etc., in which he worked much in the round in furnishings and pedestals; all are examples of his work in this direction.

The third thing to be noted as between Cellini and Fabergé is their jewellery. The Russian craftsman was, of course, chiefly concerned with impersonal objects for the table or vitrine, and articles to be *carried about* on the person, not with objects *to adorn* the person. Why this was so is of paramount interest. We have already said something about it in Chapter I and there will be more in Chapter V. So far, let it be noted, we have been discussing impersonal objects only, both as regards Cellini and Fabergé.

Fabergé's jewellery must always give way to his impersonal objects, not because it is insignificant, but for the reason that his work in impersonal objects was on such a scale of quality and quantity that it completely overshadowed his work in objects for personal adornment. This present record is concerned with the latter, but not to the point of illustration, because it has not been possible to bring together anything like a sufficient number of illustrations to convey any adequate idea of them.

For a painter, immortality is always possible; not so for the jeweller. Sooner or later his work is dispersed, through the greed of man. By far the greater part of Fabergé's jewellery had been worn, as was natural, in Russia, and was therefore in that country at the time of the Revolution. Shortly after the establishment of the new regime all jewellery in private possession was confiscated by the State and broken up, and by the irony of circumstance it was Agathon Fabergé, Carl Fabergé's second son, who was set to value the heap—'a mountain', he called it. when he related the tragic story while staying with me in Hampstead in the autumn of 1937—of precious stones resulting.

The holocaust of the last great war did the rest. But for all these tragic happenings, there must be many examples of Fabergé's jewellery in England, in the possession of some people perhaps who do not know what it is they hold. Anyhow I have found only very few examples: two, a pink enamelled gold coin of the time of Catherine the Great, set as a brooch and surrounded by diamonds and cabochon emeralds and a gold locket in the possession of Mrs. John Piper and Mrs. Constance Sturrock; a royal blue enamelled brooch in the possession of Mrs. Michael Pugh; a star sapphire and diamond brooch in the possession of Messrs. S. J. Phillips; a 'mecca-stone' and diamond pendant and a white opal enamel and diamond locket in the possession of my wife, Mrs. Dorothy Bainbridge. I am therefore reduced to words, a very poor substitute for illustrations, to give some idea of Fabergé's work as a setter of precious stones.[1]

As jeweller to the Court, Fabergé had under his care the examination and maintenance of the Russian Crown jewels housed in the Diamond Room—in Russian, 'Brillyantovaya Kómnata'—in the Winter Palace. It was also his duty to carry out the instructions of the Tsar in the making of articles of jewellery commemorating intimate family, as well as State, occasions.

As an instance of the former, there was the *sautoir* of pearls which Alexander III presented to the Princess Alix of Hesse to commemorate her betrothal to the Tsarevitch, afterwards Nicholas II. Fabergé brought together a collection of pearls for this purpose and in competition with the jewellers of the world, it was the one chosen by the Tsar. In November 1937 I asked Agathon Fabergé what was the value in money of this *sautoir*, and he replied: 'When it was brought together it was of the value of 250,000 gold roubles. It was the largest single transaction my father ever had with the two Tsars.'[2]

As examples of jewellery to commemorate State occasions, there were the large number of brooches and pendants with Imperial emblem designs made for the Coronation of the Tsar Nicholas II, and the brooches made to commemorate the Tercentenary of Romanoff rule in 1913, in diamonds, different stones of colour and pearls, following motifs of the Imperial crown and emblems, all different, of course, and presented to each of the Grand Duchesses and ladies of the Court. It is to be noted that the designs for the latter were based on the original drawings which the Tsarina Alexandra Feodorovna herself prepared and sent to Fabergé for elaboration.

These jewels are just two examples of many similar commissions which came his way as jeweller to the Court, when the designs of the objects had to be based on some national emblem and in which he displayed the craftsmanship peculiar to him. In the metal settings of all Fabergé's jewellery there is a clean-cut sharpness and brightness which is a characteristic of his work as controlled by August and Albert Holmström, his chief jewellery workmasters. This adds to the brilliance of the stones and is in evidence in all his jewellery whether for State, ceremonial, or family occasions, from brooches to tiaras.

[1] Since writing this it has been my good fortune to see the amethyst and diamond brooch in the possession of Karsavina, the famous Russian ballerina of Tsarist times, which I have described in Chapter I and chosen to illustrate in Plate 4. This is not only a jewel of historic and romantic interest but a typical example of the fine setting of Fabergé. I have also found two aquamarine and diamond brooches in the possession of Mrs. Hirst and an aquamarine drop on gold chain in the possession of Lady Studd.

[2] Recently when I mentioned this to a well-known jeweller he expressed surprise. He said, 'I should have thought it was far and away higher than this'. Nothing could bring out more clearly than this that the worth of Fabergé's work lies in craftsmanship and not in precious stones.

PLATE 53

SALT BOX. In form of a miniature chair in gold and nephrite. Chair (back and front) in translucent pale apricot enamel with classical motifs in warm sepia enamel surrounded by small pearls. The seat in same enamels forms the lid of a nephrite box used to contain salt in the bread and salt ceremony of welcome. Height: 3 inches.
(*Privately owned.*)

MINIATURE XVIII-CENTURY CABINET. In gold and cornelian, with inset enamelled pieces. Top portion, with lid in engraved rock crystal, apparently designed to contain cigarettes. Measurements: $3\frac{1}{2}$ in. $\times$ $5\frac{1}{4}$ in. $\times$ $1\frac{7}{8}$ in.
(*Privately owned.*)

PLATE 54

BONBONNIÈRE. In rock crystal mounted with finely chased gold border. Centre in moss-agate surrounded by diamonds.

BONBONNIÈRE. In rock crystal mounted with borders of translucent red, green, blue, white and pale orange enamels and diamonds. On opening the box, the outer edge of the gold mounting is seen completely covered by stripes of translucent green and red enamels separated by white enamel dots.

BONBONNIÈRE. In cornelian in form of a snail. Lid in chased gold, white and cobalt blue enamels with moss-agate centre surrounded by diamonds. Cabochon ruby thumb-piece.

BONBONNIÈRE. In translucent pink enamel on gold, adorned, top and bottom, with classical motifs in warm sepia enamel, bordered with white opaque and translucent red and green enamels.

(The four objects, which are shown to approx. actual size, are reproduced by courtesy of Mrs. Alexander S. Schaffer.)

PLATE 55

IMPERIAL RUSSIAN EASTER EGG

Made up of a platinum network in which are set innumerable square-cut precious stones of colour, the main feature of which is a set of panels, framed with opaque white enamel and pearls pinned by five diamonds, to give a floral effect. The egg is encompassed by bands of pearls lined with opaque white enamel, and scrolls of diamonds. At the round end is a moonstone. The 'surprise' inside consists of a cameo representing the five Imperial children as portrayed above. The reverse side of the cameo is illustrated in Plate 51. Length of egg: $3\frac{3}{4}$ inches. Width: $2\frac{1}{2}$ inches. Height of cameo and stand: 3 inches.

(*From Queen Mary's Collection.*)

PLATE 56

IMPERIAL RUSSIAN EASTER EGG

In pink enamel quartered by rose-diamonds, decorated with lilies of the valley in pearls and rose-diamonds, with green gold and green enamel leaves. The 'surprise', consisting of three miniatures of the Tsar Nicholas II and two of his children set in rose-diamonds, is drawn from egg, and returned by means of the gold-mounted pearl button at the side. Height of egg: 6⅙ inches; height including miniatures: 8⅛ inches. Presented by Nicholas II to the Tsarina on April 5th, 1898, as engraved on the reverse of the miniatures. An illustration of the egg with the 'surprise' extended is shown in Plate 52.

(By courtesy of Messrs. Wartski.)

Apropos of this it is interesting to say that one day when Agathon Fabergé and I were looking into the window of a London jeweller he spotted a tiara of diamonds: 'That is one of ours', he said. He was right. Among literally hundreds of jewels in that window it stood out, not only on account of the size and brilliance of the stones themselves, but on account of the sharpness of the setting, which not only held the stones in position, but enhanced their brilliance. But it is not in such objects of jewellery that you find the real Fabergé. And here Cellini must again come into the picture.

Mr. H. Clifford Smith, M.A., in his book *Jewellery*, when speaking of Cellini, says this: 'It is the desire for harmony and beauty in execution rather than the display of wealth that characterizes the best productions of the Renaissance, whose true value lies not in their intrinsic but in their real artistic worth. . . .'

It is in this principle that you have the key note to which everything made by Fabergé, whether personal or impersonal, was attuned.

And then colour. In the jewellery of the Renaissance there is colour, 'colour in combination is now for the first time the desideratum', says Mr. Granville Fell in the *Connoisseur* of July, 1935. It is the same with the jewellery of Fabergé, when he was left to his own devices, in fact colour was not only to be desired, but eminently necessary.

Harmony and beauty in execution, colour. So far so good; the two craftsmen are at one. But now in our estimate of them, they must part company.

When we speak of a piece of jewellery 'in the style of Cellini' we mean something after the shape of a hanging lamp, or basket of flowers. There are the two chains in gold and enamel by which the lamp, the jewel itself, is suspended. The jewel consists of scroll work, opposing curves and volutes, and various details following architectural motifs and shapes of flowers, etc., with precious stones mostly table cut and set in square collets, in its outer area, the whole making a very elegant formation, delicately enamelled in all colours, in the centre of which there is usually some small figure in the round, often enamelled white opaque. From this jewel hang tassels in the way of baroque pearls or precious stones set in square collets.

Whatever Cellini did otherwise in the way of more solid pieces for personal adornment, such as his cope-clasp for Clement VII and the Leda and Swan cap-brooch attributed to him, it is the form of jewel I have attempted to describe which is in the generally accepted tradition of Cellini's manner.

Such jewels in their delicate tracery are beautiful things, but ethereal, and more fitted to adorn fairy sprites than women who are corporeal. They neither take away from, nor enhance the latter's charms. As works of art they fulfil their purpose equally well by hanging them on the wall.

Now turn to Fabergé and let us quote from Roger de Piles, *Cours de peinture par principes*, 1708:

'Nature in herself is unseemly an he who copies servilely without artifice will always produce something poor and of a mean taste. What is called "load in colour and lights" can only proceed from a profound knowledge in the values of colours and from an admirable industry, which makes the painted objects appear more true, if I may say so, than the real ones.'

57

This was written for painters, but we can with advantage adapt it to our purpose. For Fabergé, a woman was exquisitely furnished with her own beauty of form, of line, of colour; therefore if you dared to deck her out it must be done with great discretion, never forgetting it was flesh and blood you were adorning, and above all, that there must be no material price upon her head. Thus he adorned her with delicate shades of meaning in stones of rare beauty but little worth, like tourmaline, aquamarine, moonstone, Siberian amethyst, rock-crystal and such like, but especially with chalcedony of the translucent kind which, resting on the body, takes on the colouring of the flesh and which he called 'mecca-stone'.

These stones, round, oval and square, sometimes equal to the area of half-a-crown, sometimes slightly *bombé*, sometimes heavily so, *en cabochon* if you prefer, surrounded quite simply with small diamonds, rubies or emeralds, he set as brooches and pendants. Sometimes the stone hung in solitary glory, unadorned, from a setting of small diamonds and larger ones, in design after the geometrical, classical French, '*art nouveau*' and so on.

Here you have the *alpha* and *omega* of the art of Fabergé so far as jewels are concerned. Extend the idea to flower-brooches, tiaras, necklaces, hat-pins, earrings and cloak clasps, especially cloak clasps, for many of them were extraordinarily rich, and from time to time substitute flat, convex or concave surfaces of translucent enamel for the stones named, never forgetting the inexpensive brooches, quite simple little things at ten pounds or so, and you see Carl Fabergé adorning women.

In other words, he gave woman 'load in colour and lights', enhancing her charm and curve with objects rich in colour and roundness. So bedecked, she appeared more appealing than when without adornment.

As examples of the art of Fabergé I can mention the objects of jewellery made for Dr. Emanuel Nobel, the petrol king, of Stockholm, and nephew of Alfred Nobel of 'Nobel Prize' fame. He was a man for whom the jubilees and anniversaries of his directors and staff meant nothing if not suitably commemorated by some object from Fabergé. Like Mr. Henry van Gilse van der Pals, a Dutchman, and his half-brother, Mr. Max Othmar Neuscheller, a Swiss, other notable customers of Fabergé, he was a man of very original ideas.

For Dr. Nobel a dinner party was no dinner at all unless the ladies present were suitably rewarded. On one of these occasions, wishing to recall a Russian winter, he conceived the idea of giving all the ladies present an icicle. Fabergé carried this out in pendants and brooches in rock-crystal with a mat surface adorned with small diamonds in frost design.

In stressing the idea of stones of rare beauty but *little* worth, I need not remind the reader that there *are* great occasions calling for stones of rare beauty and *great* worth, but as concerns Fabergé, always he prefers stones of colour. There was the blue diamond of first water which the Craftsman showed to the last Tsar: 'I will give it to the Empress if she likes it', said the Tsar, 'to commemorate the tenth birthday of the Tsarevitch'. But the Empress said, 'We cannot afford it'.

Talking of stones of rare beauty and great worth there was the case of Madame Barbara Kelch, *née* Bazanoff. Even in Russia she was exceptional. Owning gold mines in Siberia and very rich, as a Fabergé customer she can be compared to Cellini's Madonna Porzia. It was for Madame Kelch that Fabergé made one of his most interesting and massive sets of table silver ranging from the smallest coffee spoons to large jardinières. It was in Gothic style to harmonize with the decorations of the dining-room. It was for Madame Kelch, too, that Fabergé from time to time made Easter eggs, almost as elaborate as those made for the Imperial Family (very few families enjoyed a similar privilege, that of Youssoup-off being one). But these purchases were small compared with those of the largest and rarest precious stones Fabergé could find for her. These were her speciality and her collection at the end of the Tsarist régime must have been literally of enormous value. One of her best pieces made by Fabergé was a necklace of diamonds, the centre stone of which weighed thirty carats and the rest little less.

When thinking of 'load in colour and lights' one cannot help reminding one-self of the dressmaker's efforts in these directions. 'Load in colour' is most certainly his business, but of 'lights' one cannot help feeling very doubtful, that is if what he has already accomplished is any criterion of what is to come. Fascinated, and rightly so, by the roundness of the figure, he conceived the idea long ago that in all dresses there must be a bulge somewhere. He gave it to us in the bustle, when a woman from behind had the appearance of a horse with swishing upstanding tail, then came the pouter-pigeon effect, somewhat embarrassing. In the 'leg of mutton' sleeve he quite frankly reminded us of the beauty of the roasted joint, and now he has given us two bulges on each shoulder when a woman, especially from behind, looks like nothing more than a wooden toy soldier. I would most humbly beg of him for the future to stick to the simple, pure line of the figure.*

Before we pass to the last comparison between Fabergé and Cellini, it will be of interest, I think, that something should be said about Fabergé's connection with the Russian Crown Jewels, especially as we have already mentioned this vast collection of precious stones brought together by the Empresses and Emperors of Russia, chiefly by Catherine the Great, who sent her emissaries abroad everywhere in search of the finest stones.

Publicity and propaganda, those two arch-fiends, have raised the fame of these Crown jewels to such a pinnacle that it has come to be believed that they surpass all others. In size there is little doubt that they take first place, but for purity, brilliance and colour, there is still less doubt that the palm must be given to those in the possession of the Maharajahs of India.

What I have to say about the Russian Crown Jewels was given to me at first hand by Agathon Fabergé during the four months he stayed with me in Hampstead in 1937.

He, of course, is best known to the outside world and to philatelists in particular, as having brought together the unique collection of Russian, Finnish and Polish postage stamps, but there is hardly any artistic interest for which he has not a flair, from Toby jugs to pictures. In the House of Fabergé he had a special place as a connoisseur of precious stones, and in all things appertaining to

* I do not address these remarks to the many women who practise this art, for the reason, at any rate in my view, that they work wonders in what is still a man-ridden occupation.

these he gave his father his closest support, therefore it was natural that in the maintenance of the Crown jewels it was Agathon who was chiefly concerned.

I propose only to touch upon two matters of special interest, first, the fact that the replicas in miniature of the Imperial Crown, the Sceptre and the Orb, the work of Fabergé, which were exhibited in the Hermitage Museum of the Winter Palace, in Tsarist times, were the only works to have had the honour of being placed there during the lifetime of the maker.

Secondly, the record of the Crown jewels during the most critical period of their history, that is, at the close of the Tsarist régime, and the beginning of the Soviet.

By 1913 it had become clear to Agathon that the jewels should be thoroughly overhauled and recatalogued. The Tsar's permission was obtained; and early in January 1914, he began the work, one which required the most painstaking care, as the setting of every stone had to be minutely examined. He worked on a system, from lesser to greater, beginning with the objects of lowest value such as the diadems, necklaces, etc., coming, semi-finally, to the Regalia, the Cross and Chain of St. Andrew, the Orb, the Sceptre, and last of all, the Imperial Crowns.

Having finished the examination of the Orb with its magnificent blue sapphire of 47 carats, he came to the Sceptre in which is set the world-renowned Orloff Diamond of 193 carats,* a stone of the finest bluish white from the Golconda Mine in India. This stone once served as one of the eyes of an Indian Buddha, from which it was stolen by a French soldier at the beginning of the Eighteenth Century. Later it came into the possession of the Shah-Nadir of Persia. After this prince's death the gem once again was stolen. It passed into the hands of one Lazareff, a simple merchant from Tulfa. By him it was taken to Russia, concealed in a gash in his thigh, bought by Grigori Orloff and given by him to Catherine the Great on her saint's day. By her it was set in the Imperial Sceptre of Russia and there it remains to this day as a possession of the Soviet Government and worth a fabulous sum.

As I have said, Agathon had reached the Sceptre. He felt the stone, found it loose in its setting, gave it a push from behind with his thumb, and out jumped one of the most precious of all diamonds into the palm of his hand.

This was thrill enough, but just at the moment when the Imperial Crowns were set in position for examination, the telephone rang and at the other end was His Excellency, Nicholai Nicholaivitch Nowosselsky, the chief of the Cameral Department of the Cabinet of the Tsar: 'The examination of the jewels must cease at once', he said. 'All of them are to be packed in boxes and sent under guard to Moscow.' This was in the summer of 1914, a few weeks before the beginning of the first world war. When relating this, Agathon turned to me and said: 'Was this an omen, some foreboding of what was to come? The only Crown jewels which were sent to Moscow unexamined were the Imperial Crowns, the most significant of all.'

The jewels were packed in eight or nine boxes and stored in the Kremlin in

---

* Since writing, Agathon Fabergé has informed me that the weight of the Orloff diamond is 193 carats plus a fraction of a carat.

Moscow, and there they remained for the duration of the war. After the Revolution they were still there, intact.

When the Soviet had established the new régime, the boxes were unpacked and the whole of the jewels were placed on exhibition in Moscow, where they could be viewed by the Russian people. Millions saw them. In lightning flashes from tens of thousands of facets, the stones conveyed their message: 'Power has now passed to us.'*

The stones which had at one time hypnotized the Romanoffs, and which had been stored by them with religious care long after this influence had vanished, were, by the irony of Fate, now made to hypnotize the whole nation and to be the corner stones upon which the new régime was to be built. It makes one think.

But we are not finished with Agathon and the Crown jewels. In time they became a millstone round his neck. Leaving his home at Levaschova on the Finnish border, either by compulsion or otherwise, he established himself in the early years of the Soviet régime in Leningrad (formerly St. Petersburg and Petrograd) in a top flat. Here he brought some of his treasures and the place became known as 'The Little Hermitage'.

It was from here that he was arrested and imprisoned for one and a half years by the Soviet authorities. Released, he returned to his flat only to be arrested once again and imprisoned for another nine months. It is a curious fact that during the periods of his imprisonment, his wife and flat remained unmolested, his treasure untouched. When I asked Agathon why he had been arrested, he shrugged his shoulders and said: 'Why? I wonder. I don't know.'

And now the most curious thing of all. Recovering from the effects of his last imprisonment, he received a call from a peasant in sheepskin with a message from Trotsky asking him to go to Moscow to form part of the Commission to value the Regalia and Crown jewels. Excusing himself, he refused the invitation on account of his health. In a month's time a gentleman arrived in a bowler hat bearing the same message, and he again refused the invitation. Finally, about 3 a.m. one morning there were three sharp raps on the door. His wife went into hysterics and he went to the door. Standing on the threshold were two Red soldiers. They handed him a letter from Trotsky couched in the most friendly terms and again extending the invitation. This time he accepted, provided that comfortable arrangements were made for the journey for himself, his wife and boy—provided, also, that they were properly and comfortably housed in Moscow.

Thus it was that Agathon found himself confronted once more, and for the last time, with the Crown jewels. Even now, the artist in him was supreme, for he refused to undertake the work, certainly one of the most arduous that has ever come the way of a jeweller, unless a full-size photograph was taken of every piece and the weight of every stone and pearl was included in the catalogue to be prepared.

* Dr. Armand Hammer, in his book *The Quest of the Romanoff Treasure*, gives an interesting personal account of this public display. Mr. J. A. Waite, of the British Consular Service, has given me an account of the private display of the jewels before members of the Diplomatic and Consular Services accredited to Russia, which probably took place in 1926.

Agathon remained in Moscow from the autumn of 1921 until the spring of 1923, working with the Commission, and finally the catalogue was published. This catalogue is the authoritative record of the jewels and is now in the possession of the Soviet authorities. I saw a copy of it in New York in 1937 in the possession of Dr. Armand Hammer, and can vouch for it as being a most remarkable work.

With the exception of the Nuptial Crown, used for the coronation of all the Grand Duchesses at their marriage ceremony, which was sold in London some years ago, the Crown jewels, so far as I know, are still intact in the possession of the Soviet Government. One thing is certain: should at any time any of them be stolen or missing, the fact that each piece is minutely photographed in its actual size and catalogued precisely, will help vastly in recovery.

Thus far with Agathon Fabergé and the Crown jewels. But another headache was in store for him and that was the 'mountain', as he called it, of loose diamonds, the result of the breaking up of the jewellery in private possession and confiscated by the Soviet Government, to which I have already referred. The diamonds, as they were released from their setting, were washed and placed on the table in lots of from 18 to 20 lbs., forming a heap which was continually growing. This heap it was Agathon's job to reduce by sorting and packeting. When I asked him for particulars he simply threw up his hands.

Before leaving the Crown jewels, justice demands that something should be said about their safe-keeping by the Romanoffs. A popular idea pictures the scions of the Imperial house as wallowing from their youth upwards in a glory of barbaric splendour, with jewels on their heads, diamonds on their fingers and rubies on their toes; something after the fashion of the noblemen of France and England at the Field of the Cloth of Gold when in the words of Du Bellay 'they carried the price of woodland, watermill and pasture on their backs'.[1]

Their experience in the art of living was vast and no matter what is puzzling in it, we can deduce much. Curiously enough it is the sterner side, the art of restraint, of which we learn most. Peter set the example by harnessing the whole family in disciplinary traces and Nicholas II confirmed it by his simple way of life.

Between these two we find Marie Feodorovna, the wife of Paul I, who never slept on a proper bed until the last year of her life, but used a divan made up for her every night so that she might be ready for work or anything else at any time. Alexander I and Nicholas I slept on small camp-beds in similar austere fashion. The latter did not even use a blanket, but merely tossed over him his soldier's cloak.

All the young male members of the family were required to rise at 6 a.m. and say their prayers, all had to go through the discipline of the army.[2]

As we follow their history we find them caring less and less for a scintillating mass of precious stones, and by the time Alexander III had come to the throne the hypnotizing power they exercised had almost ceased. When his son, Nicholas II, succeeded him, it had completely vanished.

Now the point in all this, it seems to me, is that although the Romanoffs

[1] *Jewellery*, by H. Clifford Smith, M.A.
[2] *Once a Grand Duke*, by The Grand Duke Alexander Mihailovitch.

lived in circumstances unparalleled almost in history, surrounded by wealth, privileges and favours enough to have driven them to perdition every day had they been so inclined, they did not take this road so glitteringly set before them, and it is a point very moot indeed whether, given such conditions of living, we should have come out nearly so well.

One thing above all else stands to their high credit. A creation of standards, which Demos may well note for his own edification. The behaviour of the Romanoffs in regard to the Crown jewels was exemplary. Whilst for some 200 years these were under their trusteeship, they were housed and maintained with the utmost care. No piece was allowed to leave the Diamond Room in the Winter Palace, except under the most rigorous surveillance and regulations, even the Tsarina herself, if I remember aright what Agathon Fabergé told me, being subjected to the strict routine of taking out and redepositing.

Mr. A. Polovtsoff, in his little book *Russian Exhibition Gossip*, which embodied the stories of some of the objects shown at the Exhibition of Russian Art held in London in 1935, prefaces these stories with what he calls *A Few Truisms*. Addressing himself to the objects on view, he asks:

'How about the poor things themselves? What will they feel about the degree of appreciation they elicit? They have been brought from a number of various lands and hung on walls or stuck in glass cases so as to be studied and criticized, admired or spurned. They assume, of course, an air of unruffled complacency while being peered at, for they are mostly gentlefolks' belongings and know how to behave. But at night, when the visitors have departed and the doors are safely locked, do they indulge in a secret life of their own and do they exchange their impressions of the day? So called inanimate objects have souls (we all know that), therefore they cannot but be endowed with all the attributes of a soul: tempers, amiable or vicious, moods, reactions and so forth, and so on. Do they tell each other stories of former days, of the days when what is now the past for them used to be actuality? Do they keep up a stately conversation, comparing what was the custom then to what seems to be the custom now, inasmuch as they are able to judge through the glasses of their cases?

'It would perhaps be worth while trying to overhear their gossip. If the people were described in whose lives they have played a part, those remnants of the past would acquire a new meaning. . . . Eavesdropping is an exciting occupation and leads to many discoveries. When indulged in and recorded on paper it makes up stories.'

Mr. Polovtsoff's stories do not concern us at the moment; stories of the jasper cane-knob which the Empress Elizabeth Petrovna gave to her husband, Count Razumovsky, of Levitsky's portrait of Khrapovitsky, Catherine the Great's secretary, and so on. What we are here concerned with are the Russian Crown jewels. They were not, of course, shown at the Exhibition, at that time being safely in the Kremlin in Moscow. We should like to know what was happening to them, packed in their eight-nine boxes, while on their journey thither in the summer of 1914. How did they feel, and what were they talking about between themselves?

What a subject for a biographer with 'historic imagination'! In the hands of such a man what could not the Crown of the Empress Marie Feodorovna be made to say to the Crown of the last Empress Alexandra Feodorovna and what secrets could not this Empress's favourite diadem of pearls and diamonds be made to unfold to that in diamonds of the wife of Alexander I! And above all what admonishments could not the Crown of Catherine the Great in pearls and diamonds surmounted by that magnificent spinel ruby of 415 carats, be made to administer to the whole collection of jewels!

Unfortunately I am not so gifted. I must content myself with actuality and say this. Whatever these jewels may have said to one another on their fateful journey to Moscow in the summer of 1914, it is a fact that they were packed by Imperialism, so called, and unpacked by Bolshevism, so called, and put to the same purpose as before.

And with that, let us pass finally to Cellini and Fabergé.

When all has been said about both of them, it is their unceasing activity which grips you in the end. The restless spirit of the Renaissance hovering from place to place and the Russian Craftsman tied to his stool and counter in St. Petersburg, were both of them men of action in the first degree.

Activity is the touchstone of success. It is a necessity to the goldsmith to instil activity into all his wares and by so doing develop a state of activity in others. Working as he does in miniature in the precious metals, restricted as he is to a limited field, greater brilliance in craftsmanship is demanded of him, if he is to succeed, than from any other worker in the arts, and in this he has been generally more successful than any other craftsman. His very achievements rouse you and evoke delight. Even if they are not to your taste, you cannot withhold admiration.

The goldsmith gives you no time for tears, no time to idle. If you are panting for the waterbrook and the everlasting hills, then you must go to someone whose affair this is. Not that repose and dignity are outside his province, and so far as these concern Fabergé, you have only to look at the smoky rock-crystal goblet in Plate 7 to be assured of this.

But he would much sooner have you rouse yourself to be up and doing, and certainly three-quarters of all Fabergé did has this rousing effect. It is Petersburg all over again. It is as though he says to you: 'For the life of me I would not hurt you, but do let me do something to take you out of yourself. Whatever your particular misery, I want to break the vicious circle, and to detach you I will even outcraft my craftsmanship if only I can amaze you by the sight of it and set you going another way, even if only for half an hour.'

Yes, surprise is the potent word now, and you see his highest effort in the realm of surprise in his Imperial Easter Eggs, to the story of which I have devoted a special place. These are goldsmithery *in excelsis*.

Collectors should take this lesson to heart, and remember that just so far as they jumble their objects together, thus far do they take all meaning out of them. Each piece is one of quality, made with an infinity of care, and wrought with intent to be a surprise to some one particular person.

To display them in twos and threes, or in sixes at most, in pigeon-holes or small compartments behind a panel in the wall, to be lit up at will when there is a feeling of downheartedness coming on, is to follow the lead the Craftsman himself has given. Instead of a crude and nauseating mass of chalcedony, jade, jasper, aventurine-quartz, rhodonite, agate, lapis-lazuli and enamel they will assume their rightful aspects and evoke delight. If, on the other hand, collectors keep their quartz objects hidden away in drawers, I suggest to them they might just as well sell them, buy stocks and shares and be thoroughly miserable. But better still, allow them to be distributed between the various National Museums and exhibited in appropriate groups. What a sight for many sore eyes if groups of the Easter Eggs, of the animals, of the flowers, and of the clocks, cigarette cases, boxes and figurines could be put on public exhibition and thus reveal to the world the amazing genius of an artist-craftsman. I believe it to be a fact that there is not one single piece of Fabergé's work in any museum anywhere and mainly for the reason that it is Nineteenth, not Eighteenth Century work. I except, of course, the three pieces previously mentioned, still, I hope, in the Hermitage Museum in Leningrad, and the Buddha in the National Museum, Bangkok.*

And so we come to an end, arrived, I hope, a little nearer to the understanding of Fabergé than when we began. Let us repeat. With a handful of his contemporaries, he became the spokesman of the great patrons and cultured men and women of the end of the Nineteenth and the beginning of the Twentieth Centuries, and as the medium through which so much good will was broadcast and happiness bestowed, he made himself well-nigh indispensable to his generation.

He achieved this end through craftsmanship. His materials were of the earth's rarest products and these are costly. But, and here was the saving grace, by reason of his craftsmanship he freed the giver from the stain of the unforgivable, that by which the recipient is put under a pecuniary obligation. In fact his craftsmanship became so cunning that the cost of the materials employed was more often than not wiped out altogether.

It is when this happens that you arrive at the ideal gift for your sovereign lord the King, whoever and wherever he may be.

* Since writing this I have heard from Mr. Marvin C. Ross, Curator of Mediaeval and Subsequent Decorative Arts at The Walters Art Gallery, Baltimore, Maryland, U.S.A., that this Art Gallery possesses a collection of Fabergé objects, some of which were acquired by the Walters family when, with Princess Cantacuzène (née Grant), they visited Fabergé's establishment in St. Petersburg about 1900. Others were purchased by Mr. Walters through Mr. Alexander Polovtsoff in the U.S.A. in 1930. Two of the objects are illustrated in Plate 43.

I am also informed by Mr. Victor Hammer of New York, that Mrs. Lillian T. Pratt of Fredericksburg, Virginia, died in the autumn of 1947 and left her Fabergé collection, including four Imperial Easter Eggs and many other pieces (a truly munificent gift) to the Virginia Museum of Fine Arts. Three of these eggs are illustrated in Plates 49, 58 and 67.

CHAPTER IV

THE IMPERIAL RUSSIAN EASTER EGGS

IT is natural that collectors of Fabergé wares in his heyday should have had a better knowledge of his work and been in a position to form a truer estimate of the Craftsman than the collectors of to-day. The House of Fabergé was then in active production, and objects of every kind, as they came from its workshops, were to be found not only in St. Petersburg, Moscow, Odessa and Kieff, but throughout the world.

Nevertheless, certain objects were strictly hidden from public view. Such were the Imperial Easter Eggs made for the Tsars Alexander III and Nicholas II. These were a personal matter solely between the Tsars and the Craftsman. Fabergé himself never mentioned them in my hearing, and his staff preserved a discreet silence on the subject. Only once were they publicly displayed and that at the *Exposition Internationale Universelle* in Paris in 1900 when at the express wish of the Empress Alexandra Feodorovna and the Dowager Empress Marie Feodorovna they were shown with the rest of the Fabergé exhibits. But that was nearly half a century ago.

Now, by the irony of circumstance, the first Fabergé productions which came to general notice after the death of the Craftsman were these identical Imperial Easter Eggs. A number of them were purchased in Russia subsequent to the Revolution and were brought to London or taken to New York.* In a few years' time certain examples were shown at the Russian Exhibition in London in 1935 and for the first time on record, Fabergé received attention from the English daily and weekly Press, and particular emphasis was laid on the Imperial Easter Eggs.

Therein was calamity. The inevitable followed. Here were 'miracles of dainty expensiveness', 'gorgeous affairs', etc., and the Craftsman was designated 'rather a melancholy joke'. This was 'Imperialism gone crazy', and it was repeated that no wonder the Romanoffs came to a tragic end.

To the bleak, barren, and forlorn world of 1935, already on the downward slope which led to such tragic events, and within four short years of the great catastrophe, these Imperial Easter Eggs were considered 'wonderful, but, of course, not of our world to-day'.

Over ten years have passed since these dismal folk so expressed themselves. Years in which 'all the worlds that ever were' have been shattered beyond recognition. One thing we should have learned, that to detach the works of any man from the times in which they were made and sit in judgment upon them from the

---

* I refer the reader to Dr. Armand Hammer's book *The Quest of the Romanoff Treasure*, published in New York in 1936, in which he gives an illuminating account of his nine years' sojourn in Russia, dating from 1921, during which time he became possessed of eleven of these Imperial Easter Eggs and several hundreds of other Fabergé pieces.

juridical bench of our latter-day experience can be a very dangerous and misleading business, unless in giving our verdict we allow a proper understanding of their period and the conditions of creative activity to guide us.

Substantially where these critics failed was in not appreciating the fact that Fabergé was above all else a goldsmith and like all such he was limited by the conditions of his craft. Goldsmithery is a hard taskmaster. In practice, as the great masters of the Renaissance well knew, it makes the most exacting demands on the skill and the integrity of the artist. There can be no beating about the bush in what he has to do. He can take no liberties as with brush or chisel, or extend himself, unfettered, in works of large proportions and dimensions. He must subject himself to the severest discipline; he must be precise and confine himself wholly to the purpose.

No one in daily contact with Fabergé could fail to see that he had learned this lesson. His every act was a demonstration of the fact. To trespass unreasonably upon his time, to subject him to some inane remark, to irritate his sense of the fitness of things was to expose yourself to instant attack. One of the Grand Duchesses once enquired of him: 'And what new eggs have you this year, Mr. Fabergé?' 'This year, Your Highness, we have square ones!' was his reply. This was said without any intention of rudeness or injury. His mind was sharpened to a point rarely reached by man, and if you would get on with him it behoved you to bestir yourself.

In the Imperial Easter Eggs you see Fabergé at his best. Here is manifested his activity and his genius for envisaging his object in its minutest details to arouse your faculty of wonderment. It is quite safe to say that nothing which has so far come from a goldsmith's workshop surpasses these productions in craftsmanship and ingenuity. But that is the least one can say about them. They are supreme examples of understanding. Significance is the thing you must bear in mind if you are to appreciate on what the Craftsman's mind was focussed.

It is to his abiding credit that Fabergé conceived the egg in its right place, as a symbol; that is, he restored to it the meaning with which the ancients originally invested it. For him, as for them, the egg as a symbol was not concerned with the scheme of things beyond the grave, it was bound up irrevocably with things that are living. It was the 'Here and Now' which occupied his attention, the best that can be got out of the Earth we tread, before we can hope to have any conception of what the high Heaven beyond the skies has in store for us.

The history of the egg as a symbol is far too long to be recounted here. Plutarch in his *Table Talks* (Book II, Quest. III) asks the eternal question: 'Which of the two came first, the hen or the egg?' And there is a fund of information on the subject in the works of which I annex a list for those specially interested. The most I can do here is to summarize.

The philosophers of antiquity put it as follows. In the beginning, they declared, the egg was the origin of all things, and it was therefore the symbol of the Creation, the work of the Supreme Divinity. Nothing existed outside this Divinity. He, controlling matter, having left it in a state of chaos and darkness, unperceived, undistinguishable, undiscoverable, unknowable, sunk entirely in sleep, by degrees,

67

by mere thought, re-fashioned it in the shape of an egg and having permeated it with His goodness, separated from it the elements and made use of it to shape the universe, when solitude, chaos and gloom gave place to a great multitude of various creatures in which matter was set in motion, quickened, took on light, form and colour and resulted in that most astonishing manifestation—*Life*.

Whether you turn to the mundane egg of the ancient Persians ; to the Greeks and the egg of Orpheus; to the Egyptians and their divinity, Keph or Emeph, represented in human form, having on its head a sparrowhawk with an egg emerging from its mouth; or to the Hindoos and the Golden Egg of Brahma, the interpretation of the symbol is the same.

Plutarch (*Opera Moralia.* 'On Isis and Osiris' Translation: Monsieur l'Abbé Batteux) goes into some interesting details of the philosophy of the ancient Persians which are worth repeating in full:

'Ormuzd, born of the most pure light, and Ahriman of the darkness, are mutually at war with each other. The former produced six gods, Benevolence, Truth, Order, Wisdom, Abundance, Worthy Joy. The latter, in the same way produced six, counteracting the first six.

'Ormuzd, having made himself three times larger, raised himself above the sun, as much as the sun is above the earth, and he decked the heavens with stars, among which Sirius was set as a sentinel in the heavens, or the vanguard of the stars. He produced besides this, twenty-four other gods, who were put into an egg.

'Those created by Ahriman, also to the number of twenty-four, perforated the egg, and mingled evil with good. But there will come a time betokened by destiny, when Ahriman, after having brought plague and famine, will himself be completely destroyed; then the Earth, without any inequality, will be the abode of men, all happy, speaking the same language, living under the same law.'

However one may gasp at the extravagance of the fantasy with which these ancients brought the whole existing universe within their purview, they came back solidly to the earth on which they lived, to the fullness of it, the fertility, the richness, the order, the nature of it, and the divinity within it.

If their creed was anything it was: 'Life and hope, here and now.' And every year they renewed their faith by eating eggs. They dyed them in various colours, chiefly red, their favourite colour, and gave them as presents one to the other at the festival of the New Year, celebrated at the Spring Equinox.

As M. Court de Gebelin says in his *Monde Primitif:*

'It was so pleasing to have survived the preceding vicissitudes and all the deadly eventualities which incessantly carry off a portion of humanity that people could do no less than congratulate each other for being still among the number of those living, and mutually to wish each other a year free from calamities rich in all kinds of favours and prosperity. . . . Thus were drawn closer together the ties which bound them each to the other, and these mutual good wishes were so many guarantees to assist each other and to work for the common good.'

That is the story of the egg as told by the ancients. We proceed to the continuation as recorded in the writings and sayings of travellers, chroniclers and men of learning from the Thirteenth Century to the present day. Here again one can only summarize.

Man began by perceiving that the egg was the one perfect thing in the universe, encasing as it does the germ of life in a container pleasing both to sight and to touch. As time went on he began to consider its significance and its specific attributes, and used it to symbolize that which at the time was best suited to his race, his aspirations, his interests and his creed. It was in this way that the proportion of humanity which became Christian (and it is this proportion with which we are in particular concerned) took it over as symbolic of the Resurrection and of the Life beyond the grave.

It does not seem to have occurred to them at any time that, by so doing, the earth would be left without any symbol at all by which they might be encouraged to give some attention to present realities. In any case the acceptance of it was done very half-heartedly, for there is no evidence that at any time the egg was given any high place in the religious ceremonies of the Christian Church.

To-day we all know where it stands. As a symbol, grown men and women have put it aside altogether, both celestially and terrestrially. The children alone keep it alive. If you should ask them, they will tell you it stands for fun, for all that is joyous, delightful and free. But the way in which it is regarded by the present-day Chinese remains as of old, for to them as for the ancients, the egg is a symbol of life. When a baby is born, it is customary for the parents to distribute red-coloured eggs in even numbers among their friends and relatives. And newly-married couples are sometimes asked: 'When shall we have your red eggs to eat' (Lionel Giles, M.A., D.Litt. Late Keeper of Oriental Printed Books and Manuscripts, British Museum).

Having this historical source as their background, we can come to the Imperial Russian Easter Eggs, knowing where we stand. As I have said before, Fabergé never at any time discussed them with me, but that is no reason for thinking that he looked upon them as of small account. In fact you may be quite sure that the less he said about anything the greater consideration he gave to it. Like everything else, in his view, these eggs had their purpose. What you see you may like or you may not like, according to your personal taste. But that is beside the point. Like everything else in Russia, it is what you do *not* see which counts.

Fortunately Carl Fabergé was a very simple but very sagacious person. As such, no man knew better than he that no one can really tell another much, and that more often than not words go in at one ear and out at the other. If ever a man relied on gesture it was he, and he reduced it to such an art that you were a poor reader of human nature indeed if he did not become an open book to you. What therefore I have to say about the Easter Eggs I gathered from the whole man as I knew him. The facts are supplied by Eugène and Agathon Fabergé.

69

When in 1883 (this is the nearest approximation to a date which Eugène Fabergé is able to give) Carl Fabergé first proposed to Alexander III that for the next Easter gift for the Tsarina he should make an egg with some special 'surprise' in it, the Tsar was all agog to know about it. But Fabergé kept his secret and, loving a joke, he produced what was to all appearance an ordinary hen's egg. It was of gold enamelled opaque white, and on being opened revealed a yolk also of gold. The yolk opened, and inside was a chicken made in gold of different shades; within the chicken was a model of the Imperial crown, and inside this hung a tiny ruby egg.

This pleased the Tsar so greatly that he gave the Craftsman a standing order for an egg every Easter, and a bargain was struck between Emperor and Craftsman. The latter was given a free hand to make whatever took his fancy, and the former was to ask no questions, the one stipulation being that each egg must have some surprise inside it. But Fabergé's tactics in exciting or kindling the curiosity of his Imperial patron were so successful that at last Alexander was unable to keep his pledge and eagerly asked what the next year's surprise was to be. Knowing full well how to speak to princes, the Craftsman's only reply was 'Your Majesty will be content'.

Taking 1883 as the correct year when the proposal was made to the Tsar Alexander III, and 1884 as the year when the first egg was delivered, and calculating one egg per year during this Emperor's reign and two each year during the reign of Nicholas II,[1] including those made for the Easter of 1917, then in all Fabergé must have made fifty-seven of these Imperial Easter Eggs: eleven to the order of Alexander III, all of which the Tsar presented to his wife, the Empress Marie Feodorovna (the Danish Princess Dagmar, sister of Queen Alexandra), and forty-six to the order of Nicholas II. Of these forty-six, the Tsar gave forty-four to the Empress Alexandra Feodorovna, his wife, and the Dowager Empress Marie, his mother; one to each every year.[2]

As befitted such exclusive objects, the delivery of them was ceremonial. From all the information I have been able to gather those made for Alexander III were delivered personally by the Craftsman to the Emperor, but when Nicholas II came to the throne and there were two eggs to be delivered on the same Easter Eve, one to the Emperor for presentation to the Empress and the other to the Dowager Empress on behalf of the Emperor, it was not always possible for Fabergé to make delivery himself. At these times he himself delivered the one to the Emperor and the other to the Dowager Empress on behalf of the Emperor was taken by one of his chief assistants.

In later years, when his sons had grown up, it was they who assisted their father and so it was that in 1912 the Tsar Nicholas II, being then in residence at the Livadia Palace near Yalta, Eugène Fabergé travelled the whole of Russia from St. Petersburg to Sebastopol taking the egg destined for the Empress, the one in lapis lazuli, inside of which is the double-headed eagle in diamonds framing the miniature of the Tsarevitch Alexis. (See Plate 49.)

[1] See Chapter I, page 14.

[2] Refer to the activities of Workmaster Perchin, Chapter VII (page 123). If 1886 was the date of the making of the first egg then in all Fabergé must have produced only fifty-four.

At Sebastopol Eugène was met by Prince Vladimir Orloff (this Prince always drove the Emperor) in one of the Imperial automobiles, and driven via the beautiful Baydary Pass to Yalta, a journey taking some four hours. Here Eugène says he 'changed his clothes' and was then driven by the Prince to the Livadia Palace where he was received by the Emperor who expressed himself as delighted with the egg. The Tsar Nicholas II always intimated when audiences were at an end by rising and walking to a window and he followed his usual routine in this case when he took Eugène by the elbow and conducting him to a window pointed out the magnificent view over Yalta and the Black Sea, at the same time directing Eugène to convey 'sincere compliments' and 'best thanks' to his father.

On Easter Eve of the same year Carl Fabergé himself, on behalf of the Tsar, delivered the companion egg to the Dowager Empress in St. Petersburg. The principal decorations of this egg are military emblems and double-headed eagles on a guilloché background of emerald-green enamel framed in ruby-coloured enamel. In Empire style, the motifs symbolize the war which Russia waged against Napoleon, commemorated on its one-hundredth anniversary. Inside the egg there is a folding screen of signed miniatures by Vassily Zuieff portraying members of the regiments of which the Dowager Empress was Colonel-in-Chief.

In the May and June numbers of *The Connoisseur*, 1934, I have given many illustrations of the Imperial Easter Eggs, but in this present record there is only space to note a limited number of them. One of the most significant is that made in commemoration of the Tercentenary of Romanoff rule and presented by the Tsar Nicholas II to the Tsarina Alexandra Feodorovna, Easter 1913. This is one of Fabergé's most elaborate pieces. On the outside are miniatures of all the Tsars of the House of Romanoff, framed amid Russian eagles in chased gold on a background of white enamel. The pedestal represents the Russian Imperial Shield in porphyry, set with precious stones and gold. Inside the egg is a globe of blued steel with two maps of the Russian Empire inset in gold; one of the year 1613, the other 1913. There is no record that this egg ever left Russia, maybe it is in the possession of the Soviet Government, or in some private possession there, or perhaps it has been destroyed.[1]

Another example is that made to commemorate the Bicentenary in 1903 of the City of St. Petersburg. It is of gold superbly chased and adorned with brilliants and rubies. The miniatures are of Peter the Great, Peter the Great's house, Nicholas II and the Winter Palace.[2] It encloses a gold model on sapphire pedestal of Falconet's statue to Peter the Great. This egg was presented to the Tsarina Alexandra Feodorovna by the Tsar Nicholas II, Easter 1903. (See Plate 50.)

A third egg and also presented to the Tsarina, at Easter 1914, is remarkable for one or two reasons. For one it is the last of the joyous eggs presented to the Tsarina Alexandra Feodorovna. The idea seems to have struck the Craftsman that he would enclose the Imperial children in a cage of delight. Hyper-sensitive

---

[1] The author regrets extremely that he is unable to illustrate this important example owing to the fact that no suitable photograph exists.
[2] Miniatures by Vassily Zuieff.

as he was, perhaps he knew that never again after the year 1914, was real joy to come to them again. Who can tell! Be this as it may, for the first and only time Fabergé made use of a cage-like jewel, the main feature of which is a number of panels set with small square-cut precious stones of colour to give an effect of flowers, with a framing of white enamel and pearls. The egg enshrines the 'surprise', a cameo representing the five Imperial children in monochrome enamel supported on a small stand in gold, white opaque and green enamels adorned with pearls and diamonds. The names of the children appear on the back of the cameo in Russian characters. This egg is in the possession of Queen Mary, and as one of the most personal it is fitting it should be so. By Her Majesty's gracious permission I am able to reproduce it for the first time. (See Plates 51 and 55.)

The companion egg to this, presented to the Dowager Empress Marie Feodorovna, is equally joyous. In short it is an epitome of the arts of peace, executed in French classic style and in most lavish manner. It is illustrated in Plate 57.

By 1915 Russia was at war with Germany and the Imperial Easter Eggs from now onwards and up to the final tragedy, surely the most wicked yet to have overtaken any Royal House at the hands of a responsible Government, become symbols of war. Austerity becomes more and more the order of the day, both as regards design and the materials employed.

This is to be seen in the Red Cross Egg presented to the Dowager Empress in 1915. It is in white enamel without any precious stones, encompassed by the words in Russian characters, 'Greater love hath no man than this, that a man lay down his life for his friends'; two red crosses bear the years '1914' and '1915', the first in commemoration of the beginning of the war, the other marking the year of its presentation by the Tsar Nicholas II to his mother the Dowager Empress Marie. On mother-of-pearl panels forming a screen of gold and enamel within the egg, are portraits in miniature of the Tsarina Alexandra Feodorovna (middle of the screen) and her four daughters the Grand Duchesses Olga, Tatiana, Maria and Anastasia. Each wears the uniform of the Red Cross of which organisation in Russia the Empress was President. The Red Cross symbol surmounts the individual frames. (See Plate 58.)

When we reach the Easter of 1916 fate begins to show her hand both as regards Russia and the Imperial Family. The Tsar Nicholas II is at the front and he telegraphs to Fabergé to deliver this year's egg on his behalf to the Tsarina at Tsarskoe-Selo. On Easter Eve Eugène Fabergé again acts for his father and for the last time. Received by the Empress, who was surrounded by her five children, he hands to her what must be the most austere of any object made by Fabergé for the Imperial Family, an egg made of blackened steel with the Empress's initials in gold.* As far as Eugène remembers the egg was poised on four shrapnel which rested on a block of nephrite (or steel?). Inside is an easel, also in steel, which bears a square miniature by Zuieff representing the Tsar with the Tsarevitch in conversation with the staff generals at the front. Where this egg is to-day is not known, I have never heard of it as being in England or America and can only assume it is still in Russia if it has escaped destruction.

* An interesting cigarette case in blackened steel is illustrated in Plate 126.

The companion egg, adorned with motifs of the military Georgian Cross, inside of which are miniatures of the Tsar Nicholas II and the Tsarevitch, and made for presentation to the Dowager Empress, was delivered to her on Easter Eve 1916 in St. Petersburg by the Craftsman himself. This egg, and most rightly so, is in the possession of the Grand Duchess Xenia, daughter of the Tsar Alexander III. These two Fabergé objects were the last to be delivered to the Imperial Family.

Regardless of events, fast moving to their terrible climax, Fabergé continued with the making of the two eggs for Easter 1917, but by the time Easter Eve arrived the Tsar, with the Tsarina and their five children, were prisoners in the Alexander Palace, Tsarskoe-Selo, and it is to the everlasting shame of the Provisional Government that delivery of them was not allowed.[1] Where they are to-day and what they were made of I have not been able to find out, but Eugène Fabergé tells me that so far as his memory goes one of them was in Karelian birch.

In Plates 52, 56, and 59-68, various other of the Imperial Eggs are reproduced. Because they are not described in the script it must not be thought that they are in any way the less remarkable. The fact is that everyone of these Imperial Easter Eggs calls for a chapter to itself, but unfortunately for this there is not space enough.[2]

That is the bare record of the Imperial Easter Eggs. Now we come to the purpose they served, and one cannot reiterate too often that in the making of 'Fabergé' objects it was with purpose all the time, purpose to serve an immediate present, mundane to a degree, and never with an eye to posterity. In the Easter eggs there can be no mistake as to the Craftsman's intention; it is evident to all. Never at any time did he invest these with a celestial meaning. They were always of the earth, earthy, as you may see from the 'surprises' contained within the eggs— a coronation coach, a Siberian train, miniatures of the Imperial family, a basket of spring flowers, a strutting peacock, a gliding swan, and so on. Never did he confuse the symbolism of the egg with that of the cross.

After this, let us visit the Winter Palace, St. Petersburg, on Sunday, March 1 13, 1881, immediately after the assassination of the Tsar Alexander II, and recall the words of the Grand Duke Alexander Michailovitch in *Once a Grand Duke*.

'The Emperor lay on the couch near the desk. He was unconscious. Three doctors were fussing around, but science was obviously helpless. It was a question of minutes. He presented a terrific sight, his right leg torn off, his left leg shattered, innumerable wounds all over his head and face. One eye shut, the other expressionless. . . . The agony lasted forty-five minutes.'

So died Alexander II, the easy-going, soft-hearted, liberal-minded and courageous Tsar, who emancipated the serfs, and the reign of Alexander III, his son, began.

[1] The author does not know the whereabouts of the Dowager Empress Marie at Easter 1917. There is no evidence that she ever received the egg which had been made for her.

[2] I have often been asked what the Tsars paid for each of these eggs. To settle the question I asked Agathon Fabergé and received the following cable from him on October 1st, 1947: 'Eggs price about 30,000 roubles'.

There was nothing of good omen in the terrible passing at which the new Tsar and his wife had both been witnesses. As he led her away to the waiting carriage, and so to his first meeting with his ministers, her mind cannot but have been filled with an agonising foreboding. By the time they had driven away to the acclamation of the people, an awful vision must have taken shape in her mind. Add another numeral, and the dead man might be the colossus now sitting by her side.

That was in 1881. Two years afterwards, Fabergé made his proposal to the Emperor, and during the passage of those two years the Empress cannot have known an hour's real peace. Then things began to take a brighter turn. It was Easter, and the spring of the year, with everything quickening to new life. Alexander was a Romanoff, and as such he had that which all his family possessed, the flair for giving the right thing to the right person at the right moment. In his view the right moment was Easter, the right thing an Easter egg, and the right person the Empress. The Cross, the symbol of the Christians' immortality, was on high. For Alexander that was something fixed and immovable.

But there was another thing needed, and Alexander wanted it there and then, and very badly. His excitement when he attempted to back out of his agreement with the Craftsman is evidence enough of this. And the excitement of one without sympathy of any sort 'with exquisite refinement and studied elegance', but of a very purposeful colossus who gloried in the idea of being of the same rough texture as the majority of his subjects.

For the time being things went more happily in Russia, but Alexander wanted, above all else, happiness for the Empress. And Fabergé had found him the means to obtain it. Surprise! And surprise and wonder so fraught with astonishment and delight that it would break the bonds of the agony which bound the Empress. For half an hour, at any rate, it would ease her nervous strain and direct her thoughts towards a brighter future.

What matter to the Emperor the cost? What matter the form of the surprise? What matter the diamonds, the rubies, and the pearls, so long as he could gain his end? With surprise a new beginning would be made, and with a new beginning would be life, and with life would come hope, the very core of life.

There is no other way to understanding the purport of the Imperial Easter Eggs. All the circumstances agree. Therefore whenever we see them we should not make the mistake of detaching them in our minds from the times in which they were made. We will continue to call them 'wonderful', but we will not say 'Such things, of course, are not of our world of to-day'. We will not see them as 'miracles of dainty expensiveness' but as objects of significance. With Alexander, we will open wide both our eyes. With one, we will see a right leg torn off, a left leg shattered, innumerable wounds all over head and face. One eye shut, the other expressionless. And with our other eye we will see a basketful of spring flowers.

A last word about marks. Those eggs the main feature of which is essentially jeweller's work bear neither maker's mark nor State hall-marks stamped upon them, such for example as the rock-crystal egg with frost design (Plate 61) and the 'cage-like jewel' (Plate 55). Sometimes in such cases the engraved name of FABERGÉ, in Latin characters, appears on the egg, sometimes on the 'surprise' only, sometimes on both. For instance, the rock-crystal egg, as above, is not engraved on the egg but is engraved on the bottom of the 'surprise', a basketful of flowers, 'FABERGÉ 1913'. In the case of the 'cage-like' egg, the egg itself is engraved 'C. FABERGÉ', and the 'surprise', the cameo, is engraved 'G. FABERGÉ' (the G. is an error).

All such egg-jewels were made in the workshop of Holmström, father, and later his son, the chief jewellery-workmasters of the firm. It is of interest to note that in the making of the 'cage-like' egg the Holmströms did not require to call in any help from the workshops of other crafts except in the case of the enamelling of the 'surprise'. In the case of the rock-crystal egg, the only work for which the Holmströms were not responsible was that of the lapidaries on the egg, pedestal and cacholong flowers, and the engraving of the internal frost-flowers.

So much for jeweller's work. Those eggs in which goldsmith's work predominates were made in the workshop of Perchin and later of Wigström. Although marks are stamped on these eggs, there is no uniformity in such. A perfect marking would be (1) name of firm in Russian characters, (2) workmaster's initials, (3) Russian State hall-mark of fineness of precious metal, (4) mark of the St. Petersburg assay office or of the woman's head with *kokoshnik* which was later adopted throughout Russia as the mark of all the assay offices; but these by no means always appear.

Sometimes it is the name of the firm only; sometimes the firm's name and State hall-mark of fineness; sometimes the initials of the workmaster and the State hall-mark of fineness; sometimes the name of the firm and the initials of the workmaster, and so on—there is no regularity.

The most interesting thing is that in the case of some eggs made throughout of gold, no State standard mark of fineness appears, whereas sometimes when silver is used a perfect delight seems to have been taken in making it plainly evident that a metal of less rarity has been employed by giving prominence to the silver-standard mark. The plain truth is that marking and hall-marking did not interest Fabergé one bit. The matter is gone into in more detail in the last chapter of this record.

To return to the workshops for a moment. Those of Perchin, Wigström and Holmström, were the only ones responsible for the making of the Imperial Easter eggs.* Another workmaster, Hollming, may now and again have made some small trinket as part of the internal 'surprise', but certainly he took no part in the making of the eggs.

Some of the eggs which bear the marks of Perchin or Wigström were executed on a foundation of stone, such as nephrite, jasper, etc. This stone part was cut in one of the lapidaries' workshops supervised by the workmaster Woerffel. Although in many cases, as in that of the Coach egg (Plate 89), the whole work, that of the egg and the 'surprise' (except the enamelling, which was always done by the enamellers, Petroff or Boitzoff), was done in the one workshop of Perchin or Wigström, there were, however, times when the work on the egg itself was executed by Perchin or Wigström, and the 'surprise', because it was purely jeweller's work, was carried out in the workshop of Holmström. Such a case is that of the egg containing the double-headed eagle in diamonds (Plate 49), an

---

* If any of the eggs were made previous to 1886 then, as well as Holmström, Workmaster Kollin may have been the maker.

exquisite example of jeweller's work, set as it is, both back and front, with brilliants.

In preparing this chapter I have consulted the following sources of information:

Travels in Georgia, Persia, Armenia, Ancient Babylon, during the years 1817, 1818, 1819, 1820, by Sir Robert Ker Porter. 1821.

Principal Navigations, Voyages, etc., of the English Nation, by Richard Hakluyt. 1599.

Popular Antiquities of Great Britain, from material collected by John Brand, F.S.A., with very large corrections and additions, by W. Carew Hazlitt. 1870.

Archæologia, of Miscellaneous tracts relating to Antiquity, published by the Society of Antiquaries, Vol. XV. 1805.

Monde Primitif, by M. Court de Gebelin. MDCCLXXVI.

Travels in Asia Minor, by Richard Chandler, D.D. MDCCLXXVI.

The English Dialect Dictionary. Published by Henry Frowde. 1902.

Yorkshire Wit, Character, Folklore, etc., by R. Blakeborough. 1911.

Brockett's *Glossary of North Country Words*. MDCCCXXIX.

The Local Historians' Table Book, by M. A. Richardson. MDCCCXLIV.

Clavis Calendaria, by John Brady. 1814.

A Glossary of Principal Words used in Teesdale. MDCCCXLIX.

Dictionary of Phrase and Fable, by C. Cobham Brewer, LL.D.

The Gods of India, by Rev. E. Osborn Martin. MCMXIV.

The Customs of Mankind, by Lillian Eichler.

Encyclopædia Britannica, Eleventh Ed.: References: 'Brahmin,' p. 378.

    ,,   ,,   ,,   ,,   ,,   'Cross,' p. 506.

    ,,   ,,   ,,   ,,   ,,   'Easter,' p. 828.

Gentleman's Magazine. July 1783.

Origines Juridiciales. Dugdale. p. 276.

A View of Northumberland, by W. Hutchinson. MDCCLXXVIII.

Oriental Sports, by Thomas Hyde, D.D.

Standard Dictionary of the English Language, Funk and Wagnall Company, New York.

Webster's New International Dictionary. Second Edition, unabridged.

Herodotus, Book III. 96. (Translation, A. D. Godley.)

Histoire des Usages, by Father Carmeli.

Histoire des Causes Premières, by l'Abbé Batteux.

Plutarch. *Opera Moralia*. 'On Isis and Osiris.'

    ,,   ,,   ,,   Table Talks—'Which of the two came first, the hen or the egg?' Book II. Quest. III.

PLATE 57

IMPERIAL RUSSIAN EASTER EGG

In gold with eight opalescent pink enamelled miniatures recalling the Muses by Vassily Zuieff, framed in pearls and diamonds. The egg is further adorned with symbols, in variously coloured golds, pertaining to music, the plastic and dramatic arts, literature and science and ornamented with quatre-foil and laurel ribbon motifs in diamonds. A table-top diamond bears the crown and monogram of the Dowager Empress Marie. Another shows the date 1914. The 'surprise' is not known. Height: $4\frac{3}{4}$ inches.

(*Collection of Mrs. Merriweather Post.*)

PLATE 58

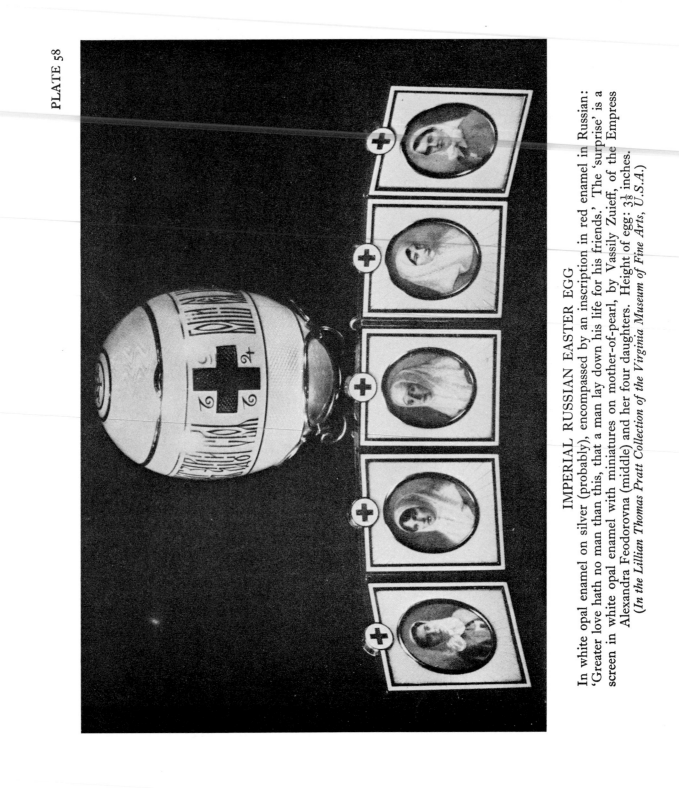

IMPERIAL RUSSIAN EASTER EGG

In white opal enamel on silver (probably), encompassed by an inscription in red enamel in Russian: 'Greater love hath no man than this, that a man lay down his life for his friends.' The 'surprise' is a screen in white opal enamel with miniatures on mother-of-pearl, by Vassily Zuieff, of the Empress Alexandra Feodorovna (middle) and her four daughters. Height of egg: 3⅛ inches.
(In the Lillian Thomas Pratt Collection of the Virginia Museum of Fine Arts, U.S.A.)

PLATE 59

IMPERIAL RUSSIAN EASTER EGG

The body of this egg is enamelled a rich ruby colour ornamented with garlands of variously coloured golds and bow knots in diamonds. It is crowned with an extraordinary table-top diamond, gem encircled. Visible through another diamond at the base of the egg, when held to the light, is a portrait in miniature of the Grand Duke Georg, younger brother of the Tsar, Nicholas II. Four 'surprises' are revealed on opening the four pearl-bordered doors around the egg. These consist of miniature views, by Krijitski, of the mountain retreat in the Caucasus where the Grand Duke, because of ill-health, spent the greater part of his life. Each of the doors bears a diamond-set numeral of the year 1893 when the egg was presented to the Empress Marie Feodorovna by the Tsar, Alexander III.

Height: $3\frac{5}{8}$ inches.

(Collection of Dr. Armand Hammer.)

PLATE 60

IMPERIAL RUSSIAN EASTER EGG

In mat opaque mauve enamel this egg is latticed with diamond ribbons. It is surmounted with a large diamond showing the year 1906, when it was presented to
the Tsarina Alexandra Feodorovna by the Tsar Nicholas II. Lifted from the egg
by a handle of water-lilies in four tones of gold, a large aquamarine serves as a lake
with lilies on which an automatic swan rests. Lifted from the aquamarine and
set in motion by means of a tiny device beneath one wing, gold webbed feet guide
the little figure along its course. Head and neck are proudly raised, then lowered,
and wings are spread to disclose each feather separately. Height: 4 inches.
(Privately owned.)

PLATE 61

IMPERIAL RUSSIAN EASTER EGG

In rock crystal with frost flowers engraved on inside and executed in tiny rose-diamonds on outside. Each half of egg bordered with diamonds. A moonstone surmounts the egg, showing date 1913, when it was presented to the Dowager Empress Marie Feodorovna. Rock crystal pedestal ornamented with diamonds. Inside is a basketful of spring flowers. Basket of platinum wholly set with rose-diamonds. Flowers in white cacholong with olivine and gold centres, leaves in light green jade, stalks in gold. Length of egg: 4 inches. Height of basket: $3\frac{1}{4}$ inches.
(Collection of Mr. Bryan Ledbrook.)

PLATE 62

IMPERIAL RUSSIAN EASTER EGG

This egg, serving as a clock, is in pink enamel with hours in rose-diamonds, on a background of pink and white enamels. It surmounts a colonnade of jadeite on a base of jadeite and pink enamel, borders and garlands in variously coloured gold. The four little silver gilt figures sitting at the base are allegories of the four daughters of the Tsar Nicholas II, that which surmounts the egg is an allegory of the Tsarevitch. Height: 11¼ inches. Presented to the Tsarina Alexandra Feodorovna by the Tsar Nicholas II.

(From Queen Mary's Collection.)

PLATE 63

IMPERIAL RUSSIAN EASTER EGG

In nephrite adorned with pansies enamelled violet-rose set with diamonds, supported on a swirl of leaves in silver gilt set with diamonds. Inside is a folding easel with heart-shaped medallion in white opal enamel set with diamonds and eleven quarter-inch miniatures of the sons and daughters of the Empress Marie Feodorovna, their consorts and children. Miniatures covered by ruby enamelled lids, bearing monograms and all released at same time by pressing a button. Height of egg: 5¾ inches. Presented by the Tsar Nicholas II to his mother the Dowager Empress Marie Feodorovna in 1899.
(Collection of Dr. Armand Hammer.)

PLATE 64

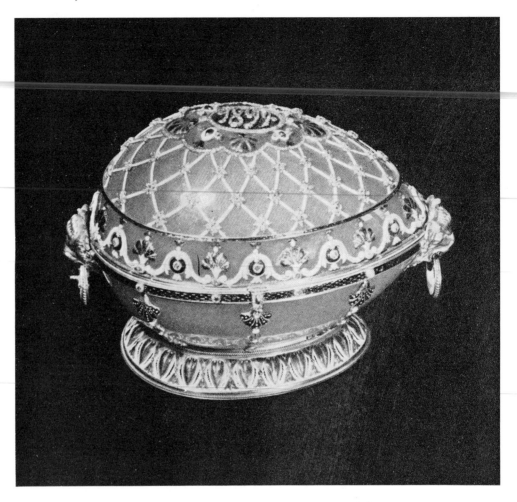

IMPERIAL RUSSIAN EASTER EGG
In milky agate, in Renaissance style, in emerald, ruby, lapis-blue and opaque
white enamels, mounted horizontally on a gold enamelled base. Date 1894 in
diamonds on a ruby enamelled background surrounded by diamonds. Height:
$3\frac{3}{4}$ inches. Inside 'surprise' not known. The last Easter egg presented by the
Tsar Alexander III to the Empress Marie Feodorovna.
(By courtesy of A la Vieille Russie.)

PLATE 65

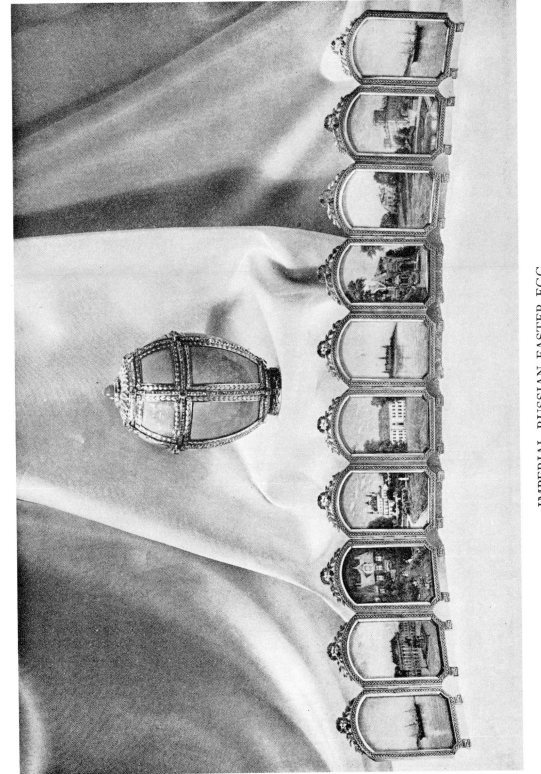

IMPERIAL RUSSIAN EASTER EGG

Presented by the Tsar Alexander III to his wife the Empress Marie Feodorovna. In translucent pink enamel surmounted by a star sapphire and mounted with gold leaf, diamond and emerald borders. Inside is a screen of miniatures by Krijitsky, dated 1891, depicting palaces and houses in which the Empress lived when Princess Dagmar of Denmark. End views show the yachts 'Standart' and 'Poliarnaya Svesda'. Height of egg: 4 inches.
(*Collection of Mr. and Mrs. Nicholas H. Ludwig.*)

PLATE 66

IMPERIAL RUSSIAN EASTER EGG. In rock crystal with engraved border and monogram of the Empress Marie Feodorovna on a pedestal of silver gilt. Inside, a tree in gold with flowers in enamel and precious stones. On the tree sits a peacock in gold, richly enamelled, which when wound up and placed on a table struts about, spreading and closing its tail, and moving its head. Presented to the Dowager Empress Marie Feodorovna by the Tsar Nicholas II in 1908.
(*By courtesy of Messrs. Wartski.*)

PLATE 67

IMPERIAL RUSSIAN EASTER EGG

In gold, engraved ornaments. Surmounting egg is a pelican, in enamel and diamonds, feeding her young (emblem of a mother's love). When taken from its stand and extended (as illustrated in the succeeding Plate No. 68), it forms a screen of miniatures on ivory by Zehngraf representing the Institutions of the Empress Marie, wife of Paul I. These institutions, founded in 1797 for the education of girls of the nobility, were eventually controlled by a Department of State called The Department of the Empress Marie, which was still in existence at the close of the Tsarist régime. Height of egg: 4⅛ inches. Presented by the Tsar Nicholas II to his mother, the Dowager Empress Marie Feodorovna, in 1897.

(In the Lillian Thomas Pratt Collection of the Virginia Museum of Fine Arts, U.S.A.)

PLATE 68

IMPERIAL RUSSIAN EASTER EGG. View showing the egg extended, a description of which is attached to the preceding Plate 67, which shows the complete egg.

PLATE 69

HIPPOPOTAMUS CIGAR LIGHTER
In nephrite. Length: 7 inches (approximately). Formerly in the possession of King Edward
VII and possibly returned to giver by Queen Alexandra as a souvenir of the King.
(*By courtesy of Messrs. Berry-Hill.*)

PLATE 70

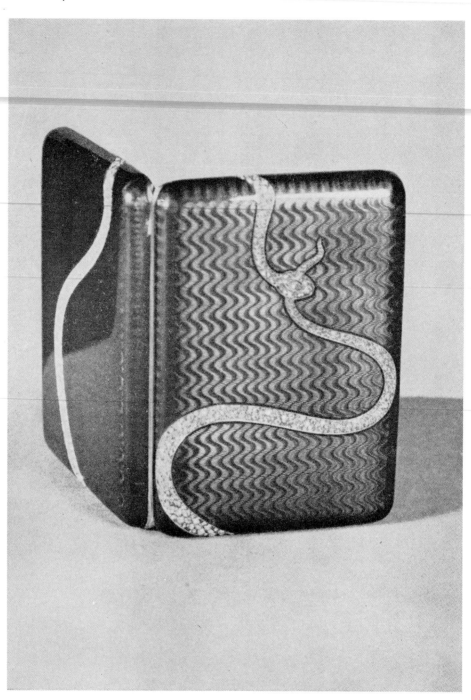

CIGARETTE CASE
In royal blue enamel on gold. Snake in diamonds. Diamond thumb-piece.
Length: 3¼ inches. Width: 2⅝ inches.
(Formerly in possession of King Edward VII, now in Queen Alexandra's Collection.)

PLATE 71

IKON, MADONNA AND CHILD

In polished and mat silver. The backgrounds of the 8 medallions encircling the Madonna's halo, together with portions of the Child's halo, and the two bottom corner pieces of Ikon, are all in mat opaque green enamel. Height: 3 feet 2½ inches. Width: 2 feet 9 inches.

(*In the possession of the Duke of Norfolk, K.G.*)

PLATE 72

BUDDHA

Body, rose quartz; head and hands dark grey chalcedony; belt, translucent white enamel studded with cabochon rubies and rose-diamonds; tongue, ruby; earrings, diamonds; stand, light green jade. Total height, figure and stand: 6⅛ inches. The head, hands and tongue are so delicately balanced, the slightest touch sets them in motion.
(From Queen Mary's Collection.)

PLATE 73

CHIMPANZEE. In chalcedony. Ruby eyes. Height: 3⅜ inches.
(From the Collection of Lady de Grey (Marchioness of Ripon), by courtesy of the late Lady Juliet Duff, now in the possession of Messrs. Wartski.)

Left to right facing photograph: CHIMPANZEE. In agate. Green sapphire eyes.
FROG (cigarette lighter). In nephrite. Diamond eyes. 3⅝ inches high.
LAUGHING DOG. In agate. Diamond eyes.
(From Queen Alexandra's Collection.)

PLATE 74

FLAMINGO. In rose quartz. Legs in gold.
Eyes in green sapphires. Stand in light
green jade.
(*From Queen Alexandra's Collection.*)

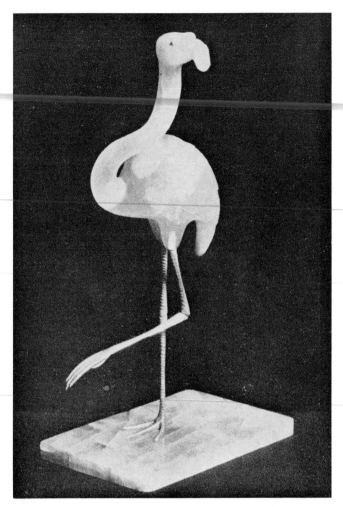

FROG. In jadeite. Diamond eyes. Height:
$3\frac{9}{16}$ inches. Width: 5 inches.
(*From the Collection of the late Lady Juliet Duff.*)

PLATE 75

JAPANESE DWARF TREE

In mat gold. Tulips opaque white enamel with rose-diamonds and gold centres, leaves in nephrite, stalks in gold. Jardinière in rhodonite with gold feet on white jade stand. Height: 4½ inches. Width: 4 inches.

(Formerly in the possession of Lady De Grey (Marchioness of Ripon), now in the possession of Messrs. Tessiers.)

PLATE 76

GROUP OF BIRDS

Back row, left to right: Hornbill in black agate; beak, yellow agate; eyes, diamonds; gold claws. Owl in labradorite; eye, diamond. Pouter Pigeon in grey chalcedony; ruby eyes.

Front row, left to right: Owl in striated bluish white agate; ruby eyes. Kingfisher in chrysophrase; ruby eyes; gold claws and beak. Pelican in beige agate; ruby eyes; gold claws. Hornbill in obsidian; diamond eyes. The approximate height of the figures is 2–2½ inches.

(From the Collection of the late Lady Juliet Duff.)

PLATE 77

GROUP OF ELEPHANTS
Back row, left to right: In nephrite; diamond eyes. In bloodstone; ruby eyes.
Front row, left to right: In jasper; diamond eyes. In nephrite; ruby eyes. In mauve chalcedony;
diamond eyes.
(*From the Collection of the late Lady Juliet Duff.*)

PLATE 78

FLOWERS IN MINIATURE

ORANGE TREE. Flower in opaque white enamel on gold, diamond centre. Fruit in orange enamel on gold. Leaves in nephrite. Vase in rock crystal.

CONVOLVULUS. Flowers in various colours of enamel on gold, diamond centres. Leaves in nephrite. Pole in white enamel. Tub and stand in white jade. Stalks in gold.

STRAWBERRY. Flower in pearls and diamonds. Berries in strawberry enamel on gold. Leaves in jadeite. Stalk in gold. Vase in rock crystal.

(From the Collection of the late Lady Sackville, by courtesy of Mr. Nigel Nicolson. The centre subject is from Queen Mary's Collection.)

PLATE 79

FLOWERS IN MINIATURE
Particulars not available.
*(From the Collection of the late Lady Sackville, now in the possession of Messrs.
Spink & Son.)*

PLATE 80

FOUR ELEPHANTS (*left to right*). In rhodonite; obsidian with houdah in gold, opaque white enamel and rubies. Total height: $2\frac{13}{16}$ inches; nephrite; lapis-lazuli. BEAR in obsidian. All eyes rose-diamonds.
(*Formerly property of Countess Torby, now in Collection of Lady Zia Wernher.*)

FRENCH BULLDOG. In jasper. Diamond eyes.
Collar, white opal enamel. Height: $3\frac{3}{4}$ inches.
Length: $5\frac{1}{4}$ inches.
(*From Queen Alexandra's Collection.*)

PLATE 81

CHERRY. Blossom in white opaque enamel on gold, with diamond centres. Berries in purpurine. Leaves in nephrite. Stems in gold. Height: $5\frac{1}{8}$ inches.
HOLLY. Berries in purpurine. Leaves in nephrite. Stem in gold. Height: $6\frac{1}{4}$ inches.
(From Queen Alexandra's Collection.)

PLATE 82

ROSE BUDS. Flowers in pink and green enamel on gold. Leaves in nephrite. Stalk in green enamel on gold. Vase in rock crystal.

PHILADELPHUS. Flowers in white chalcedony, gold and green sapphires. Leaves in nephrite. Stalk in gold. Vase in rock crystal.

JAPANESE DWARF CONIFER. Tree in gold. Pot in jadeite on aventurine-quartz stand.

RASPBERRY. Four berries in rhodonite. Two berries in green jade. Stalk in gold. Leaves in nephrite. Vase in rock crystal.
(From Queen Alexandra's Collection.)

PLATE 83

ROWAN TREE
Berries in purpurine. Leaves in nephrite. Stem in gold. Vase in rock crystal. Height:
9 inches.
(*From Queen Alexandra's Collection.*)

PLATE 84

CHRYSANTHEMUM. Flowers in yellow and mauve enamels on gold. Leaves in nephrite. Stalk in gold. Vase in rock crystal. Height: 10 inches.
(*From Queen Alexandra's Collection.*)

BLEEDING HEART. Flowers in rhodonite and white chalcedony. Leaves in nephrite. Stalk in gold. Vase in rock crystal. Height: $7\frac{3}{4}$ inches.
(*From Queen Alexandra's Collection.*)

PLATE 85

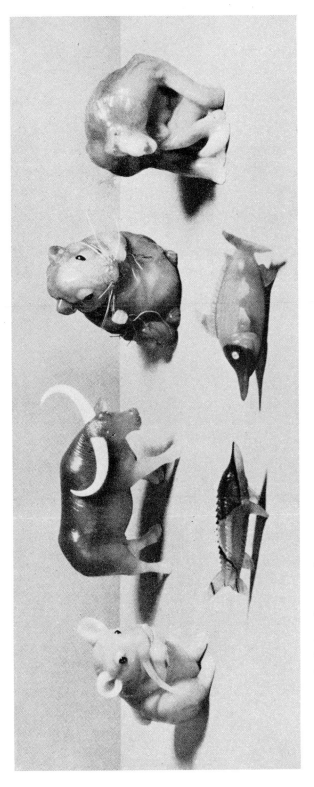

Left to right facing photograph:

MOUSE. In grey chalcedony. Sapphire eyes.
BUFFALO. In grey chalcedony. Ruby eyes. Ivory horns.
DORMOUSE. In grey chalcedony. Cabochon sapphire eyes. Gold whiskers.
BABOON. In grey chalcedony. Diamond eyes.
STURGEON. In blue and pink agate. Diamond eyes.
SWORDFISH. In blue and pink agate. Diamond eyes.

(From Queen Alexandra's Collection.)

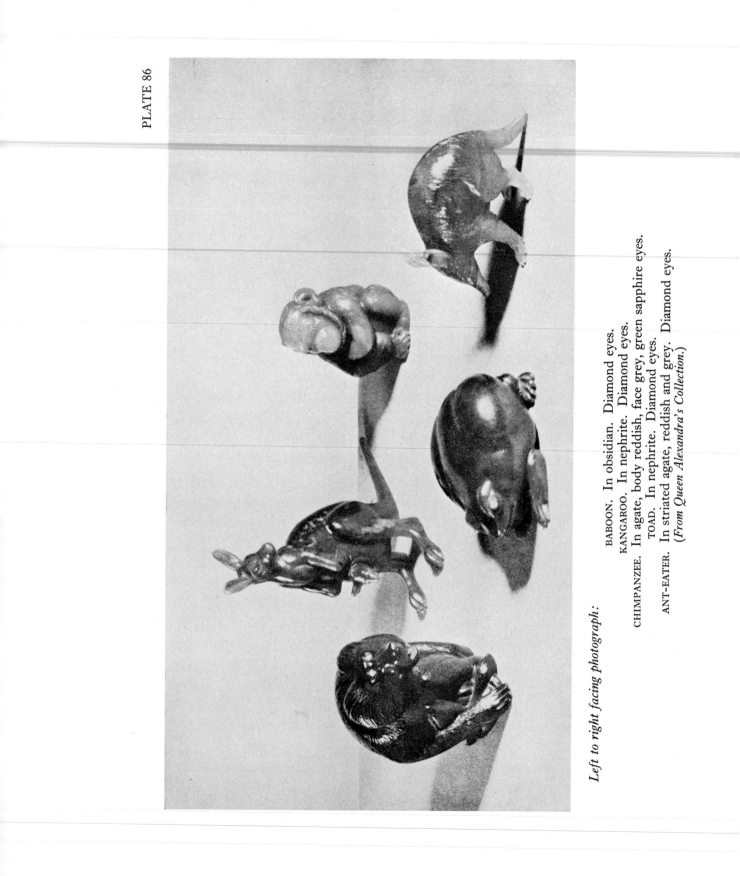

PLATE 86

Left to right facing photograph:

BABOON. In obsidian. Diamond eyes.

KANGAROO. In nephrite. Diamond eyes.

CHIMPANZEE. In agate, body reddish, face grey, green sapphire eyes.

TOAD. In nephrite. Diamond eyes.

ANT-EATER. In striated agate, reddish and grey. Diamond eyes.

(From Queen Alexandra's Collection.)

PLATE 87

MINIATURE FRAME. In translucent pink enamel. Miniature of Queen Alexandra with Duke of Clarence as a baby.
(*From Queen Alexandra's Collection.*)

MINIATURE FRAME. In translucent dark mauve enamel, with floral sheaf in green, red, yellow and white gold. Miniature of the Tsarina Marie Feodorovna.
(*From Queen Alexandra's Collection.*)

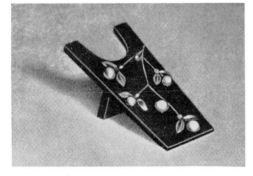

NEPHRITE PEN-REST. Mounted with mistletoe in gold and pearls. Curiously enough the very delicate gold stalk is marked. This pen-rest was in daily use by King George V.
(*From Queen Mary's Collection.*)

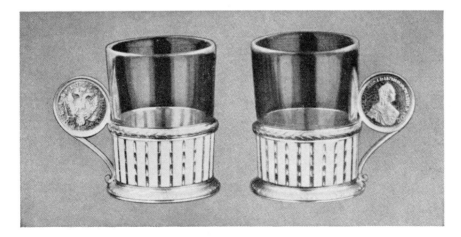

TWO OF A SET OF SIX LIQUEUR GLASSES. In holders of gold and opaque white enamel. Handles, gold roubles 1756, enamelled red. Measurements: $1\frac{3}{4}$ inches high $\times$ 2 inches wide.
(*Privately owned.*)

PLATE 88

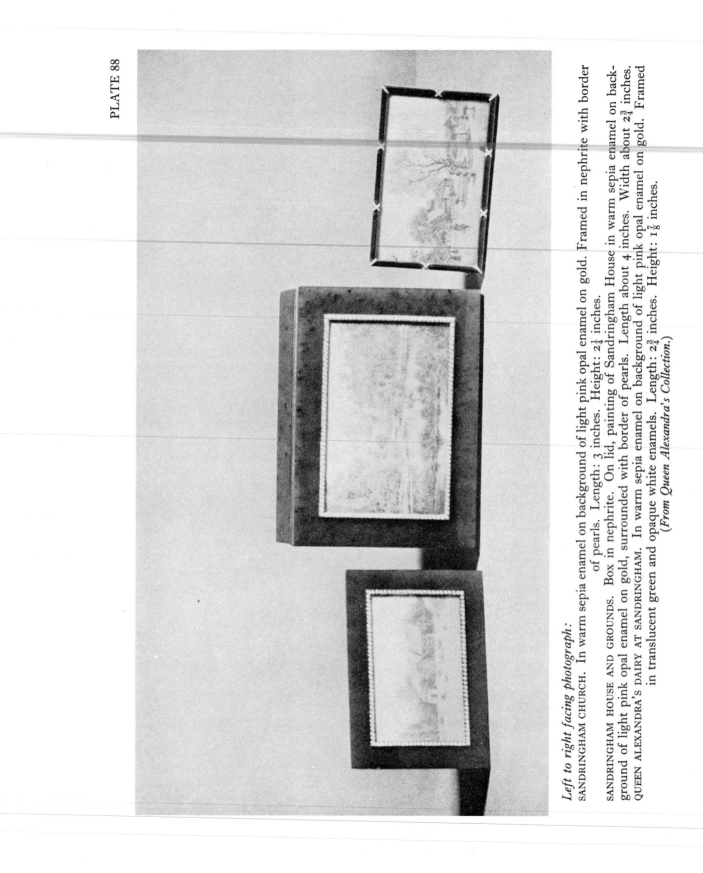

Left to right facing photograph:

SANDRINGHAM CHURCH. In warm sepia enamel on background of light pink opal enamel on gold. Framed in nephrite with border of pearls. Length: 3 inches. Height: 2¼ inches.

SANDRINGHAM HOUSE AND GROUNDS. Box in nephrite. On lid, painting of Sandringham House in warm sepia enamel on background of light pink opal enamel on gold, surrounded with border of pearls. Length about 4 inches. Width about 2¾ inches.

QUEEN ALEXANDRA'S DAIRY AT SANDRINGHAM. In warm sepia enamel on background of light pink opal enamel on gold. Framed in translucent green and opaque white enamels. Length: 2¾ inches. Height: 1⅞ inches.

(From Queen Alexandra's Collection.)

Juvenal, *Satyr VI*.

Ovid. *Ars Amandi*.

Pliny. *Hist. Nat. Books XIX and XXIV*. Ch. VII. and Ch. II.

Original Sanskrit Texts, by Dr. J. Muir. Vol. IV.

Travels in Various Countries, by Dr. E. D. Clarke. MDCCCXVI.

Ordo Baptizandi, etc., ex Rituali Romano Jussu Pauli Quinti edito; pro Anglia Hibernia and Scotia, 1657.

CHAPTER V

FABERGÉ IN THE EDWARDIAN ERA AND THE
SANDRINGHAM FABERGÉ ANIMALS AND FLOWERS

'TO-DAY is the Queen's birthday', or alternatively, 'To-day is the birthday of Her Majesty the Queen'. So ran the Court Circular on December 1st for every year during the reign of King Edward VII.

When those words appeared there had been no First Great War, no Russian Revolution, no Second Great War. Edwardianism was then in full flood with its wassails, its symposia, its *fêtes champêtres* and its pageants.

Volumes have been written about King Edward, but for him very few words will here suffice.

The doctrine of this vital King, Edwardianism as we call it, has been sneered at and belittled as savouring of gauds and feathers, but was nevertheless something which asserted itself at a time which has come to be known as the Edwardian Era, and no period is thus clearly defined without the occurrence of some remarkable phenomenon during its existence.

It was a time of awakening when this land of ours threw off her Victorian cloak of over-seriousness and looked around.* As at some picture show for the first time in many years she reviewed scene by scene her heritage, her loveliness, her dances and music, her sports and pastimes and all those simple, joyous manners and customs handed down to her through storm and sunshine, as being of much account, and of which we should be justly proud. And more. It was a time in which she took stock. Rebounds are but strokes of fate to restore our sanity and balance. It then became manifest that pain is not the only thing necessary to salvation, as some to-day would have us believe; there are other things equally necessary to make our blood course, and sometimes boil.

But above and over all were the institutions of the land. It was to these that the King restored all things that were rightly due to them, holding them aloft as things of good report and lasting account and here for our protection. And of all the institutions the one which most touched his heart, and in case this may pass for sentimental cant, let me say instead, that which mostly satisfied his sense of what had to be upheld beyond a peradventure, was the Majesty of the Queen Consort of England.

* This is by no means to decry the Victorian Era. Any writer who did this would show himself completely ignorant of one of the greatest phases of English history. This record of Fabergé is concerned with the exchange of gifts. In order to give a true and clear picture, the writer has taken the reader back to Elizabethan times, and has made an attempt to show in what way those then living made good and where they erred. It occurs to the writer, as he corrects the proofs, that perhaps he may be criticised for limiting himself too much to the bad points of the Victorians and not making a note of those things in which they excelled. His apology, if one is called for, is that as a Victorian himself he was living too near to the times of the great Queen to feel that an account of an excellence, which was common knowledge, was necessary.

I speak as a very humble citizen, but I can do so with some authority because I know at first hand. 'We must not make any duplicates!' the words with which the King prefaced every meeting with him, ring in my ears to-day as they rang forty years ago.

But I go too fast. So back to the beginning: 'To-day is the Queen's birthday.' On this day the Queenhood of Her Majesty was celebrated with all things appertaining to it, by will and command of the King.

It was Queen Alexandra's Pageant and the setting was Sandringham, the home of the Royal Family.

When many were abed, for at Sandringham clocks were then always kept half an hour in advance of Greenwich time, a Highlander would go round the house putting 'life and mettle' into the day with strathspey and reel, and maids were around with dustpan and brush making ready. The bells pealed out from Sandringham Church, from Kings Lynn, from far away St. George's Chapel and the Parish Church at Windsor, in an awakening crescendo to the day. London took up the call, with all main thoroughfares beflagged, as well as the Mansion House, the Bank of England, the Royal Exchange, the Houses of Parliament and all Government offices. A Royal Salute was fired at the Horse Guards end of St. James's Park and answered from the Long Walk, Windsor Park, from Edinburgh Castle and Kingstown, from all the forts of Malta, from Toronto, Ottawa and all military stations in Canada and from His Majesty's ships, dressed 'over all', at Portsmouth, Plymouth, Devonport, Sheerness and all other naval and military stations throughout the world.

In the meantime, at Sandringham telegrams of congratulation were pouring in from all quarters of the globe; the Lord Mayor of London sent congratulations from the citizens of London; the King (except when the birthday fell on a Sunday or he was indisposed) went shooting with the Prince of Wales and the male members of the house-party; the Queen, the Princess of Wales and ladies of the party joining them for luncheon in the woods. All the school children of the seven parishes on the Royal estate, some 600 to 1,000, were the Queen's guests at tea. The celebrations ended with a dinner-party given by the King and Queen.

Next morning in *The Times* this appeared: 'The magnificent collection of birthday gifts was displayed in the salon and was much admired by the house party.' (*The Times*, December 3rd, 1907.)

For ourselves we should have expressed it differently, for long after the salvos had ceased, these birthday gifts, or at any rate most of them, were still there, in the same vitrines in which Queen Alexandra had left them, to serve as an indestructible expression in rare stones, enamel and gold, of the affection in which she was held.

Not all the Queen's birthday gifts came from Fabergé, but it would be true to say that a great part of them did; so much so that when she died they were found to include one of the largest collections of Fabergé's work in existence.

Why King Edward took such particular interest in the bringing together of

79

this collection, and why his homage to his Queen took the form of Fabergé objects, are nothing less than matters of English History. These two questions can only be considered in relation to the King himself and to what happened in England long before he was even thought of. As to King Edward, I cannot do better than take the reader to Lord Ponsonby's book, *Henry Ponsonby*.

Henry Ponsonby, as we all know, was Private Secretary to Queen Victoria, and in this book Lord Ponsonby makes many references to King Edward when Prince of Wales, especially in Chapter V, which he devotes to 'The Queen and the Prince of Wales'. What evolved and maintained the Victorian era is not our present business, but what process produced the man whose name was to be given to the succeeding one is plainly to be seen from a study of these pages.

When one reads of the endeavours of the great Victorian figures and of the great Queen herself to set the Prince in the straight and narrow way, it is surprising that they could not see that they themselves were the main cause of his dissent from the doctrine of over-seriousness. In nothing was this more apparent than in the matter of the exchange of gifts.

From 1871, that is when as Prince of Wales he was thirty years of age, and in subsequent years, it became a pressing question of State how to find serious work for him to do. The Arts and Sciences, Philanthropy, the Army, India and Ireland, all came into purview in the correspondence between the Queen, the Prime Minister, the Foreign Secretary, the Lord Privy Seal, the Permanent Under-Secretary of State and the Queen's Private Secretary.

'We should seek to give him a central aim and purpose', said Mr. Gladstone. 'If the Queen really desired his opinion (Foreign Affairs), sent for him and consulted him, he would probably get amused and interested', said Lord Granville. . . . 'All this will not prevent my doing anything in my power to co-operate.' Lord Halifax thought 'He might not have the same temptations in Ireland'. Mr. Francis Knollys, the Prince's Private Secretary, reported: 'The first political party here was, I think, altogether a great success and I hope it will induce H.R.H. to continue to ask the leading men on both sides to Sandringham.' And Sir Julian Pauncefote, the Permanent Under-Secretary at the Foreign Office, put it like this: 'I have accordingly sent to him all despatches of real interest whether marked "secret" or not. I hope I may continue to do so as I think it most important at this critical juncture that he should see what cards are in the hands of the players in the great European game . . . '; and 'Quite right to let H.R.H. know what is going on . . .' said Sir Henry Ponsonby.

All this makes a wonderful, human picture, the great Victorian gentlemen, for they were all that, administering their doses with a bedside manner full of anxiety for their Royal patient, the Prince always civil and courteous to them all, and showing the greatest deference to his mother on public occasions but dodging all private discussions with her; the great Queen herself reproving him and at times delivering her admonishments by roundabout methods but solicitous for his welfare to a degree during his severe illness in 1872 at Sandringham and taking charge there with an iron hand; and lastly Sir Henry Ponsonby with his 'acute sense of humour' and 'ready recognition of the ridiculous', cementing all differences as best he could.

But for us this is background only. Our central figure was very conscious of the important part played by the goldsmith, jeweller and lapidary in the general scheme of things, a matter sorely neglected not only in all records of King Edward himself, but of many other notable people. The goldsmith it would appear is here to deliver his treasures like milk in the morning supplied by a beneficent Providence.

As Prince of Wales, his journeyings to Germany, Russia and India, do not concern us, but what does are the numerous occasions on which His Royal Highness opened bridges, museums, public buildings and so on. At these times it was the custom to reward him and the Princess of Wales, who generally accompanied him, with something by way of presentation, and on one of these occasions a certain mayor and municipality conceived the idea of giving them a piece of dining-room furniture in the shape of a sideboard. This way of thinking so well in accord with the high thinking of the time seems then to have prevailed throughout the country, and in the course of time His Royal Highness became possessed of one of the finest collections extant of such examples, in oak and mahogany. As the pantechnicons arrived at Marlborough House he must have said many times: 'What next!'

But the Prince had other friends, the 'Smart Set' as they have been called, who were equally desirous of doing him a good turn. They were largely active in fields of sport, racing, shooting, hunting and so forth. Like the golf fiend and the bridge fiend, they lived to flourish their activities in the same atmosphere of over-seriousness. They conveyed their 'humble duty' by means of some object very dear to them, and expressing their own limitations to a T, according to the special preference which attracted them. Some, with great daring, presented him with walking-stick handles. In this way the Prince became possessed of a collection of trophies which in time became so distressing that something had to be done about it.

Here you have two 'overloads' which the Prince was carrying with great restraint and courtesy. He could not very well open an exhibition for the enlightenment of mayors and municipalities, but he could take his personal friends in hand and set them an example. And it was the coming of Fabergé which gave him his great opportunity. By this, do not let it be thought that the Russian Craftsman was the only one who was helpful; there were craftsmen and shopkeepers in England and other countries who were doing their best in their own particular way, but the coming of Fabergé flashed like a comet through the black firmament of over-seriousness everywhere, and with such unmistakable brilliance, that it was impossible for such a vital mind as that of His Royal Highness to let it pass unrecognized.

And so began an experiment in education, not of the masses, but of the classes. King Edward, who had come through tribulation with his faculties undimmed, in turn administered his admonishments.

Whether following a practice, or on his own initiative, most likely the latter,

King Edward during his reign gave tradesmen an opportunity, from time to time, to show their wares to him at Buckingham Palace, and Fabergé, through his representative, took his turn. The King kept what he wanted and returned the rest, but a time came when he took nothing, and we all scratched our heads at 48 Dover Street where Fabergé was then established in London, in fact we came near to collapse. Fabergé had shot his bolt and the sooner we shut up shop the better, so we began to think.

And so we thought for a fortnight, when a certain Captain L. arrived. If we were bordering on prostration he was in tears: 'For a long time', he said, 'I have been searching for a certain print of a racehorse to give to the King, and now that I have found it he won't have it. Instead, he said, "Go to Fabergé's, they have a hippopotamus cigar-lighter in nephrite, if you wish to give me something give me that. The print is right enough, but I have so many of them; far better give it to some museum where it will be seen. Besides, the lighter, I am sure, is half the price, and it is amusing"!' I give an illustration of this lighter in Plate 69. So it was that a cloud lifted, and many more clouds, for as time went on it was clear that the King knew Fabergé's stock better than we did ourselves. One after the other the things went back to Buckingham Palace, but this time for the accounts of the King's friends.

That is how King Edward drove a wedge into the over-seriousness of his so-called 'Smart' friends and partly how, at the time of his death he was in possession of so many Fabergé pieces.

And here let us pay homage to Queen Alexandra's graciousness, courtliness, kindliness and happy way of doing things. There are some gestures entirely out of the range of ordinary mortals, you must be a Queen to make them. One morning shortly after the death of King Edward the Grand Duke Michael Mikhailovitch called. He was then living at Ken Wood. 'See', he said, 'what Queen Alexandra has given me as a souvenir of King Edward!' and he produced a Fabergé pocket cigar-cutter which at some time he had given to the King. It was then I heard that after the death of the King, Queen Alexandra gave back to each of his friends something which they at some time had given to him. The most noteworthy of all these souvenirs must be the cigarette case in royal blue translucent enamel on gold with an encircling snake in diamonds which Mrs. George Keppel gave to King Edward and which Queen Alexandra gave back to her as a souvenir. I say noteworthy, because it is a fine example of that for which Fabergé was famous, a large surface of enamel on a guilloché background of gold or silver. An illustration of this fine case is given in Plate 70. It is remarkable, too, as an example of the happy and sane way of doing things: for in 1936 Mrs. Keppel gave it to Queen Mary to return to Sandringham and thus keep the collection complete.

Just now I said that King Edward drove a wedge, etc. But it must not be taken that all his friends had to go through a course of training, there were some who could give even him points. Mr. Stanislas Poklewski-Koziell, for instance.

At that time he was Counsellor at the Russian Embassy, a great friend of the King, and perhaps the most prolific present-giver the world has ever seen. When he went off to country house-parties he arrived loaded with things from Fabergé;

two large suit-cases filled with them. I have no doubt that the ladies of the party scanned the list of visitors with eagerness to see if his name was included and, if so, took care to be present with aprons extended when he shook the tree. Once certainly, so I am told, he proved himself equal to King Edward. After playing cards one night at Clarges Street, he lost to the King and in paying up found himself short by one pound. On saying good-night the King turned to him and said: 'Remember, Poklewski, you owe me a pound.' Poklewski paid his debt with a box made by Fabergé, set in the lid of which was the pound.*

And there was Mr. Leopold de Rothschild. The King could teach him nothing. How he did things is best shown by his coronation gift to King George V and Queen Mary. Wishing to send Their Majesties some rare orchids for their coronation breakfast table, he ordered from Fabergé a rock-crystal vase (Plate 90*). On the morning of the coronation the gardener from the Rothschild house at Gunnersbury came to Fabergé's to arrange the flowers and away went the rare vase to Buckingham Palace, with its load of precious flowers, certainly the most refreshing of all gifts. This vase, of course, is still in the possession of Queen Mary.

Collectors may come across things enamelled in stripes in the Rothschild racing colours, dark blue and yellow, and the reason for them is as follows. The Rothschilds of Fabergé's day were 'Their Exquisitenesses' and they had, of course, a great following in the city of London. Every year just before Newmarket time, Ascot and the Derby time, lesser exquisites came westward to Fabergé's with the question, 'Have you anything suitable for a man, costing about ten pounds?' Well, frankly we hadn't. Fabergé wares were mostly made for men to give to women, unless you offered a figure of £75-£100 or so, at which price you could buy a gold cigarette case.

Then one day Mr. Arthur Levita arrived and he put his demands bluntly. 'I want something for Mr. Leopold.' A brain wave was now inevitable, so we cabled to Petersburg: 'Everything you have ever made, now make in the Rothschild racing colours, dark blue and yellow', or words to that effect. It was the first time I had put Fabergé on to mass production.

When the first consignment arrived I became so excited I ran straight off to New Court and showed it to 'Mr. Leopold', who said, 'Splendid! I will take the lot'. From this time, with the exception of Mr. James de Rothschild, no one else had a look in. Whenever he wanted to say 'Good morning!' 'I like you!' or 'Don't bother me any more!' he simply slipped a dark blue and yellow Fabergé object into his friend's pocket.

To say anything about Mr. Leopold de Rothschild is to bring Sir Ernest Cassel to mind at once for the reason that they were the two opposites: 'Mr. Leopold' the talkative, Sir Ernest the silent. One often wished he would say more, for he had a most attractive voice. No word of comment or suggestion had to escape your lips if you were to hope for any success with Sir Ernest. There was only one thing to do; lock the door and leave him very severely alone to his own devices. All he asked for was an empty table and this, some 40 inches by 30 inches, in most

* True or untrue, I include this story because it is typical of the way of the Edwardians in such matters.

hopeful silence for a shopkeeper, he would cover, adding object after object, chosen with meticulous care and taking the whole morning over the operation. Nobody took more trouble to give his Edwardian friends enjoyment than Sir Ernest and nobody was treated worse when the crash came with the first great war.

And now a Baring, the second Lord Revelstoke. Here was the hard man of plain facts and figures, the 'twice two makes four' man of the Edwardian Era. He was among the foremost of Fabergé's discerning customers. Travelling constantly between Petersburg and London nothing new happened in the workshops of the Craftsman without his knowledge. He was the first to bring to London the figurines, several of which are illustrated in Chapter VI.

With his façade of granite he looked the man in need of no one's assistance, and yet he leaned on Fabergé. And why? His Russian friends used to say of him, 'Hard! Why he is as soft as velvet!' This soft side of him was I am sure the true man. It was the romance within him which helped him to find relief in Fabergé objects. I feel equally sure at the bottom of him he was of the same mind as Deems Taylor, who says:

> 'That the light of pure reason casts grotesque shadows. That a world in which there is nothing but the letter of the law, and the logical conclusion, and the inevitable deduction, and the axiomatic fact, and the rational course of conduct is, in the last account, a ridiculous one.'

The next on the list is the old Duke of Norfolk, the last man some might think to be led away by the gewgaws of Fabergé. It fell to him to say something for which the Craftsman was for ever grateful. The occasion was as follows:

Standing on an easel at Norfolk House was an ikon of the Madonna and Child in silver, enamel and precious stones (shown in Plate 69).* The Duchess had commissioned Fabergé to make it, and after it was finished I had taken it to Norfolk House for final inspection before its journey to Arundel Castle, where it was to be given an exalted, permanent and consecrated place in the library, as an oblation to the Almighty. It was a momentous occasion for the House of Howard and with the Duchess the ladies of the House were gathered around it, picking it to pieces as it were, to make doubly sure that there should be nothing wanting about it. Now some parts of the silver had been finished with a mat surface in order to bring out the significance of other parts and one lady of the party, noticing this and only knowing silver in its polished state, made the remark that metal with such a surface could not possibly be silver. An animated discussion followed and so much so that the Duchess said, 'I will call the Duke; let him decide'.

In came the Duke with his spectacles upturned on his forehead. 'What is it, my dear?' he said, and explanations followed. 'What does Mr. Fabergé say?' he asked. And further explanations followed. 'If Mr. Fabergé says it is silver,' he said, 'then silver it must be', and with that he turned and went away.

And Mr. Alfred de Rothschild and the Marquis de Soveral, respectively the

* It was in the early spring of 1908.

exquis and the indispensable. I mention them mainly for the fact that no biographer of the Edwardians, with any sense of what is due from him, can leave them out, so part and parcel of the age were they. Neither of them were buyers of Fabergé objects to any large extent. 'Mr. Alfred' was far too entangled with everything to do with the Eighteenth Century and, besides, he was a master of nuance and was in need of no one to help him to express those delicate shades of meaning in which he excelled. The Marquis de Soveral is summed up in the fact that no dinner party given for the King and Queen was at all likely to be a complete success without him.

And the Grand Duke Michael Mikhailovitch, like all Romanoffs, equally at home on the steps of the throne or in the kitchen, and Earl Howe, the doyen of courtiers and the three honourable gentlemen, Sidney Greville, John Ward and Derek Keppel. As I recall these gentlemen I cannot but bring to mind the extraordinary feeling everybody had for Carl Fabergé, which was something bordering on affection. To further his interests was the same as furthering their own, or so it seemed, and it was the same all over the world. The remarkable thing was that people felt like this in very many cases without even having come into personal contact with him. It was almost as though he managed to enshrine in his wares some spirit of himself which gripped men willy-nilly. And it was in this sunshine that a representative lived and worked. The timely word, the helping hand, was for ever forthcoming and none gave more timely aid than the five gentlemen I have named.

And Prince Francis of Teck (who with his love for nice things I should have named long before this); Lord Colebrooke; Count Benckendorff, the Russian Ambassador; Count Mensdorff, the Austrian Ambassador; Lord Farquhar; Lord Alington; Lord Ilchester; the Marquis of Anglesey; Mr. Waldorf Astor; Lord Carnarvon; Lt.-Col. Holford; Lord Savile; Lord Lurgan; the Duke of Richmond and Gordon; the Duke of Beaufort; the Earls of Derby, Leicester, Pembroke and Montgomery, and Rosebery; Mr. Ivor Ferguson; Lord Iveagh; Mr. A. J. Balfour;* Mr. James de Rothschild; Baron Edouard de Rothschild; the Marquis de Breteuil; but I am getting into France and will soon be in Italy and Austria, overrun with names, Murats, de Béarns, Polignacs, de Broglies, de Rochefoucaulds, Doria-Pamphilis, Potenzianis, Kinskys, almost *ad infinitum*— anyhow, why should I cudgel my brain about the men? Really they did not count.

The fame of men, and of craftsmen in particular, has always been in the hands of women. And reader, please do remember that amidst all our wanderings and digressions we seek for a background to craftsmanship. Cellini had his Madonna Porzia, Wedgwood his Catherine the Great, and Fabergé Queen Alexandra and all the Edwardian great ladies. Never can there have been such a galaxy of remark-

---

* Little things of fun and fancy had slight attraction, if any, for English statesmen and politicians of the Edwardian Era. But I shall never forget Mr. Balfour's reaction when he saw Fabergé objects for the first time. It was at some political gathering, may be at Lansdowne House, and why I was there I do not remember. Some Fabergé objects were set out on a table in a corner. Mr. Balfour noticed them, stopped talking, came over and said 'What are these?' In a moment politics were forgotten and he had to be dragged away to continue the meeting.

able women, never did they so eclipse the men and never did men respond more gallantly to their enchantment.

I speak from personal acquaintance otherwise I should have nothing here to offer. One by one they all passed in procession before me at 48 Dover Street. But it is one thing to have seen them and quite another to assess them. Each one of them filled a niche of her own and there were many niches. In some way I must limit myself and I cannot do better than get right down to rock bottom.

Fabergé objects were the outward and visible sign of the spirit of the age. Nothing, whether of importance or of no importance, took place unless signalised by them. The further you departed from Fabergé the less Edwardian you became, the nearer you came to him the more so you were. That is the simple truth.

Let us take a look at the galaxy, and one cannot but chuckle at the thought that it should come the way of an old shopkeeper to take a dive, so to speak, through this Milky Way, clutching here and there in his passage at some great lady and dragging her out of the obscurity that might otherwise very well be hers but for his having made a note of her distinction.

The Duchess of Devonshire, she who at one time had been Duchess of Manchester and outstripped all with her beauty at the Court of Napoleon III and the Empress Eugénie, 'the great Dividing Line' we may call her, if there is anything in the old saying that in her time Society was divided into two parts, those who went to Devonshire House and those who did not; Consuelo, Duchess of Manchester, the first of the three sisters Yznaga of Cuba; the Countess of Mar and Kellie; Lady Gosford; the Duchesses of Portland, Marlborough, Roxburghe and Sutherland; the Countesses of Derby, Essex, Londesborough and Dudley; Mrs. Arthur Sassoon; Lady Brougham and Vaux; Mrs. Ralph Sneyd; Mrs. Ronald Greville; Lady Savile, Lady Sarah Wilson, Mrs. Neumann, Mrs. Cavendish Bentinck; Lady Helen Vincent; Lady Desborough; Mrs. Hwfa Williams; Lady Ridley; the Countesses of Ilchester, Kilmorey and Howe; the Marchioness of Lansdowne; the Duchess of Westminster and Princess Henry of Pless; Lady Alington; Lady Wimborne; the Duchess of Buccleuch; Lady Chesterfield; Lady Curzon of Kedleston; Lady Randolph Churchill; the Countess of Suffolk; Mrs. Bradley Martin; Mrs. Willie James; Mrs. Wilfrid Ashley; the Marchioness of Londonderry; Mrs. Anthony Drexel; Lady Gerard; the Marchioness of Bute; Lady Sassoon; Miss Alice de Rothschild; Lady Portarlington; Lady Mountstephen; Lady Dufferin; Lady Battersea; Madame Koch de Gooreynd; Lady Colebrooke; Lady Wernher; Mrs. Hall Walker; Mrs. Eckstein; the Duchess of Rutland; Mrs. Cassel; Miss Muriel Wilson; Lady Leslie; Mrs. Arthur James; Mrs. Hartmann; Lady Cunard; Mrs. Charles Hunter; Princess Hatzfeldt—all these ladies and more, played their part. Each one of them touched Fabergé at some point in her career.

But just to touch Fabergé was not enough, you had to cling to him and foster him if you were to stand out unassailable as a really great lady of the period. And please to remember that to be of the period did not necessarily mean that you had to dine every day at the royal table. Edwardianism spread all over the world.

And so I have the honour to present seven ladies: Lady De Grey, Mrs. George

Keppel, Mrs. Leopold de Rothschild, Lady Paget, Mrs. Sackville-West, the Countess Torby and the Grand Duchess Marie Pavlovna, better known as the Grand Duchess Vladimir.

It is more than likely that someone competent to give an opinion would give the palm to Lady De Grey. If beauty plus a poise naturally aristocratic plus an ability to appreciate all the arts, plus an attraction which drew Queen Alexandra to her from her earliest years as Princess of Wales and which equally drew the King and culminated in those happy parties at Coombe Court all through Edwardian times—if all these count, then for many Lady De Grey must be given first place. But for me there is evidence which is conclusive. Look, reader, at the illustration in colour of a Buddha in jadeite (Frontispiece). So far as I know Fabergé made only two pieces like this, the other is in rose quartz and chalcedony and now in the possession of Queen Mary, which is reproduced in Plate 72. Look at the chimpanzee illustrated in Plate 73, certainly one of the most outstanding of all Fabergé animals, and the frog (Plate 74). Look at the Japanese tree in gold (Plate 75), another outstanding example of craftsmanship, and at the group of birds reproduced in Plate 76, and of elephants in Plate 77.

Now a great number of these objects were given to Lady De Grey by Mr. Poklewski-Koziell, and he of all people not only recognized personality when he saw it and respected it, but paid homage to it by way of the finest Fabergé pieces which he could persuade the Craftsman to make especially for him. I need say no more.

If Poklewski speaks for Lady De Grey, Rudyard Kipling puts in a claim for Mrs. Sackville-West, the third Lady Sackville of Knole, for he has said this of her: 'On mature reflection *the* most wonderful person I have ever met'.* She came as a flood upon you, and it was a flood which divided and then joined up again, leaving you bound as on an island by her beauty, her charm, her enthusiasm and, most captivating of all, at any rate to one who was doing his best to send folk to heaven the Fabergé way, her full agreement with you about what to do in the Fabergé manner with birds and flowers, animals and fat *izvoschiks*. She was, I think, as much of an inspiration to Fabergé as he was to her, for he never failed to ask after her every time I went to Petersburg: 'And how is Mrs. West?' he said. I have a note of a meeting with her and her daughter on January 23rd, 1908, when she saw the Chatsworth box with a view of the house in monochrome enamel which Fabergé had just made, and ordered a similar one of Knole. On this day, too, we arranged about some flowers, in miniature, climbing poles and luxuriating in lily ponds, certain of which I reproduce in Plates 78 and 79.

And Mrs. Leopold de Rothschild. She surely was the humblest and simplest of all the Edwardian Great Ladies. In his very entertaining book *Homes, Sweet Homes*, Mr. Osbert Lancaster, dealing with the latter end of Queen Victoria's reign and 'le style Rothschild', says this: '*Objets d'art et de vertu* had been collected by rich men since the end of the Seventeenth Century; but, in the majority of cases, for their own sake; now they are feverishly sought after for the kudos they acquire for their owners and as visible evidence of enormous wealth.'

* *Pepita* by Victoria Sackville-West.

And again when speaking of the Edwardian era: 'A legion of little ornaments still required a quantity of occasional tables for their accommodation but now tended to fall into two categories—the admittedly precious and the supposedly functional. In the former were included all the usual knick-knacks, with the addition of as many specimens of the ingenious Mons. Fabergé's costly handiwork *as the owner could afford*.' The italics are mine.

We all see things in our own way and I hesitate to appear to undermine the charm of Mr. Lancaster's statement, but I must make this comment. Except in rare cases I never remember the Edwardian ladies buying anything for themselves; they received their Fabergé objects as gifts from men, and these gifts were purely for the psychological moment. When that had passed, i.e., the actual moment of the giving, they completed the mission for which they had been made.

What happened to them afterwards depended entirely upon the feeling of the ladies concerned, some took great care of them, some did not. There was a certain section of Edwardian Society, in fact a rather large one, comprising those who were not quite 'in the know' on many matters with which Society then concerned itself and who adopted a loud-voiced affectation to camouflage their ignorance. Carelessness and casualness were their armour. For them Fabergé things meant very little indeed. They did not understand them. It is no exaggeration to say that as many fine pieces, cigarette cases, *nécessaires* and so on were destroyed by them by careless handling as were ever cherished by those who understood and appreciated them as creations of a great craftsman.

As for any Edwardian lady, good, bad or indifferent, making an inordinate display on occasional tables for the sake of the kudos thereby accruing to her, the less said the better. Can anyone imagine Mrs. Leopold Rothschild who was in a position to buy up enormous quantities of kudos, attempting to enhance her social position, or trying to wreck the social status of, say, Lady De Grey, by such means?

Instead, like all good Edwardians, she made use of Fabergé objects for the purpose for which they were designed; in her case to say something to her husband.

I have some interesting notes about them both. For instance, shortly after Fabergé had modelled Persimmon for the King, I tried to persuade 'Mr. Leopold' to have St. Frusquin done. Persimmon had won the Derby for the King by a neck from St. Frusquin after one of the classic struggles of the turf, and it seemed fitting that the latter too should be immortalized, but 'Mr. Leopold' said: 'Such a luxury is all very well for the King of England, I can't afford it.'

This led me to approach 'Mrs. Leopold' and, with her help in the spring and summer of 1908 at Ascott, Fabergé modelled St. Frusquin, the staghounds Herald, Harbinger, Pilgrim and Harriet, some of the prize bulls and cows, and 'Mrs. Leopold's' French griffon 'Pixie'. St. Frusquin was cast in silver and the other models cut in stone in the Fabergé workshops in St. Petersburg and all given by 'Mrs. Leopold' to her husband. Afterwards 'Mr. Leopold' ordered from Fabergé six to twelve models of St. Frusquin in bronze which he gave away on

PLATE 89

IMPERIAL RUSSIAN EASTER EGG

In translucent lime-green enamel trellised in gold, with double-headed eagles in black enamel and rose-diamonds. A large table-top diamond crowns the egg, with another at the point dated 1897 when it was presented to the Empress Alexandra Feodorovna by Nicholas II. Inside is a working model of the Coronation coach in yellow gold, translucent red enamel and rose-diamonds, with interior upholstery in translucent red enamel. Height of egg: 5 inches. Length of coach: $3\frac{11}{16}$ inches.

(By courtesy of Messrs. Wartski.)

PLATE 90

VASE IN ROCK CRYSTAL
Engraved with the English Royal Arms and 'June XXII, MCMXI', the date
of the Coronation of Their Majesties King George V and Queen Mary. Mounted
in gold, cabochon rubies, emeralds and sapphires, opaque white and various
translucent enamels. Height: 6⅝ inches. Width: 5 inches.
(*From Queen Mary's Collection.*)

PLATE 91

CIGARETTE CASE
In translucent green enamel, probably on silver; with red and green gold
mountings. Engraved 'Marie Vladimir'. Moonstone thumb-piece.
Measurements: $3\frac{8}{10}$ in. $\times$ $2\frac{4}{10}$ in.
(*Privately owned*.)

PLATE 92

CIGARETTE CASE
With place for matches. In translucent yellow enamel on gold, moss-agate
motifs in dark brown enamel, rays in black enamel. Moonstone thumb-piece.
An outstanding example of large-surface enamelling. Engraved 'Maria Ana'
inside lid.
(*Privately owned.*)

suitable occasions. One thing sticks in my mind, St. Frusquin could not be made to stand still until his stable companion was brought out, a kitten.

And so to Mrs. George Keppel. As I have said before we seek a background to craftsmanship and to Queen Alexandra's Fabergé collection in particular. All those coming and going between Sandringham and London were fully aware of the importance which the King attached to the collection, and none more so than Mrs. Keppel who, as we shall see later, was largely instrumental in inspiring the creation of the Sandringham Fabergé animals—a truly marvellous set of models cut in different stones and portraying living animals at the Royal residence in the time of Edward VII.

Also Lady Paget, wife of General Sir Arthur Paget, an American, if I remember rightly, and charming for a certainty. It was she who put Fabergé wares on public exhibition for the first time in England. The occasion was the bazaar held in the Albert Hall on June 21st, 22nd, 23rd, 1904, in aid of the funds of the Royal Victoria Hospital for Children which Queen Alexandra attended and at Lady Paget's stall of Fabergé objects purchased a jade scent bottle and an enamel and diamond cigarette holder.

And the Grand Duchess Marie Pavlovna, better known as the Grand Duchess Vladimir. We have heard a great deal of 'The Gentlemen of Europe' but little if anything of 'The Ladies of Europe'. Well, here is one without any shadow of doubt whatever, in fact I may call her *the* Lady of Europe of her time. With Petersburg her capital city where her court outstripped that of the Empress, every other capital city knew her well and none better than London. Imperious, capable to a degree that was uncanny; without any preparation whatever, she could adapt herself to the most diverse assembly without any previous knowledge of its human components and come out of the ordeal as fresh and undaunted as when she went into it. Always the right question to ask, the search for which is the prime concern of all royal ladies, was to her as natural and easy as the intake of the breath. Many were the gifts she gave from Fabergé. As an instance I give an illustration of a cigarette case in green enamel in Plate 91 engraved 'Marie' and 'Vladimir'.

Lastly, the Countess Torby, the wife of the Grand Duke Michael Mikhailovitch, of Keele Hall, and later of Ken Wood, Hampstead. This esteemed lady collected Fabergé elephants; that is the most significant thing I can say about her, because it implies a quiet, undisturbed and jolly humour. Bound together as they were, coupled in perfect harmony, these two, he of Russia and she of Luxembourg, forged for themselves a unique place in Edwardian Society. They were representative of all that is best in English life but with just that touch of cosmopolitanism which mellowed it. In Plate 80 I illustrate some of the objects from Countess Torby's collection, by permission of Lady Zia Wernher.

So much for the background of King Edward, and Edwardians in general, to Queen Alexandra's Fabergé collection. All that has been here said should have given the reader a pretty good idea why the King paid homage to Queen Alexandra by way of Fabergé objects. December 1st was her day and on that day, for the King, the rest of the world stood still. Everything had to be done to amuse, delight and surprise her and the fulness of his own experience was enough to convince him that he could do this best by giving her Fabergé objects.

But the fact that the King had a liking for these things was by no means the sole reason for the Queen's collection of them. She herself literally adored them and never did she receive one without saying 'Oh, how lovely!' Those were her actual words. But there were other reasons.

By the time the history of England arrives at Queen Alexandra a standard is set. By law, unwritten certainly, but none the less inflexible, as with so much that is best in this fair land of ours, unless you happen to be a near relative, a very intimate friend, or represent in yourself some Dominion or Colony of the Empire or some foreign country, any ornament containing precious stones, or without, intended for the adornment of the person, whether costly or otherwise, is not acceptable to Her Majesty of England.

Instead the gift must take the form of some impersonal object for her writing table, for her vitrine, or it may be to carry about or hang on the wall of her room, but under no circumstances must there be any appearance of costliness about it. The only safe rule is to rely entirely on craftsmanship. It is not that the finest creations of nature in themselves are in any way offensive, it is man who has made them so. And it would appear that having made an idol of the precious stone, even to converting it, as near as can be, into currency itself, he is now called upon, perhaps as a punishment, to substitute for it some work of his own hands, which he can only come by through expenditure of much toil and sweat.

Be this as it may, no subject to-day is allowed to adorn the person of the Queen of England, for that is an intimate personal matter for the Queen herself. To-day we accept this as a matter of course, but there was a time when the subjects of the Queen of England vied with one another in loading her with jewels from head to toe, and what is more, Her Majesty accepted these attentions as her rightful due. Not only this, woebetide any lady who was rash enough to enter into competition with her. I refer, of course, to Her Tudor Majesty Elizabeth, to whom something more than a passing reference must be made, for just as surely as Queen Alexandra was the end of the story of the Sandringham Fabergé collection, so Queen Elizabeth was the beginning of it.

Here we can only give the beginning and end of the story, for it is a long one and one in which other arts than those of the goldsmith and stonecutter played a part. The reader can with advantage turn to the master portrait painters of the Eighteenth Century where the story is coming to an end and to Romney's *Mrs. Robinson*, Gainsborough's and Reynolds' portraits of the same lady, to Reynolds' *Mrs. Carnac* and Lawrence's *A Lady*, to Nattier's *La Comtesse de Tilliere* and *The Princesse de Rohan*, Fragonard's *The Swing*, Lancret's *La Belle Grecque* and Greuze's *Mlle Sophie Arnould*, and to Prud'hon's *Duchesse de Vicence* and *Mademoiselle Mars*, and Antoine Vestier's *Portrait of a Young Lady*, in which there is no showing of jewellery whatever. Boucher, in his portrait of *La Pompadour*, just embellishes her here and there with very unobtrusive innocent little pearls, and Mosnier, in his portrait of the *Countess Stroganoff and her Son*, gives us a few pearls to finish her sleeves.

Before we stress the extravagance of the Tudor Queen, and that we must do, we must also be fair to her, for no English Queen, before or after her, paid her footing with such largesse, and no Queen left such a lasting imprint on everything she touched.

But it is not so much Elizabeth of Merrie England, of Shakespeare, Sidney, Jonson, Bacon and Spenser, of Drake, Raleigh and her 'sweet robin' Leicester; it is not Elizabeth who came to the throne when England was in sore need of her and left her country possessed of the manor house, of domestic comfort, the chimney corner, pillows, carpets and glass windows, the middle class, grammar schools, a new literature, a sense of individual life and action, a Protestant Church and the throne raised to a height in the love of the people to which it had never previously attained; it is not Elizabeth who never mixed business and pleasure, without love or hate, with 'a finer sense than any of her counsellors of her real resources', 'never swayed by enthusiasm or by panic', who when her subjects lost their heads with the triumph of the Armada sat down to count the cost, 'who played with grave cabinets as a cat plays with a mouse', and of whom Phillip II's envoy said, 'This woman is possessed of a thousand devils'—it is not this Elizabeth of English history books whom I would present, although this is a mighty enough Elizabeth, in all conscience, to absolve her from all her sins, and they were many.

Rather is it the Elizabeth of Ivan the Terrible, 'the great Lord, King and great Duke John the son of Vasili of all Russia, of Volodimir, Moscouia and Nouogorod, King of Casan, King of Astracan, Lord of Plesko, and great prince of Smolensko, of Tver, of Vgor, Perme, Vatka, Bolgar, and of others; Lord and great Duke of Nouogorod in the lowe contrey, of Cherneegoue, of Razan, Pototsko, Rostoue, Yeroslaue, of Belozer, Lifland, Vdor, Obdor, Condence, and commander of all the land of Seeberia, and of the north partes and others', for as such he subscribed himself.

This is the Elizabeth I would hold aloft. For one thing this is the Queen more in accord with the present narrative, but mainly for the reason that she is largely forgotten, if ever she is remembered, as such. These two monarchs corresponded for over twenty years and each with an axe to grind. What concerns Elizabeth in the letters which they exchanged is free transit trade down the Volga to Persia and to the untold riches of Siberia. What concerns Ivan is his life. From England he wants doctors and apothecaries to keep him in good health, workmen to dig out gold and silver to make him rich, architects to plan fortresses, towers and palaces to keep him safe, Lady Mary Hastings, daughter of the Earl of Huntingdon, for his sixth or seventh wife and, above all, 'a league of love and friendship', 'an alliance, such that the enemies of the one should be the enemies of the other, the misfortunes of the one, the misfortunes of the other, that if one of them should be obliged to forsake his kingdom, the kingdom of the other might be free to him as his own possession'.

It is a mighty, but I think unequal, contest which they wage, these really BIG TWO. The Terrible Tsar, great lord over vast territory abounding in undeveloped resources, his throne soused in the blood of his subjects, and living in craven fear of their vengeance was no match for the Island Queen, with her Tudor craft, assured of her throne and the love of her people.

'You flowe in your maydenlie estate like a wench', writes the angered Tsar when the Queen refuses to 'kiss the Cross' and conclude a treaty with him. What seems to have incensed him still more was this. While promising him 'a welcome in England as affectionate as the most beloved ally could expect', yet as regards her seeking refuge in Russia she instructs her ambassador to declare 'that such a request on our part would lead our subjects to suppose we had some reason for fearing them, and such a supposition would breed so dangerouse a myslykynge in them towards us as might put us in perill of our estate, which thing wee know our good brother, in respect of the goodwill he protests to beare us, wold be lothe to draw us unto'.[1]

Such is the Elizabeth we should never forget when we speak of her extravagances, and these were commensurate with her achievements. 'She progressed bejewelled and bedecked, Queen of an England lush with gold and precious stones after the Spanish conquests in America.'[2] And following her example all those surrounding her, courtiers, favourites, men and women of fashion, many of her ministers even, and those possessed of title and wealth, 'progressed' with her. The men in particular, even the most virile of them, which was natural enough with a virgin Queen upon the throne, strutted around in silk and satins and the 'glitter of the jewels that spangled them from top to toe', convinced 'that to be inconspicuous was practically equivalent to not being alive'.

Soon all classes of the community were involved and Europe pointed a warning finger at a nation which could so abandon restraint in a display of extravagance and over-adornment of the person which astonished even her. Philip Stubbes writing at the time says this:

'And hereby it appeareth that no People in the World is so curiouse in new fangles as they of England be. . . . So it is verie hard to know who is noble, who is worshipfull, who is a gentleman, who is not, for . . . those which are neither of the nobylite, gentility, nor yeomanry . . . go dailie in silks, satens, damasks, taffeties and such like not withstanding that they be both base by byrthe, meane of estate, and servyle by calling. This is a great confusion and a general disorder: God be mercyfull unto us.'[3]

And as one looks around in this year of grace 1946 one cannot but be assured that God indeed has been merciful. But having given our full due to Him, it is our duty to thank that portion of ourselves 'that sturdy majority', that 'backbone of the nation', call it what you will, which stands erect in all times of our wealth, in all times of our tribulation, the monopoly of no one class of the community, whether in Elizabethan or any other times.

In our search for some background to Queen Alexandra's Fabergé collection

[1] *England and Russia*, 1553-1593. *The First Forty Years of Intercourse*, George Tolstoy. Published in St. Petersford 1875.
[2] *Jewellery*, H. Clifford Smith, M.A.
[3] *Elizabethan Pageantry*, H. K. Morse.

we have unwound many bobbins, a bobbin here, a bobbin there, and so many that we may appear disorderly, but life is like that. You must have thread enough to weave a pattern and disorder enough to make order. If we could put a flash or two upon a screen there would be no need of more ado, as it is we can only state the following facts.

Among the jewels given to Queen Elizabeth as 'Newyeres-giftes', 1571-72, are the following:

'First, one armlet or skakell of golde, all over fairely garnished with rubyes and dyamondes, haveing in the closing thereof a clocke, and in the foreparte of the same a fayre lozengie dyamonde without a foyle, hanging thereat a rounde juell fully garnished with dyamondes and perle pendant; weying 11oz. quᵃ' dim̄ and farthing golde weight. In a case of purple vellate all over embranderied with Venice golde and lyned with a greene vellat. Geven by therle Leycetor.

'Item, a juell, being a white hare of mother of pearle, having two rubies, the one behinde, and the other before in the brest, and an emerald on her forehedd, sitting upon a stocke of golde enamuled, and garnished with 3 table dyamonds, and many small rubies, with a cluster of perles pendaunte, containing 10 pearles alltogether, hanging in three small cheynes of golde; 3oz. qᵃ. Geven by the Counties of Bedforde.'

Among those for 1574-75 are the following:

'Fyrst, a doublet of white satten garnished with goldsmith's work, and sett with XVIII very fayre payre of claspes of goldsmithes worke enamuled, every pair of them set with fyve diamondes and eight rubyes, one diamonde in every payre bigger than the rest, one of the smaller dyamondes lacking, with a pasmayne of lace of damask gold, and damask silver. Geven by therle of Lecetor.'

'Item, a girdle of black vellate, the buckells and studdes of golde being broken. The same girdle set with 15 emeraldes and 3 pearles, all set in collets of golde. Geven by therle of Warwick.'

'Item, a fare juell of golde, containing three personages, as Mars, Venus, and Cupido, fully garnished with sparcks of dyamondes and rubyes, with three emeraldes, one ruby bigger than the rest, and one round perle pendaunte with shorte cheynes of gold, all 2 oz. scante. Geven by the Lady Cheyney. The same faire juell geven by her Majestie to the Lady Carye, Sir George Carye's wife.'

Such were the gifts Queen Elizabeth received from her friends and those surrounding her Court. With the exception of such items, here and there, as gold tooth picks, an 'ear-picke of gold enamuled garnished with sparcks of rubies, blue saphires and seede perle', 'a smale warming-pan of golde, garnished with smale diamonds and rubies with two ragged perles pendant', a 'sault', it is jewels every time.*

Now let us come to Queen Alexandra and her Fabergé collection. From the time King Edward VII ascended the throne, to the time of his death, she received as gifts, from the King, from her friends and from those surrounding the Court,

*The Progresses and Public Processions of Queen Elizabeth, by John Nichols, F.S.A., 1823.

among hundreds of similar objects, the following, a number of which, by the gracious permission of His Majesty, King George VI, are illustrated in Plates 74, 80-88, and 93-95 and described in the succeeding paragraphs:

A sprig of holly in a rock-crystal vase, berries in purpurine, leaves in nephrite (Siberian jade) and stalk in gold. Height 6¼ inches (Plate 81).

A sprig of the cherry tree in rock-crystal vase, flowers opaque white enamel on gold, cherries in purpurine, leaves nephrite and stalk in gold (Plate 81).

A spray of rosebuds in a rock-crystal vase, buds in pink and green enamel on gold, leaves in nephrite, stalk in gold enamelled green (Plate 82).

A spray of Philadelphus in rock-crystal vase, the flowers in white chalcedony, leaves in nephrite, stalk in gold (Plate 82).

A dwarf conifer in gold in jadeite pot on aventurine-quartz stand (Plate 82).

A sprig of raspberry in rock-crystal vase, berries in rhodonite and green jade, leaves nephrite and stalk in gold (Plate 82).

A Rowan tree sprig in rock-crystal vase, berries in purpurine, leaves in nephrite. Height 9 inches (Plate 83).

A chrysanthemum spray in square rock-crystal vase, flowers in mat yellow and purple enamels on gold, leaves in nephrite. Height 10 inches (Plate 84).

A spray of Bleeding Heart in rock-crystal vase, flowers in rhodonite and white chalcedony, leaves in nephrite, stalk in gold. Height 7¾ inches (Plate 84).

A mammoth in nephrite, with rose diamond eyes. Length 5⅛ inches, height 4⅞ inches.

A French bulldog in jasper, with rose diamond eyes. Collar in white opal enamel. Length 5¼ inches, height 3¾ inches (Plate 80).

A buffalo in grey chalcedony, with ivory horns and ruby eyes (Plate 85).

A baboon in grey chalcedony and rose diamond eyes (Plate 85).

A dormouse in grey chalcedony with sapphire eyes and gold whiskers (Plate 85).

A sturgeon in pink and blue agate with rose diamond eyes (Plate 85).

A swordfish in pink and blue agate with rose diamond eyes (Plate 85).

An owl in variously coloured agate with rose diamond eyes and gold feet. Height 4 inches.

A goose in grey agate with ruby eyes.

A kangaroo in nephrite with rose diamond eyes (Plate 86).

A pheasant in crocidolite with rose diamond eyes.

A flamingo in rose quartz, legs in gold, eyes green sapphires, on jade stand (Plate 74).

A circular gold box in translucent light pink enamel with Peter the Great's statue in warm sepia enamel on lid, ornamented with opaque white, translucent green and red enamels.

A seal consisting of a ball of chalcedony supported on a small pedestal in opaque enamel, ornamented with translucent green and red enamels.

A miniature frame in dark mauve enamel bordered with gold with miniature of the Empress Marie Feodorovna encircled with a floral sheaf in different coloured golds (Plate 87); and another in pink enamel with portrait of Queen Alexandra with the Duke of Clarence as a baby (Plate 87).

A bust of the Tsar Alexander III in topaz on a jade stand.

Painting of Sandringham Church in warm sepia enamel on a background of light pink opal enamel on gold. Framed in nephrite and border of pearls. Length 3 inches, height 2¼ inches (Plate 88).

A picture of Queen Alexandra's dairy at Sandringham in warm sepia enamel on light pink opal enamel on gold. Framed with border of translucent green and opaque white enamels. Length 2¾ inches, height 1⅞ inches (Plate 88).

Painting of Durham Cathedral in warm sepia enamel on light pink opal enamel background on gold. Framed in jadeite with chased gold border. Length 6⅛ inches, height 4⅝ inches (Plate 93).

Box in nephrite 5¼ inches long by 3⅜ inches wide and 1⅜ inches deep. With view of Houses of Parliament on lid in warm sepia enamel on a background of light pink opal enamel on gold. Bordered in chased gold (Plate 93).

A rock-crystal clock with engraved leaf border and decorations, with four arrows and bows in rubies and rose diamonds. The clock face bordered with green translucent enamel and rose diamonds.

A cigarette case in smoky rock crystal, gold rim of lid adorned with translucent green enamel and rose diamonds.

A nephrite box 5½ inches by 3 inches by 1⅜ inches. Bordered in gold, adorned with red translucent and opaque white enamels, with small Imperial crown in white, red, green and black enamels and bow in red and white enamels. Inside is a card in Queen Alexandra's handwriting 'Given by sister the Empress of Russia to Sir Arthur Ellis and left to me after his death June 1906' (Plate 94).

A nephrite bowl 6⅛ inches by 10 inches, ornamented in white opal enamel and mecca stones (Plate 95).

It is to be well noted that in the whole of Queen Alexandra's collection there is not one single item of jewellery or object of any sort to adorn the person, and on this account it can be said to be a monument to a standard of English manners and customs. Precious stones are altogether at a discount. The animals certainly have rose diamonds, tiny sapphires and rubies for their eyes, for the sake of liveliness, but these possess no monetary value whatever. In all the objects there can be seen the pattern of the Queen's royal choice. The collection is remarkable in many ways but in none more so than in showing restraint. It is that powerful injunction 'behave' which is implicit in the blood of all English men and women and which governs all their thoughts and actions.

Whether this faculty for restraint was something which the world in its wisdom thought necessary to record, who can say? But if one is to judge by events one has every reason for concluding that such was the case. When one marshals all the trends and events from the Tudor Queen to Queen Alexandra one cannot but be impressed by the fact that in the chain-like succession of those trends and events, there is presented to one's notice a movement towards a particular end.

As the time approaches for this event, there happens to be just the right King on the throne, with just the right experience behind him, just the right Queen with just the right love of simple things, such as animals and flowers, and just the right craftsman to give expression to that fortunate combination of circumstances. And it is to be remarked indeed that it was out of St. Petersburg, the new Babylon as some would have it, that came this Craftsman, who in the Nineteenth Century gave the death blow to the hypnotism of the precious stone.

But it was made certain beyond a peradventure that there should be no mishap in the course of events for Alexander III of Russia, Fabergé's greatest patron, had married the Princess Dagmar of Denmark, sister to Queen Alexandra. Thus the link-up was made complete.

And so we leave this march of destiny and give our attention to the collection itself.

To supply objects at the outset of such a task calls for the highest standard of craftsmanship and inventiveness on the part of the Craftsman, but this high standard being already achieved, the beginning was quite easy. But having made a start, easiness never came his way again. As year follows year, the greater becomes the strain to provide surprises, and surprise is of the very essence of success in such a matter. How to keep the fun going at top speed taxes to the utmost the ingenuity and nerves of the Craftsman and all concerned with him.

Here, reader, whether you like it or not, the biographer must come into the forefront of the story. Fabergé himself never saw Queen Alexandra's collection as displayed at Sandringham. It is doubtful if he ever saw King Edward, Queen Alexandra perhaps once. Far removed from England as he was, it fell to his representative to carry the load of the collection, and to carry the load meant a multitude of things.

If one is to be guided by some people there is an idea prevalent that all artists and craftsmen live and work with an eye to posterity; that there is no present purpose in their work whatsoever at the time of creation. We know this is quite untrue, and especially as regards the goldsmith. The purpose for which all the objects were made for Queen Alexandra was to express affection and great good will, of which they were merely tokens, and Fabergé worked under almost paralyzing limitations to produce them. Every object had to conform to a severe sense of decency, that is its price was strictly regulated.

If one has to give any idea of the stress and troubles of a representative working on the Queen's collection, one must be truly and bluntly outspoken and say that the limit of sale prices ranged from £15 to £50. Some of the Queen's friends were poor, and some enormously rich, but even for the latter it took an object of 'out and out' pure craftsmanship to persuade them to exceed this limit, not because their purses would not stand it, but because the Queen's favour was not for purchase by the highest bidder. The average was £30 and however you might engage yourself to produce something really ravishing or amusing in gold, enamel and rare stones, that exacting limitation rose up continually before you like a forbidding wall, saying: 'Thus far but no farther, please.'

With that sum firmly fixed in your mind you started out on your problem, to find out in what way you might please Her Majesty, and a most accommodating

Majesty she was: gentle, natural, forbearing, jolly, one might almost say rollicking Majesty, in spite of her lameness. I am told on unimpeachable authority that on one occasion when visiting a hospital she noticed a patient very dejected and down in the mouth. On being told that he was afraid he would never be able to use one of his legs again, she said to him, 'I am lame, but look what I can do', and she took a chair and moved about it with remarkable agility.

But you had not gone very far with resolving your problem before you came up against something far more subtle than limitation of price. It was Queen Mary when Princess of Wales, who made me aware of this barrier.

At a time when it seemed well to give a more personal touch to some of the Queen's objects, I sent Fabergé some pictures of Sandringham and the grounds, and in the course of time a box arrived, on the lid of which appeared Sandringham House and a part of the grounds executed in monochrome enamel. I give an illustration of it in Plate 88, but please note that the reproduction of the enamel painting does not do justice to the delicacy of the original. Earl Howe bought it and gave it to Queen Alexandra. Shortly afterwards Queen Mary called; she was then, as I say, Princess of Wales. 'What a beautiful box you have made of Sandringham for Queen Alexandra', she said. Now to have one's efforts praised, always set me off, and I had a brain wave. In a flash I saw all England in front of me in warm sepia enamel: the Palaces, the Cathedrals, Waterfalls, the Houses of Parliament and so on, *ad infinitum*. There would be enough here to keep Fabergé going until the end of King Edward's reign and well into King George's. To begin with I suggested to Her Royal Highness that we might do the palaces, like Windsor, Buckingham Palace, St. James's Palace, even Holyrood, only to be met at once with this remark. 'But they are not ours; they belong to the nation.' I thought I knew the attitude of the Royal Family pretty well, but here was a revelation of their minds which had not occurred to me.

I give an illustration of a gold box in Plate 94, showing Balmoral and Windsor Castles in enamel, one of the nicest things in the royal collection. I must say that Queen Mary's remark damped down my enthusiasm and slow minded as I am it took me quite a time to come to the conclusion that it was one thing for the Royal Family to demand and quite another to accept that which was offered. In the course of time both Buckingham Palace and Hampton Court appeared in monochrome, as small plaques, framed in nephrite, and there may have been others.

In looking back to that brain-racking, harassing, exciting time of forty years ago, when Fabergé with hundreds of his craftsmen continually exercised their minds, their ingenuity, their hands and eyes to catch hold of an idea and having caught it pared it down until it became possible to represent it in a small piece of rare stone or precious metal, I say looking back one cannot but come to the conclusion that one's worst enemy was oneself. If any one has suffered from over-seriousness certainly I have. So anxious was I to make an outstanding success of the Queen's collection that it was never out of my mind. I lived with it, slept and ate with it constantly before me.

I got it into my head that the greatest Craftsman of the age was at my beck and call, and being of the turn of mind that England was a country to immortalize, therefore at all costs that country must be represented in gold, enamel and rare stones. It was a chance that might never come again to any other living man.

And so I set about it. Poor Fabergé, how I must have sickened him with 'atmosphere'. I kept on bottling it, as it were, in London and sending it in jars to Petersburg, as much as to say: 'There you are, that is a grouse moor and those are the butts; that is Melton and the Quorn; this is Epsom Downs on Derby Day and Hampstead Heath on Bank Holiday; this is Lords and the Oval, and that is Ascot, Goodwood and Newmarket; this is Sandringham and the Queen's Dairy, and that is Chatsworth, Devonshire House, Crichel, Castle Rising and Coombe Court; this is Durham Cathedral from the railway station, Edinburgh Castle and the old town from Princes Street, for to me Scotland was all the same, the High Force, Teesdale, Bamborough Castle from the turn in the road, the Roman Wall at Borcovicus; and so on and on. Once I took him two really good North Country plum puddings which my wife had made, to prove to him that his early experiences in the Strand had been nothing but a myth. 'But these are not plum puddings', he said, and took a second helping.

And there were Cellini's 'Seasons', which 'Mr. Leopold' kept on showing me at Hamilton Place. Little groups in enamel representing Spring, Summer, Autumn and Winter. Here was inspiration enough, thrown at one almost once a week and of course similar groups sprang up in my mind representing the British Common-wealth of Nations. What could there be more pleasing for Queen Alexandra's collection! And England and Russia, for I had a mania for bringing them together in such a way. A group in lapis-lazuli, aventurine-quartz, chalcedony, jasper and other stones so intermingled and intertwined that they could never fall apart, would make, so I thought, a most significant gift for Her Majesty of England.

But here I was pressing Fabergé too hard. There is a limit to what craftsmanship can do and earn a living. He got out of it by saying he was an artist, not a prophet.

But this was not a tithe of the load one carried, self-imposed or otherwise. For instance, one often felt very much ashamed of oneself. Every year I went to Petersburg, not only to find things for the Queen and talk about new ideas for her, but loaded up with demands from all over the world. My list ran something like this: 'Do find me something very, very new—Do you think Fabergé could make me a porcupine? I'd love it if he would!—I want a crochet hook and a "love-bird" green enamel cigarette case—I want an altar-piece and a picture of the Madonna and Child—I want a *nécessaire* in raspberry-red enamel with a place for matches and cigarettes—I want some candle-sticks with owls on them—I want some gardening scissors and an elephant that walks, and do bring me back my buttons, the hat-pin and the buckle. Tell Fabergé my dressmaker's waiting for a lead— I want the moon, *do* you think it's possible to do it in translucent yellow enamel? Perhaps Fabergé could make a clock of it or something of that sort.'

I say I felt ashamed to go to Petersburg with a list like this, and not for the reason that it was mostly concerned with those little things of fun and fancy, which to the discomfiture of the more serious efforts of mankind 'slip, laughing, through Time's fingers', and which it was Fabergé's whole business to create, but because one's nature recoiled from the idea of adding to the load of a man who was already pestered almost beyond endurance to meet the home demands of the Tsar, the Tsarina, the Dowager Empress Marie Feodorovna, and all the Grand Dukes and Grand Duchesses, the Schuvaloffs, Bariatinskys, Galitzines, Kotchubeys, Zinovieffs, Benckendorffs, Stroganoffs, Troubetzkoys, Vorontzoff-Dashkoffs, Mescherskys, Elleseyeffs, Apraxins, Naryshkins, Orloffs, Lobanoff-Rostoffskys, Dolgourukis, Dolgourukoffs, Sasso-Ruffos, Demidoffs, Orloff-Davidoffs, the Bjeloselskys, the Sheremeteffs and the Youssoupoffs, to name only a few.

A good Russian, too, is a sensitive creature, hyper-sensitive. Nothing hurts him more than to say 'No' to you. To say 'Yes' is almost equally trying to him. Because things are all right on Saturday morning is no reason for concluding they will be equally so on Monday morning, is his way of thinking. And not a bad way either when one thinks of those exasperating, insufferable words, 'Go to it!' flashed into the air one Monday when a little forethought on the Saturday might have done much to save the City of London.

And so quite extraordinary situations arose during my yearly visits to St. Petersburg. Never can there have been such fencing, such *finesse*. I on my part, most anxious to get possession of the best things for London and the Queen's collection and yet without hurting the Craftsman's feelings, he on his part equally anxious not to hurt mine and wishful to meet my demands in most open-handed manner and yet wondering how he was to carry on his business in Russia, if he gave me all the best he had. Those who are fortunate enough to deal in fine things will have some fellow-feeling for a man who created everything he sold. When to this general atmosphere of hyper-sensitiveness you add the extraordinary character of the Craftsman, then it will be clear that no reasonable explanation can be offered for the situations which developed.

In general, I made it my routine to ransack the Petersburg stock from beginning to end once a year, putting aside what I considered a choice fair to both Petersburg and London, and then inviting the Craftsman to give his sanction to my taking away the pieces I had chosen. Sometimes he would take a cursory look and say 'The King and Queen won't like any of them'. This meant a change of approach and so I waited for a more auspicious occasion. It was the habit of the Craftsman every morning to walk through the offices on the way to his work, saying 'Zdrastuitye' and brushing his fingers through his side-locks. Some mornings he did the brushing less vigorously than usual and then was one's opportunity. Taking a couple of chosen objects I would go into him and say 'May I take these to London?' and more often than not he would reply, 'Why not, and have you seen this and that and the other. Take them, the Queen, I am sure, will like them all'.

But certainly the most trying situation for both of us was, I think, something which occurred on my first visit to him in 1906. The consequences of it taught me my first serious Fabergé lesson, that it was no business of mine to tout for orders, rather was it to turn customers away.

Carried away by the generosity of my reception, I felt the least I could do was to show the Craftsman I knew a thing or two, so I wrote about a dozen letters to the Crowned Heads of Europe and to those immediately surrounding them, to say that there would shortly be in London a quite astonishing selection of Fabergé objects and inviting their interest in them. At that time I did not know that to Carl Fabergé letters of any sort were very disagreeable and upsetting things or that letters of the sort I proposed writing were really shocking to him; in fact, I had not then learned the simple truth that the House of Fabergé already had far more business than it could comfortably cope with.

The more one recapitulates the idiosyncracies of Fabergé the more one realises what horse sense he had. No one knew better than he that for a creator to push the sale of his wares was the right way to push them out of existence. The only way to maintain a standard of perfection was to concentrate effort, not disseminate it, and to let each object speak for itself.

Fabergé was far too sensitive to hurt my feelings by refusing to sign the letters I put before him, but if I *would* perpetrate such abominations at any rate he could subject my handiwork to withering sarcasm, and this he promptly did, with caustic on his pen for every signature. Well for my eventual peace of mind if I had torn up those letters. Instead, I posted them.

In a week's time or so came a cable from Queen Alexandra who said she would like to see all the new things before anyone else, as she wished to find something for the King. On my return to London, Lady De Grey button-holed me on the stairs at 48 Dover Street, 'Do, please, let me see everything first', she said, 'I want to choose something for the Queen'. I was certainly beginning to feel the full weight of my indiscretion. It was no easy matter to tackle Lady De Grey, and by the time we had reached the first floor and I had closed the door I was on the point of giving way to her charm and persistence, when there was a knock on the door and I let in Chandler, the chief wardrobe-keeper to the King. 'The King's command', he said. 'Before you show anything to anyone he must see the lot, as he wants to find something for the Queen.' And so my discomfiture was complete.

But whatever a representative of Fabergé might do or might not do, he was always in trouble. It could not be otherwise. To be sandwiched between two of the moving spirits of the time was to be subjected to extraordinary emotions. The King always on the *qui vive* as regards anything to do with the Queen's collection, never losing an opportunity when at Sandringham to compel one with his dictum, 'We must not make any duplicates. We must not make any duplicates'. It was his stock command; how many times he said it I should not like to say.

And the Craftsman's 'You must think me the Creator Himself to undertake all these impossibilities'.

Working to please King Edward should have taught me one lesson, that whatever you suggested to him he would go one better. But in one's eagerness to take full advantage of the craftsmanship of Fabergé one never learned the lesson, so I was never out of one difficulty before I was plunged into another. And the biggest of all came with the proposal to model a few of the favourite animals at Sandringham and then cut them in different stones in the colours of the originals. The proposal arose thus wise:

A frequent caller at Fabergé's in London was Sir Ray Lankester, the scientist. Like the Queen, it was the models of animals, birds and fishes in different stones which interested him. It was he who suggested the idea that the owners of English pedigree animals should have models made of them and then cut in different stones the same colour as far as possible as the originals, with the object of making a national collection to be housed in one of the National Museums. However, nothing came of it, and knowing now what I did not know then, I account it a happy release for Fabergé.

Fortunately, or unfortunately, not being content to leave well alone, I let the idea smoulder in my mind, not to the extent of modelling all the pedigree animals in England, for that fantastic project was over, but I was ready to take fire at any time in a more limited way. Perhaps some of Fabergé's customers might have one of their racehorses done, or a dog or two, and so I waited for an opportunity.

I was in this frame of mind when Mrs. George Keppel called. The Queen's Fabergé collection was no uncommon topic of conversation when the friends of the King and Queen came to Fabergé's and it was while talking to Mrs. Keppel about it that I told her what had been running through my mind. 'Why not some of the favourite Sandringham animals for the Queen's collection', she said, 'if the King will give his permission'. Next day I received a telegram from Sandringham: 'The King agrees; Mr. Beck will make all arrangements', and so I took the next train to Wolferton. As usual, things were going far too well to begin with and my guardian angel was at the winning-post long before I was half-way there; for I learned from the King's agent that not only were Persimmon, the King's Derby winner, Cæsar, his favourite rough-haired terrier, and one or two of the Queen's dogs, to be done, but as Mr. Beck put it, 'the whole farmyard', heifers and bullocks, cocks and hens, turkeys, shire horses and even pigs.

At a stroke, the King had gone twenty better and this time I was really in the welter of the impossible. As I journeyed back to London I wondered how I would tell Fabergé, for as yet he knew nothing about it. How would he find stones enough? What about the cost of the venture? How about the modellers; could they be spared to work in this country for months? All the precious nonsense of portrait models in rare stones sounded well enough, but suppose the whole thing turned out a fiasco? And with the King of England, too! What then? Where would Fabergé be? And so on and so on.

I did not then know that Oliver Cromwell had said, 'A man never goes so far as when he does not know where he is going', which was exactly my case. I was only at the beginning of my 'Fabergé in Wonderland'. Nobody was to be in it to the same extent as myself. The King was to have his portion, Fabergé his but as luck would have it the beginning, the middle and the end were to be mine alone. The last-minute telegrams from Sandringham on the eve of the Queen's birthday, the midnight drives through the woods of Wolferton, with prancing horses, a royal coachman and footman all complete, the reception at Sandringham House by some important personage, as though I were some last-minute saviour of a desperate situation. 'While you are having something to eat, I will unpack your bag.' So said King George of Greece, Queen Alexandra's brother, the last time

I saw him on one of these excursions. And awakened next morning to the sound of bagpipes going round the house, as I turned over in a royal bed and wondered if the millenium had arrived.

Such happenings, and many more of a like nature, were to crowd my eleven years with Fabergé; and entirely because of him. To-day they may smack too much of exuberance and a joy in living, of downright egotism may be, but what of it? Each man, according to what was in him and to his taste, was free to take a dive into the deepest waters of adventure, for as yet 'that Phantom Uniformity' had not taken a stranglehold of the minds of men.

As I was saying, I was only then at the beginning of my 'Fabergé in Wonderland' and had not then learned how to hold my breath long enough in the flood of topsy-turvy happenings as I kept diving into them. I need not burden you, reader, with all that took place before the adventure at Sandringham was well on its way. I take you there on Sunday, December 8th, 1907.

If on that day, shortly after lunch, you had found yourself, as I did, hiding behind a hedge in the grounds of Sandringham, you would have seen the King leaving Sandringham House surrounded by his guests. He was dressed in a tight-fitting overcoat and what looked like a small cricket cap. It was very evident something was astir, for the whole party was moving at a pace as though there were no time to lose, and Cæsar, the King's terrier, added zest by rushing in and out, barking all the time. The King was holding forth, one imagined him saying, 'Now I am going to see something', without enlightening his guests what it was all about. He was on his way to Queen Alexandra's Dairy.

For months past Fabergé's artists had been hard at work modelling the animals according to the King's list: Boris Froedman-Cluzel, Frank Lutiger and others, unfortunately not now remembered. During the time they had been at work they had become what can best be described as the Sandringham Star Turn. On shooting days, by the King's command, all work ceased and he took the artists round with him and, at the usual royal gathering for luncheon, presented them to the Queen, the Prince and Princess of Wales and his guests. In many other ways he showed that spirit which was essentially his, of extracting from a situation all there was to get.

And never did he show it better than on that Sunday afternoon in December 1907, when at his command all the finished wax models were set out in the Queen's Dairy for his examination and criticism. His cosmopolitanism joined hands with his love for his home, and out of the union he contrived to stage a pageant. The incongruous combination of interests and people; the butter beautifully set out in one room of the dairy, awaiting the King's approval; in the other, artists of several nationalities keeping guard over their work and waiting, no doubt rather nervously, for the King's criticisms; the many guests, split up into groups, strolling about outside the dairy and seemingly quite in the dark about what the King was up to; the setting of the scene in the Sandringham stable-yard, with Persimmon close by in his loose-box, perhaps wondering what was afoot; and the final gesture of the King, when, standing on the steps of the dairy, he sent a message of congratulation to Carl Fabergé: 'Will you please tell Mr. Fabergé how pleased I am with all he has done for me. I have pointed out to the artists one or two places where some little alteration can be made, but otherwise I think the work splendid.'

If at that moment I had given my hat a twirl it would have circled up to heaven.

I have searched the chronicles, Rastrelli, Charles Cameron and Falconet in Russia, Rubens in England, even Cellini as he progressed from one city to another, in all the glory of Italy of the Renaissance, with the Medicis as near as can be at his beck and call, and I can find nothing which quite compares with the homely pageant on that Sunday afternoon, in the heart of England, when craftsmanship by Royal Command was given an opportunity to display itself in a manner which those who were concerned in it can never forget.

The wax models were sent to St. Petersburg and, with the exception of Persimmon which was cast in silver, cut, in the workshops of Fabergé, in different stones, the colourings and markings of which were as near as it was possible to come to those of the originals. The finished animals in their various stones were sent to London and all of them acquired by King Edward and given to Queen Alexandra for her Fabergé Collection.

So the story ends. But before we let it go, for once let us indulge ourselves. I say 'ourselves' because this chapter is essentially for Englishmen and women. Do let us make it doubly plain whence we have come and whither we go, that we have had our extravaganza and have learned a thing or two. Moreover, let us take off our hats to the Edwardians. We have heard far too much of their knick-knacks and feathers, and it is more than time that we gave them their due. Finally, therefore, let us focus our attention on two facts.

At 'Newyerstyde 1585' the Earl of Leicester gave to Queen Elizabeth 'a sable skynne, the hedd and four feete of gold fully garnished with dyamonds and rubies of sundry sorts'. On December 1st, 1908, King Edward VII gave to Queen Alexandra a shire horse in aventurine-quartz of no material worth whatever.

In Plates 96-99, by the gracious permission of His Majesty King George VI, I give an illustration of this portrait model, together with those of a shorthorn, a Clumber spaniel, King Edward's terrier 'Cæsar', Queen Alexandra's Pekingese, a turkey, a cock and a pig, all of which at one time or another were given by King Edward to Queen Alexandra and form part of the Fabergé collection of animals modelled at Sandringham.

Before we close this chapter something must be said in a general way about the animals and flowers. That Fabergé should be classed as the greatest goldsmith, silversmith and jeweller of his time, even of all time, is justifiable, for no craftsman has contributed in such varying ways to the needs and delight of so many sections of people. His silver plate, spoons, forks, trays, bowls, tea and coffee sets, were in everyday use in a large number of Russian households and his *surtouts de table* were essential to the outfit of every Grand Duke on his marriage; his Easter eggs made for the Tsars Alexander III and Nicholas II were the outstanding Easter delight of the Imperial Family; his cigarette cases in gold, silver, enamel and stone were enough in themselves to make him famous since no gentleman of Europe considered himself adequately equipped without at least three or four of them, especially those in ribbed and fluted gold of different colours; his figurines in different stones, especially those representing figures of Russian national life, for those wanting something typically Russian; his pendants and brooches of stones of colour but little intrinsic worth were sought after by every cultured woman; and his clocks, frames, ashtrays, seals, ikons, paper-weights and writing utensils of every sort were to be found everywhere all over the globe, regardless of nationality, creed or sex.

Here is achievement rich enough for any man and yet does not take account of the animals and flowers. Whether the palm for craftsmanship should be given to the Easter eggs, to the figurines, the cigarette cases, the animals or the flowers, is not the present point. At the moment what we are after is to fix which of these creations (I use this word but I do not like it because it is presenting man with a power he does not possess; in point of fact it has now become jargon, and, to the ordinary mind out to learn something, smacks of deception, quackery and preciousness) has given the greatest delight.

You, reader, must rely on me when I tell you they are the animals and flowers, and you must lean on me still further when I say that it is women who have for the most part been attracted by them: Queen Alexandra and all the ladies of her period, regardless of nationality. What is more, it is the knowing ladies of to-day who continue to be attracted by them.

There is something in this continuity of feminine appreciation which the opposite sex may very well note, and which to my mind goes to the very core of the condemnation of these animals and flowers by the higher artistic critics as being merely copies of nature, and not works of art and therefore to be poohpoohed.

By this time in the world's history there is every justification for laying it down as axiomatic that 'Feminine and Masculine', 'Female and Male' are tantamount to saying 'The Quick and the Dead'. That everything quickening in life is vested in the female requires no demonstration, as for the male, there can be no better proof that his activities are towards death and destruction than the fact that after thousands of years of his rule the outstanding question to-day is not, what progress are we going to make, but how soon will the earth be totally destroyed?*

When to his lust for destroying everything which falls within his grasp you add his arrogance, then you begin to understand the male in reference to those matters of art which we have at present under view, and it is his arrogance which in the last resort is his downfall. When you offer him an acanthus leaf border in gold, he acclaims it at once. 'Here is art', he says, 'and the man who originated the design a creator.' But when you confront him with a representation of the whole plant in gold, jade and enamel, he says, 'Take it away! Take it away! Take it away!'

The fact that in the border the leaves have been cut out of their original setting and then arranged in a long line one after the other camouflages their natural

* Refer to the two concluding lines of Goethe's "Faust":

Das Ewig-Weibliche
Zieht uns hinan

Bayard Taylor says: 'I can find no English equivalent for *Ewig-Weibliche* except 'woman-soul' . . .'
Sir Theodore Martin speaks of 'the feminine element . . . in the Divine Being . . .'

origin and an erroneous impression is given that something has been made which has never existed before. With the whole plant, or a good portion of it, it is a different matter, the thing is too blatantly what it is, a copy of nature. There can be no excuse here whatever for claiming that a new thing has been made and therefore it must be damned as a work of art.

Such it would appear is the attitude of the male. The female does not concern herself with such mysteries, instinctively she goes straight for that in which is crystallized the most truth and liveliness, that is the whole plant, or a good portion of it.

It is only when you acknowledge that mankind can create nothing new, that all that it can do is to discover, or rather, uncover, that which already exists that confusion is swept away, and if the leaf border is a work of art then so much more is the representation of the whole plant which entails vastly more delicate handiwork and insight to bring out all that is inherently alive in it. It is in this way of thinking that you avoid the hundred and one byeways of 'the curious', 'the old', 'the tortuous' and 'the lifeless', so dear to the male mind.

What I can say only with difficulty, Charles Morgan, when reviewing Mr. Geoffrey Bickersteth's book, *The Golden World of King Lear*, states with remarkable clarity. He says: 'Art exists not to instruct or persuade the mind, but to *impregnate the imagination*—to "get the curtain up"!' The italics are mine.

To take the two examples again, there can be no doubt which of them is the most successful in this direction. It is the whole plant or a good portion of it.

Like all men, Carl Fabergé was not wholly masculine, just as no woman is wholly feminine. Like so many, if not all, male geniuses he had in him very much more than a streak of the feminine; in his case I should say about half of him, and it is this which accounts more than anything else for the liveliness which is to be found in all the work which has come from his workshops.

So successful was he with his flowers that it behoves collectors to see that they get the right thing, for they have been imitated, not in great numbers but to such an extent as to call for care when purchasing them.[1] No one can object to following the example of another, since we all build on work which has gone before, but in the cases to which I refer, the imitating was done with malice aforethought, the flowers in every case being stamped on the gold stalk with the forged mark of Fabergé and the Russian hall-mark for gold. In doing this the imitator over-shot his aim because Fabergé by no means marked all his flowers. The Japanese tree illustrated in Plate 75 is not marked at all, and here one might expect to see marks, because the whole tree is in gold.[2]

The collector of Fabergé flowers must forget hall-marks and makers' marks altogether, and if he is not sufficiently acquainted with their chief characteristics which *in toto* make up something which to the experienced eye can be seen at a

[1] An all-round word of warning must be given. The first sales period since the death of Carl Fabergé can now be said to be over and genuine pieces are now in short supply. Collectors who have not developed a Fabergé sense of their own should be guided by the advice of dealers of repute especially in regard to more important objects.

[2] The same applies to flowers, Plates 37-39.

glance, then let him seek guidance. If words can convey anything I can give him this help. Always keep in mind the superb finish of the original natural flower, and keep the critical sense at this pitch. Examine the stalks minutely and note that for the most part they have a 'shin bone' in them, sometimes more than one; where there is no shin bone they are evenly lined, even if sometimes the lines are hardly to be seen. Let him notice that the surface of the stalks is, in varying degree, mat. Let him examine the back of the leaves as well as the front and take note that the veinings are correspondingly ribbed on the back. Of the flower blooms, one can only say that their delicacy is indescribable, the only thing he can do is to take a microscope and on bended knee saturate himself with their unending detail.

If to this he will add a little knowledge of their habits, then he must acknowledge that however you may play tricks with animals, you cannot be funny with flowers. They are the perfection of all created things. Absolute autocrats, you cannot subordinate them, they will do nothing for you except in their own sweet way. Even if you torture them and by scientific process retard their growth, they will outwit their torturers and blossom more luxuriantly than ever; and if you would represent them, you must do so petal for petal, pistil for pistil, and leaf for leaf. You must take no liberties.

To conventionalise them, by splitting them up and simplifying them according to some artistic principle for decorative ends, is to take all truth out of them. To mass them, and by vigorous touches give some general impression of form and colour, is to murder them.

So equipped, the collector can then turn to the Fabergé flowers with some assurance that he knows what he is after, and in them he will find this, *that the delicacy and intricacy of the natural flower has been faithfully reproduced up to the point where further reproduction is no longer possible owing to the limitations of the materials employed and the mechanical devices necessary. For instance, the jade leaves have just so much body more than the natural to allow them to bear the collet by which they are permanently fixed to the stem. And this more is to be noted, that where greater nearness to the delicacy of the natural flower might have been attained in some one direction, this greater delicacy has not been attempted because it could only have been done at the expense of another part which could not have been so treated.*

The effect of this is to convey the impression that the workmanship throughout is sustained at the highest pitch possible, which is in fact the truth, and which in turn gives a sense of fullness, completeness and richness, and nothing of unevenness, meagreness or thinness, and which is all to the joy of the beholder.

In other words, it is our old friend 'substance' back again, which is at the bottom of all Fabergé's work. Here is an artistic triumph somewhat akin to understatement in the hands of a literary genius.

So much for the flowers. Much that has been said about them applies in general to the animals. Again they are copies of nature modelled in the most recognisable poses of the natural animals. Unlike the Chinese which are superb examples of the 'tortuous' and the 'curious' in art, they are healthy looking, natural, pleasing creatures. The outstanding quality about them is that they appear alive and in accordance with their natural bent. Put one or two of them together and this is very evident and amusing. Some are magnificently aloof and others for ever poking into the affairs of their neighbour. The amusement in arranging and rearranging them in groups is never ending and this in a large measure is their attraction, and the reason that no one can possess too many of them.

Again the question arises how to recognize them, and again, like the flowers, it is a matter of living with them.* A tip here and there is all I can do to help. Fatness and finish are two good words to start with. Fabergé had the Shakespearean outlook, all his animals are well fed. He was an excellent man of business although so unbusinesslike. Who is going to buy a lean, sad thing when he can have a fat and jolly one? Therefore he went for fatness wherever and whenever possible. His elephants are his classic example, he played on their bulk and concertina-fashion pushed them together making them fatter still. This is why so many people collected them and do still. Of them all, it is those in rock-crystal which I think are the most attractive. What more amusing, satisfying and unique than a collection of them, from the largest to the smallest? To-day it would be without price.

And then there is the frog, especially a large one with a gloriously distended stomach and a smile on his face. Here is the Fabergé Falstaff and a cure for all ills. I give an illustration in Plate 73.

As I relate these things it is brought home to me that I was wrong in describing the animals as merely copies of nature, Fabergé put his joke into so many of them. And the same with the flowers, where the Craftsman came to a most artistic full-stop when the delicacy of nature became too ephemeral for him religiously to follow.

And all the birds, the owls, kingfishers, kiwis, and the fishes. What of these? Well, the same as for all Fabergé models of living creatures, all have had a good meal and are comfortable looking. And so we get back once again to our old friend 'substance'. And two other things; the workmanship, top and bottom equally, is without blemish, never slip-shod or hastily passed over. Every model is highly polished and right down to the bottom of every carved line, only very rarely was a model left semi-polished.

And lastly 'the rights of the material'. Here Fabergé triumphed again. Whether each stone was chosen first and then a suitable animal modelled to meet its peculiar characteristics, or whether vice versa, is difficult to say. Perhaps both methods were employed and personally I should say that it was more often the former, for no lapidary was happier in finding the right bit of a stone for the head, the right bit for the tail, and so on.

On page 28 I have repeated a little story about King George V and as I bring to mind the triumphs of Fabergé—his care for 'the rights of the material', his avoidance of anything slip-shod, the fine fitting of hinges and last but not least his determination that whenever possible his objects should serve some useful purpose—I am once again reminded of His Majesty and the fact that no one appreciated these things more than he did and no one took a greater delight to

*The animals being of stone did not require to be hall-marked. A very few are now found to be engraved, FABERGÉ, but no reliance for identification purposes should be placed on such engraving.

point them out to others. Moreover, he never lost an opportunity to remind those responsible for the care of his Fabergé possessions that they must be careful how they handled them. In plate 89 I give an illustration of a small pen-rest which was always on His Majesty's writing table.

As I conclude this chapter let me remind the reader that the why and wherefore of all craftsmen, in the main, is made evident by means of their works and not by the words of a biographer. But for the fact that so many Fabergé pieces have been well housed and cared for in England and the U.S.A., no record would have been possible. In this caretaking many people have been concerned, but in particular we are indebted to the English Royal Family. When it is borne in mind that the greater part of the many Fabergé objects in their possession, a large number of a very fragile nature, have been cared for by them during the reigns of four English Monarchs and subjected, in that time, to all kinds of accidents arising from examination, re-arranging, dusting, etc., let alone the hazards of two great wars, it is a remarkable fact that the objects are still in mint condition.

But there is something else to be remarked. As I have said before, the whole purpose for which Fabergé objects were made was achieved at the moment of their presentation by one person to another. There was never any intention that any of them should necessarily serve as objects of craftsmanship for the enlightenment and enjoyment of posterity. And yet it is just this, which was never intended, which has happened, and I have been given ample opportunity to acquaint myself with this fact. Not only have I been given a ready access to Fabergé collections everywhere, but I have been privileged to examine them in the presence of their owners. In this way, as I have seen each collection so I have come to new knowledge of how Fabergé still works on the minds of men and women, and the record of his life has benefited accordingly.

In this willingness to be of service the English Royal Family have been most gracious. Whenever they have given me permission to see their collections they have made a point of being present themselves at the examination. As I have mentioned in a former chapter, it has been my privilege from time to time to examine, in company with Queen Mary, every piece included in her collection—an examination made vastly more inspiring by the knowledgeable comments expressed by Her Majesty on the history and significance of individual pieces. In my humble opinion Queen Mary herself is the greatest surviving connoisseur of Fabergé's craftsmanship.

In Plates 112 and 120-125 we see a number of Fabergé cigarette cases from the Collection of King George VI. On November 1st, 1948, His Majesty, in company with Her Majesty the Queen, received me at Buckingham Palace when Fabergé and his work was the subject of discussion, with special emphasis on His Majesty's collection of Fabergé cigarette cases.

Laid out on a white cloth on a table the cases which the King had chosen for reproduction were all ready for examination and at once His Majesty went into all particulars about them, referring from time to time to an album in which each case was catalogued with a photograph and all details about it, who had presented it and so on.

For a biographer of Fabergé here was a moment. I felt like a prospector who,

PLATE 93

VIEW OF DURHAM CATHEDRAL. In warm sepia enamel on light pink opal enamel background on gold. Framed in jadeite, with chased gold border. Length: 6⅛ inches. Height: 4⅝ inches.
(*From Queen Alexandra's Collection.*)

BOX. In nephrite, chased gold borders. On lid a view of Houses of Parliament in warm sepia enamel on background of light pink opal enamel on gold. Length: 5¼ inches. Width: 3⅜ inches. Depth: 1⅜ inches.
(*From Queen Alexandra's Collection.*)

PLATE 94

BONBONNIÈRE. In light pink opal enamel on gold, bordered with opaque white enamel. Leaves in green enamel and rose-diamonds and rose flowers in opaque white and pink enamels. Views of Windsor and Balmoral Castles in warm sepia enamel. Diameter: 2¼ inches.
(*From Queen Alexandra's Collection.*)

BOX. In nephrite bordered with red translucent and opaque white enamels on gold. Imperial emblem in white, red, green and black enamels. Given by the Empress Marie Feodorovna to Sir Arthur Ellis and by him left to Queen Alexandra in 1906. Length: 5½ inches. Width: 3 inches. Depth: 1⅜ inches.
(*From Queen Alexandra's Collection.*)

PLATE 95

BOWL

In nephrite, mounts in white opal enamel on silver studded with mecca stones of varied
colours; rims in gold. Total height: 6⅛ inches. Total width: 10 inches.
(*From Queen Alexandra's Collection.*)

PLATE 96

SHIRE HORSE, PORTRAIT MODEL
Modelled at Sandringham and cut in St. Petersburg in aventurine-quartz. Sapphire eyes.
Length: 7 inches. Height: 6 inches.
(From Queen Alexandra's Collection.)

PLATE 97

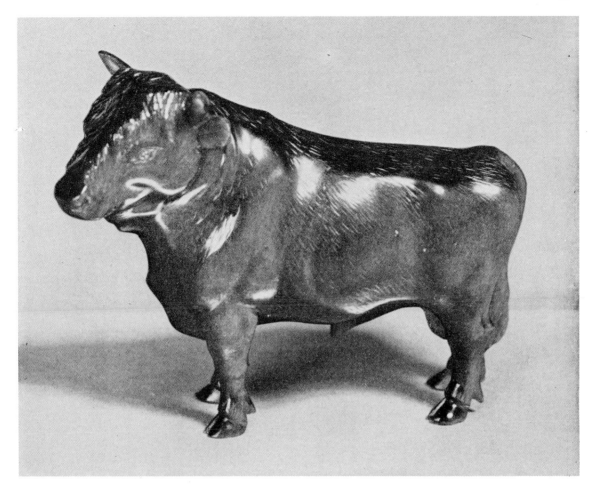

SHORTHORN BULL, PORTRAIT MODEL
Modelled at Sandringham and cut in St. Peterburg in obsidian. Ruby eyes.
Length: $4\frac{1}{4}$ inches. Height: $3\frac{1}{8}$ inches.
(*From Queen Alexandra's Collection.*)

PLATE 98

CAESAR, PORTRAIT MODEL. King Edward VII's rough-haired terrier. Modelled at Sandringham and cut in St. Petersburg in white chalcedony. Ruby eyes. 'I belong to the King' on collar of brown enamel on gold. Length: $2\frac{5}{8}$ inches. Height: 2 inches.

CLUMBER SPANIEL, PORTRAIT MODEL. Modelled at Sandringham and cut in St. Petersburg in greenish grey chalcedony. Ruby eyes. Length: 4 inches. Height: 2 inches.

COCK, PORTRAIT MODEL. Modelled at Sandringham and cut in St. Petersburg in obsidian, jasper, purpurine. Claws gold. Eyes diamonds.

TURKEY, PORTRAIT MODEL. Modelled at Sandringham and cut in St. Petersburg in obsidian, lapis-lazuli, purpurine. Claws gold. Eyes diamonds. Length: $3\frac{1}{4}$ inches. Height: 4 inches.

(The above objects are from Queen Alexandra's Collection.)

PLATE 99

QUEEN ALEXANDRA'S FAVOURITE PEKINGESE, PORTRAIT MODELS. Modelled at Sandringham and cut in stone in St. Petersburg. One on left in light blue beryl. Diamond eyes. Length: $4\frac{1}{2}$ inches. Height: $2\frac{5}{8}$ inches. The other in cream-grey translucent chalcedony. Diamond eyes. Length: 4 inches. Height: $3\frac{1}{8}$ inches.

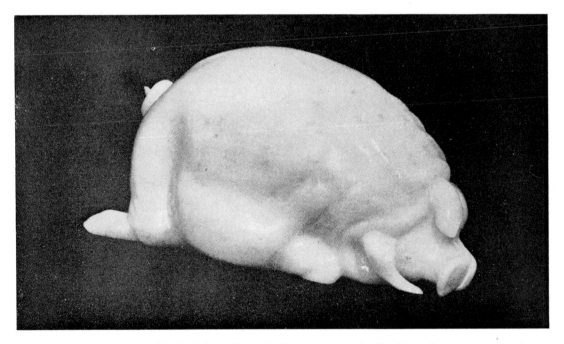

PIG, PORTRAIT MODEL. Modelled at Sandringham and cut in St. Petersburg in aventurine-quartz. Diamond eyes. Length: 6 inches. Height: $2\frac{3}{4}$ inches.
(*The above objects are from Queen Alexandra's Collection.*)

PLATE 100

Fig. 1. COSSACK (*Cherkéss*). Height: 8½ inches. Engraved 'Fabergé 1915'.

Fig. 2. COSSACK (*Cherkéss*). Back view.

Fig. 3. DRIVER OF PUBLIC VEHICLE (*izvoschik*). Height: 4 inches.

Fig. 4. STREET PEDLAR (*raznoschik*). Height: about 4 inches. (*Privately owned.*)

PLATE 101

Fig. 1. PEASANT (*mujik*). Height: 4½ inches.
(*Collection of Sir William Seeds, K.C.M.G.*)

Fig. 2. COSSACK BODYGUARD OF THE DOWAGER EMPRESS MARIE FEODOROVNA. Approximate height: 6 inches.
(*By courtesy of Hammer Galleries.*)

PLATE 102

KOVSH. In yellow striated agate. Handle in gold and three cabochon sapphires. Workmaster Kollin (E.K.). Total height: 2½ inches. (*From Queen Mary's Collection.*)

KOVSH. In jadeite, gold, and gold rouble enamelled red. Workmaster Kollin (E.K.). (*From Queen Alexandra's Collection.*)

BASKET. In purpurine; handle, border and ribbon bows in gold; 2 emeralds. Length: 3½ inches. Workmaster Kollin (E.K.). (*By courtesy of Messrs. Tessiers.*)

PLATE 103

CIGARETTE CASE
With tinder and place for matches, in gold. Style Louis XIV.
Measurements: $3\frac{15}{16}$ in. $\times$ $2\frac{3}{4}$ in. $\times$ $\frac{5}{8}$ in.
(*From H.R.H. Princess Marina's Collection.*)

PLATE 104

BOX. In translucent yellow enamel on gold mounted with red and green gold borders and garlands. Monogram of Nicholas II and crown in diamonds. Measurements: $3\frac{1}{4}$ in. square $\times$ 1 in. deep.
(*From H.M. Queen Elizabeth, the Queen Mother's Collection.*)

CIGARETTE CASE. With place for matches. In two coloured golds and opaque white enamel. Measurements: $3\frac{7}{8}$ in. $\times$ $2\frac{1}{2}$ in. $\times$ $\frac{5}{8}$ in.
(*By courtesy of Messrs. Wartski.*)

PLATE 105

CIGARETTE CASE. Gold, guilloché surface, bordered with opaque white and translucent blue-enamels. Double-headed eagle in diamonds, emerald eyes. Miniature of Tsar Nicholas II covered by a baquette diamond. Thumb-piece, rose-diamonds. Measurements: $3\frac{3}{8}$ in. $\times$ $2\frac{1}{4}$ in. $\times$ $\frac{1}{2}$ in.
(*By courtesy of Messrs. Tessiers.*)

CIGARETTE BOX. In nephrite, bordered in chased gold. Miniature of Tsar Alexander II, surrounded by diamonds, crown in rubies and diamonds. Measurements: $3\frac{11}{16}$ in. $\times$ $2\frac{5}{16}$ in. $\times$ $\frac{7}{8}$ in.
(*From Queen Mary's Collection.*)

PLATE 106

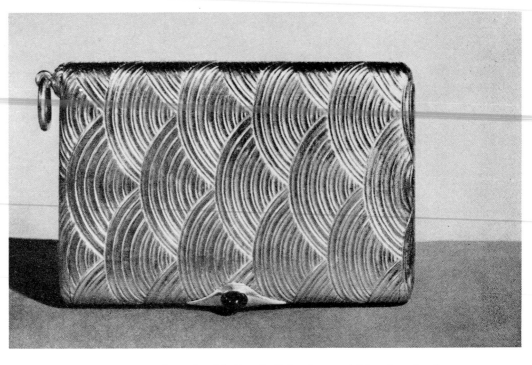

CIGARETTE CASE. In red gold, fluted. Cabochon sapphire thumb-piece.
(*By courtesy of Messrs. Berry-Hill.*)

CIGARETTE CASE. In three coloured golds in rough cast, set with rubies, sapphires, emeralds and diamonds.
(*By courtesy of Messrs. Berry-Hill.*)

PLATE 107

CIGARETTE CASE. In gold and opaque white enamel, bordered with green enamel and rose-diamond leaves. Basket of flowers in rose-diamonds. Diamond thumb-piece. Measurements: $3\frac{2}{10}$ in. $\times$ $1\frac{3}{4}$ in.
(*Collection of Mr. Michael Pugh.*)

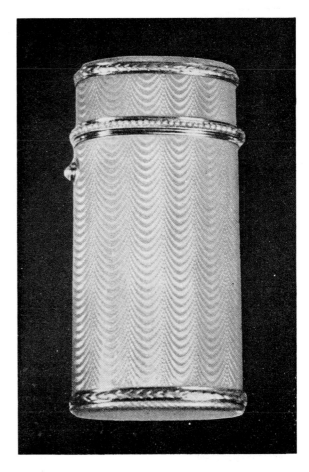

CIGARETTE CASE. In enamel, typically Fabergé, showing large surface enamelling on guilloché background of silver, mounted with chiselled gold leaf borders, and set with pearls.
(*By courtesy of A la Vieille Russie.*)

PLATE 108

CIGARETTE CASE. Gold, guilloché surface striped in opaque white enamel. Monogram
and thumb-piece in rose-diamonds.
(Collection of Mrs. H. T. De Vere Clifton.)

CIGARETTE CASE. Gold, striped in opaque dark blue enamel, bordered with opaque white
enamel. Monogram and thumb-piece in rose-diamonds. Note the fine sharp finish.
(Collection of Mrs. H. T. De Vere Clifton.)

after much toil, strikes oil and at a gush. Here in front of me was just what I wanted and in number enough to carry my point.

Throughout this record it has been my endeavour to put forward the fact that Fabergé, like all good craftsmen, was concerned in making objects to serve a useful purpose and in doing this he did not forget that this purpose was equally concerned in giving pleasure and 'procuring a good'.* The Imperial Easter Eggs are examples of objects possessing the two latter qualities. The Fabergé cigarette cases possess all three qualities. In some, the giving of pleasure and 'procuring a good' predominate and come under the heading of what may be called 'museum pieces'. Of these Queen Mary and other collectors have allowed me to reproduce outstanding examples.

But what I have wanted all along has been more examples of cigarette cases which give pleasure and 'procure a good' but at the same time serve a useful purpose. My point being, of course, that to say, as some do, that Fabergé was only concerned in the making of gew-gaws and knick-knacks is nonsense. And it is the King's cigarette cases which give me this long-desired opportunity. They include those which belonged to King Edward VII and King George V, as well as those given to and collected by King George VI. With the exception of four all of them are suitable for daily use, and His Majesty tells me he gives each one of them a turn. The four exceptions include the one in rhodonite, Plate 112; another in nephrite, Plate 120; a third in red enamel, Plate 121; and the fourth in opaque pink enamel, with a mat surface, Plate 122. Particulars of these four cases appear in the captions.

But the subject of cigarette cases was not the only one interesting the King. The right way to display Fabergé objects has long been a pet obsession of mine. I have said something about it on pages 64 and 65. To listen to His Majesty, bringing up this same matter and expressing himself strongly, was something to give much satisfaction. Nothing to be done to confuse the eye, but everything to bring out the full value of the form and colour of each single piece. That was the burden of his remarks, and it is something which should have been said long ago.

In Plates 37, 104 and 114, I have illustrated several objects from the Queen's Collection, and Her Majesty had many things to tell me about them, especially with reference to her Fabergé flowers, the delicacy of the finish of the ears of corn (Plate 37) and the simple beauty of her buttercups. But to a biographer of Fabergé, always on the *qui vive* to find out in what way collectors are affected by his objects, one remark of Her Majesty stood out alone.

Taking up one of the King's cigarette cases, the Queen caressed it for a moment and then said this: 'There is one thing about all Fabergé pieces, they are so satisfying'. What has taken me the whole of Chapter III to convey, Her Majesty here puts into a dozen words.

---

* 'Utility . . . includes not only the power to satisfy want, to give pleasure, to procure a good or ward off an evil, but to serve any purpose of man, society or the State . . . .' *Political Economy* by J. M. Gregory. Ch. 2—p. 33.

CHAPTER VI

THE FABERGÉ FIGURINES IN RUSSIAN STONES OF COLOUR

ONE of the main purposes, if not the main purpose itself, of this record of Fabergé is to make it clear that what gives his wares their attraction is something not French but Russian, a something which can best be expressed by the word 'substance'. It is precisely the same thing which Russian dancing possesses as compared with that of the West. Here is substance at every step, indeed 'guts' is a good word for it. There is nothing mean and miserly about it, nothing thin. Full of verve, it is pervaded with a well-rounded, fat, realistic vitality imparting the utmost satisfaction to the beholder. Who of us is not roused when we recall the lively rhythms of the mazurka, with its decisive stamp, and the utmost abandon with which it brings home to us a romping display of well-being. And this is not to forget that the mazurka is Polish. It is what Russia puts into it which counts.

In exactly the same way it is so with Fabergé wares. The style of ornamentation is purely accidental and has nothing whatever to do with the achievement; it can be French, Italian, or what have you; it is the performance which counts.

So far I have put forward this Russian idiom of Fabergé in varying ways, by words, by illustration, by persuasion. But all of these have called for corresponding effort on the part of the reader to rise to the occasion, to look through and through, to probe for something often hidden below the surface, and it is quite possible that my assertions may not have helped very much to that end. It is well, therefore, that Fabergé himself should come right out into the open and to the assistance of any wobblers, and as he comes out let it be as though he himself says: 'Away with words, I will show you.'

Thus we are directed to the Fabergé figurines in different stones of colour representing types of Russian national life. And in the illustrations which I give I am convinced that there will not be one dissenting voice. Everybody will say at once 'Now, these are *completely* Russian!' And I suggest that the only reason for this is that the appearance of these figures is one which has come to be commonly associated with Russia, one to which everyone has grown accustomed and cannot fail instantly to recognize.

But different appearances can have the same underlying reality. And this it is which so many who have so far assessed the work of Fabergé have failed to appreciate. His genius consisted in having given so many appearances to one and the same reality and that Russian. At the one end of his achievements are his productions in the French classic styles and at the other these figurines of national Russian types.

This, of course, is saying something which has already been said before, only in a different way, but it is so important that it is worth this repetition. And I would remind all readers that to reiterate is something which in itself is peculiarly

Russian. It is as though Russia has always known she was a little difficult and that no one can understand her at one hearing.

During Agathon Fabergé's stay with me in Hampstead in 1937 we talked about these figurines, and what follows is the result of many conversations with him.

The history of their origin is the same as that of many other works by Fabergé, namely, that the idea first took shape in the mind of one of his customers, in this case, the Grand Duke Nicholai Nicholaivitch. He asked for a caricature of Queen Victoria. Fabergé replied that he was sorry he could not do this, but Her Majesty being a little woman he could make her a little smaller, and perhaps a little stouter, and he could place a crown upon her head. This little figurine in jadeite I remember seeing years ago in a shop window in London, but I eventually lost sight of it and am wondering where it is to-day. Perhaps the present owner may recognise this description if it should come his or her way.

It then occurred to Fabergé that such figures might be made more attractive by building them up with different stones of colour, rather than cutting them from a single stone, and so came into being the Russian national types, the subject of this chapter. In doing this Fabergé carved and made permanent a phase of history in stone.

Figure No. 1 (Plate 109) is that of a carpenter (*plotnik*). Face and hands are in rhodonite; hair and beard in brown Siberian jasper; eyes in sapphires; shirt in purpurine; trousers in lapis lazuli; apron in white quartz; shoes in black Siberian jasper; axe in silver, marked 'ФАБЕРЖЕ, H.W.91,' mountings in gold.

Figure No. 2 (Plate 109): Peasant from the Ukraine (*hohol*). Face and hands in cacholong; eyes in sapphires; hair in coffee jasper; shirt in white quartz; overcoat in brown Caucasian obsidian; trousers in lapis lazuli; boots in black jasper; hat in black jasper and brown Caucasian obsidian; sash in purpurine; mountings in gold and enamel.

Figure No. 3 (Plate 109): Houseman (*dwornik*). Face in rhodonite; eyes in sapphires; jerkin in grey Caucasian obsidian; shirt in lapis lazuli; hair, hat and boots in black Siberian jasper; apron in white quartz; trousers in jasper from Kalgan; broom in gold. Hat engraved: 'DWORNIK. 24 MORSKAIA' in Russian characters; broom marked 'H.W. ФАБЕРЖЕ.'

Figure No. 4 (Plate 110): Peasant (*mujik*). Face in Siberian jasper; hair and beard in rhodonite; eyes in sapphires; overcoat bordered in Brown Caucasian obsidian; dress in rhodonite; hat in black jasper; belt in purpurine; glove in light brown Siberian jasper; stick in silver gilt, marked 'H.W.88'.

Figure No. 5 (Plate 110): Labourer (*zemlekop*). Blouse in purpurine; trousers in lapis lazuli; shoes in grey Caucasian obsidian; hat in black jasper; face and hand in cacholong; hair and beard in brown Caucasian obsidian; eyes in sapphires; shovel in silver gilt.

Figure No. 6 (Plate 110): Nobleman (*boyarin*). Coat in purpurine, the borders and collar in brown Caucasian obsidian, mountings in gold; hat in brown Caucasian obsidian and nephrite; shoes in nephrite; face in Siberian jasper; hands in cacholong; beard and hair in Siberian jasper; eyes in sapphires; staff in oxidized silver with gold top and ferrule.

Figures Nos. 7 and 8 (Plate 100): Cossack (*cherkéss*—native of Caucasia) built up of different Siberian stones as those already described.

Figure No. 9 (Plate 100): Driver of public vehicles (*izvoshchik*), built up of different Siberian stones as already described.

Figure No. 10 (Plate 100): Street pedlar (*raznoschik*) built up of different Siberian stones as those already described.

Figure No. 11 (Plate 101): Peasant (*mujik*). Jacket in grey jasper and purpurine; breeches in lapis lazuli; stockings in cacholong; shoes in rhodonite; face and hands in rhodonite; hair and moustache in coffee jasper; eyes in sapphires; balalaika in silver gilt, marked '88. H.W.,' engraved ' ФАБЕРЖЕ '. Seat in Siberian jasper.

Figure No. 12 (Plate 101): Cossack bodyguard of the Dowager Empress Marie Feodorovna. Both the last Empress Alexandra Feodorovna, and the Dowager Empress Marie on every occasion when out riding in their sleighs or motor cars were attended by a personal bodyguard, a Cossack. The Tsar Nicholas II commissioned Fabergé to make stone models of these guards. They were to be portraits from life, the two Cossacks attending at the Fabergé studios where they were modelled in wax. The figurine of the bodyguard of the last Empress I have not been able to trace.

The overcoat of the figurine of Dowager Empress's bodyguard is in green jasper, bordered with brown Caucasian obsidian and braided in gold with double-headed eagles in black enamel; hat and boots in black jasper and gold; belt in purpurine; face and hands in cacholong; hair, beard and moustache in grey jasper; eyes of sapphires; and medals in gold and different enamels. The soles of the boots are engraved 'Fabergé, 1912. N.N. Pustinikov, Kamer-Kazak since 1894'.

From this it appears that Pustinikov, at the time the figurine was made, had been in the service of the Dowager Empress for eighteen years.

Fabergé made other figures following the same technique—including a policeman (*gorodowoi*); a soldier of the Preobrashensky regiment (*soldat*); a coachman of the nobility (*barskikutcher*), which are in the possession of Sir William Seeds. Some three or four models of drivers of public vehicles (*izvoshchik*) were also made, of which the Edwardian Lady Sackville always took one about with her as a mascot. Lady Edward Reid has one as illustrated (Plate 100, figure 3). Agathon Fabergé told me of two figurines he possesses, a peasant and his wife, two of the finest made, he said, but from all accounts not more than thirty of these Russian types were made in all.

In addition to the figurines referred to there were a few models of English types: a Yeoman of the Guard, in the Sandringham collection; a policeman and may be, two others. Then a few taken from *Alice in Wonderland*, the Mad Hatter, Alice herself and others, perhaps half-a-dozen. Where are these last I wonder?

Taking all into consideration it appears likely that a total of not more than forty to fifty figurines were made. The scarcity of them, plus their unique craftsmanship, make them of much worth both artistically and monetarily, and rare pieces for a collector.

Because four of the figurines illustrated are marked H.W. on the metal accessories does not mean that Wigström put together the stone parts of the figurines. This was done by the lapidaries in Karl Woerffel's workshops where, in every probability, the parts were cut. I say 'in every probability' because both Kremleff and Derbysheff may have had a hand in this work.

In the same way many birds in stone have gold claws which are marked H.W. (as well as the initials of Fabergé in Russian characters), but Wigström did not cut the birds, he only made and fixed the claws. So with the figurines, it was Wigström's job only to make and fix the metal accessories.

CHAPTER VII

THE WORKMASTERS OF FABERGÉ

THE idea that 'team work' is the cure for all ills is very strongly held to-day, so strongly indeed, that where there is any work to be done the doing, we are told, should never be in the hands of one man, but many. In other words that there should be an element of sacrifice, of sharing, in everything that we do, that each one of us is a cog in a great wheel, that if we fail to do our 'bit' we are not adding our quota, etc.

Throughout the ages this has always been the battle-cry of dominating spirits and dominating societies placed in a dominant position. Their exhortation has been 'Collect yourselves together for this great good work and be quick about it. It's up to you!' To this gospel which they have preached there has always been one exception, under no circumstances must it apply to themselves. Nothing, of course, must interfere with their single course; their ambitions are for themselves, to be shared by no one.

Of course, much of what I have said is pure extravaganza, but I put it in this way to bring out the fact that in the glorious world in which we live it is *infinite difference* which is the keynote of the Divine Creator's scheme (F. W. Rolfe in *Hadrian VII*), and nowhere is there more convincing evidence of this than in the world of art and craftsmanship. Handel did not hunt around for a host to share with him the pain and joy of bringing into the world the Hallelujah Chorus; he sat down and did it himself.

And so with Fabergé. This keynote of infinite difference rose to a dominance in his House; it gripped your faculties and played upon your emotions. Whatever there was in you to rise to the occasion, rose, making everything you did a particular event, an opportunity for giving of the best within you. And this was made possible, *not* by team work. No man in the House of Fabergé was a cog in a wheel. There was something much more majestic about the path he trod, for he moved in an orbit of his own, unmolested, but kept to his course by a centre of attraction which was Fabergé himself.

This Craftsman had many qualities, but over and above all was his understanding of human nature. And no one knew better than he that where art and craftsmanship are concerned man cannot but be anything else but greedy, selfish and even cruel if he is to rise to any height in his trade; there can be no question of sharing or sacrifice if he is to use his faculties to the best advantage.

So it became the high principle in the House of Fabergé that the work on any one object should be carried through from start to finish in one workshop and, if possible, by one pair of hands. Of course this principle could not always be strictly adhered to. Some of the objects required to be enamelled and that was a very expert work calling for the enameller, others required the attentions of the lapidary, but in the end each object was returned to the craftsman mainly concerned, for finishing, and even with its dressings he could still say 'That is my child, I brought it into the world'.

I have iterated and reiterated the fact that the success of the House of Fabergé was due to many dominant factors all working to the same end, but there was something predominant. Fabergé knew how to handle men. I have also said that the master-craftsman always gave one the impression of actually doing nothing, or at any rate very little. He never fussed, never rang bells, never issued instructions to cover behaviour or action under certain circumstances, never called in anyone to take down a letter, because he had none to dictate and in short he never did anything which the average business man thinks essential, and simply, for one thing, because he was not a business man.

For another, and here is the plum. If you are to pull out *the* one thing, here it is. Fabergé knew how to generate 'atmosphere', the right atmosphere which never staled. Not only had it quality but quantity for it permeated the whole establishment, every nook and corner of the workshops, of the offices and studios and shop. No need for the workman to run to his workmaster for every little thing; no need for the artist to be always troubling the Craftsman, this magic atmosphere surrounded him all the time, the very breath of his nostrils. And if you happened to be engaged abroad, you bottled some and took it with you. It saved you many a cable and much writing for instructions. No wonder Carl Fabergé often gave one the impression that he was doing nothing at all, except to be quiet, for no man can give out as he did unless he continually replenishes his stock.

We are nearing the end of this record and I have something to say and here is the best place to say it. Throughout the story I have avoided anything in the manner or language of the æsthete; from time to time I may have fallen but generally I have done my best to keep faith with this determination. It would have been so easy to say 'Fabergé inspired everyone associated with him' and simply to leave it at that. But would anyone have been any the wiser? Would these words have left the fount of all the powers of Fabergé splashing in gay display for all eyes to see for the looking? Most assuredly not.

It is my business to present the Craftsman as I and all those working for him saw him in St. Petersburg and to account for the fairy tale which he succeeded in building up. I cannot do this by employing words which have come to have no value at all except to leave the mind of a reader floating aimlessly around in a celestial haze.*

And here I am in a difficulty. A writer and critic of renown tells me that it is not my business to account for anything at all, but simply to tell the story and leave it at that, 'to illustrate the mystery inherent in mortal things'. Doubtless there are mysteries, for which we cannot yet account, but that is no reason why we

* Mr. C. K. Ogden reviewing *Language in Society* by M. M. Lewis, reminds us that over three centuries ago Comenius observed that 'men commonly do not speak but babble; . . . and that not only the common folk do this but even the half-educated also, and what is more to be grieved at, the well-educated themselves for the most part'.

should not account for those for which there is a ready and reasonable explanation, especially if it is a quite practical, happy and mundane, one. At any rate by so doing we shall have all the less to contend with, and our agony will be so much the less prolonged.

And so my friend I have to say that there was no mystery whatever about Fabergé, but there was magic and this lay in his sense of the value of limitation.

If I have a quarrel with to-day it is this, that there is little if any sense of this value. Whatever comes under purview the whole must be discussed, if it is the body, then it involves the entrails, the liver and the kidneys. We possess these dreadful organs, so why not bring them in? The same with music; there is discord in the world, then why not bring it in, even to a lot of it and out of all proportion. The same with news, speed and of course love, not a little but a tremendous lot of it, even to embrace the whole world. 'Partake of all these to the full and the rest will be added unto you' is the idea. And it is the last mentioned which concerns this story.

Fabergé did not love the whole of mankind, because that was not physically possible for him, but he did love his neighbour even as himself. It was on one's lips many times to say to him 'Mr. Fabergé you really must not go as far as that, you will ruin your business'.* When I said just now that Fabergé generated atmosphere, I was not quite happy in the way I put it. Rather should I have said that he was always doing something which so captivated the hearts of those working for him that they reacted at once and gave tit for tat, with the result that not only were thousands of beautiful things scattered all the world over, but, and this is to be well remarked, every one of these things possessed the same characteristics, although each of them was largely the product of a separate pair of hands.

Now unless I was convinced that we were growing up, that at last we realize that it is quite possible to push things so far we may put too great a strain on the Fairy Queen, making her powerless to wave her wand any more, that it is unreasonable to explain away all the accidents, coincidences and fairy-tale happenings by reference to the supernatural, or something not controlled within the confines of the earth we tread, I should certainly feel that in saying what I have said that I had 'let down', dreadfully, a romantic story, one of the greatest of fairy-tales.

As it is, my conviction, supported by the many concrete examples of the behaviour of Fabergé, gives me daring enough to cite him as a superb example of the developed heart and 'the relaxed will'. This, the gospel of Mr. E. M. Forster, is doubtless known to the reader, and, it will be seen, has some meaning in reference to Fabergé from what I have already said about him in previous chapters.

When the Craftsman in 1900 removed his House to 24 Morskaya many things accrued, but of all the benefits which were to sustain the firm until the débâcle in 1918, those accruing from the arrangements for housing the workshops under the same roof as all the other activities were far and away the most outstanding.

* From time to time there were men who took advantage of his simplicity and kindly nature, and rather largely too, but such actions he regarded as matters of little consequence.

The nearness of the designers to the Head of the House had always been provided for in previous homes of the firm, if not to the full, at any rate to some extent. Now there was space, not merely for the artists working 'in the flat', but for the sculptors working 'in the round', for not only did each object require its sketch, and in colour, but the more important were modelled in wax or some plastic material before any work was begun upon it.

And talking of designers reminds me that from time to time I have seen articles labelled as 'Designed by Carl Fabergé', in sales catalogues and shop windows. This statement can be literally true of a large number of pieces, especially the more important which originated with Fabergé and were elaborated in the studios, but it is of course not true of every single object made in the Fabergé workshops. It would have been a physical impossibility for any one man to do this. François Birbaum, the chief designer, and those working with him, were responsible for very many, but it was a *sine qua non* that these should be submitted to the head of the House before further work was continued upon them and that the last elaborated sketch was further submitted for examination in every detail.

The manner of submission was always something to watch as it was also when it concerned the workmasters. It was purely Russian, and well worth a moment's notice now. For generations we have made a habit of misjudging the Russian, no name has been bad enough for him—the Beast, the Bear. 'Scratch a Russian . . .' we say, and so on. As a fact he is the most sensitive, courteous, and gentle of creatures. One thing above all we have never given him credit for is that he lives much nearer to nature than does the Anglo-Saxon. He is far and away more digni-fied, far and away simpler and nearer both to the niceties and the crudities of life, and therefore much more of a realist.

All this he puts plainly before us in his appellations. Carl Gustavovitch, Elizabeth Petrovna, he says. Carl the son of Gustav, Elizabeth the daughter of Peter. Could anything be more natural, more dignified, simpler and full of comradeship? It was his innate sense of comradeship, I am sure, which made the Russian such an easy prey to his present rulers.

There is something in all this far too subtle for the Englishman. One has only to think for a moment what would happen in England if a clerk went into his manager's office and instead of saying 'Oh, sir, may I have a day off to-morrow?' said 'Oh, Charles, the son of Edward, may I, etc., etc.?' to realise what a gulf separates the Anglo-Saxon and the Russian.

And so, as I have said, there was always something to watch when Birbaum went in to Fabergé with his designs. He did not take a step into the Holy of Holies, or the Lion's Den; there was nothing of 'sir' or 'chief' about his entrance and after-behaviour. His demeanour throughout was of the very essence of Carl-Gustavovitchism or Elizabeth-Petrovnaism, whichever is preferred, if I may manufacture a word to express the ease, the impersonality, the naturalness, the informality of these interviews, the doing of nothing to endanger benefit to the object chiefly concerned. And, of course, on the part of the Head of the House there was Carl-Gustavovitchism at its high water mark.

All this was true of all meetings between Fabergé and all the artists and work-

117

masters. I choose Birbaum for my example because after Carl Fabergé I put him at the top. Nobody had a bigger say in deciding the eventual shape and colouring of Fabergé objects than he. As I think of him I see a rather frail man of medium height with a moustache and neat Vandyke beard, a quiet gentle man of a fine humour, much after the pattern of Fabergé himself. The last I heard of him was that he was making cream cheeses in Switzerland.

And now for the workmasters. If the removal to 24 Morskaya did a lot for the designers and modellers it did much more for the workmasters.

This is the high spot in the Fabergé story. And in saying this I have a feeling that some readers may have lost interest in my high spots, that they are tired of the iteration and reiteration of my philosophies and ethical excursions and that they have borne with me so long only in the hope that at long last I would release myself from my obsessions, get down to business and launch out into something really substantial on the artistry of Fabergé, a dissertation in the accepted way in suitable language on line and form and colour and style and all the rest of it, as handed to me by the Craftsman himself.

If such readers there be, then with all respect to them I have to say they are doomed to disappointment. Dr. Johnson has told us that the right person to write of any man is the man himself. But if the man himself happens to be a Fabergé who in no circumstances whatever could be persuaded to put pen to paper, then if there is to be a biographer his story must be true to life. All of which means that I must represent Fabergé as he presented himself to me, however exasperating that may be. And Fabergé could be very exasperating.

In the chapter on the Art and Craft of Fabergé and to some extent in other chapters, I have given an account of what I conceive to be the attraction of the artistry of Fabergé and the purpose for which he worked. None of this I must say was handed to me by Fabergé specifically by word of mouth. Although we spent hours at a stretch together, there was never any discussion on art; he never picked up a piece of his own and expatiated upon it, he never talked of Russia and her influence upon him, in fact he never talked at all of anything which concerned his work. All was by gesture, but gesture with such meaning that there could be no mistake about what he wished to convey.

As an artist and craftsman, Fabergé was silent. It was only when you came to the humanitarian in him that he was articulate. Here were embers for ever burning, which only needed fanning by some silly remark or recapitulation of some mean or selfishly possessive behaviour to turn them not into a roaring blaze but into a flame intensely hot and sharp and often hissing like that from a Bunsen burner. It was then he took intense delight to perplex you with his irony and cut you to pieces with his sarcasm. At the same time tell him a story of some struggling man who had descended to some highly improper action to get a loaf of bread and he would veer as quick as lightning. 'But men must live', he would say.

Here is the high spot right enough. No need for me to offer any apology. I should only lie if I did. What has really worried me throughout this record is the complete inadequacy of my pen to bring home to the reader the full significance of Fabergé and all his works, and it comes up at the moment more forcibly than ever. I have before me as near as it is possible for any man to hope for, if not a perfect example, at any rate a most outstanding example of a sane way of living and working and one which not only resulted in a success never before achieved in the history of goldsmithery, but might very well be the standard for universal practice in all walks of life—I have all this, and yet all I can say by way of accounting for it is that the whole art and success of Fabergé sprang from and was cradled in his humanity.

This is true and the right way of saying it, but it has nothing about it likely to arrest for a moment any one who deplores those ways of life which are inhuman, and who does not? All this I am inclined to believe is the natural outcome of the injunctions of one's literary betters. To say anything in the right way, that is in the way which has been coined as the best way, is the wrong way. Once said, this best way of saying anything must never be repeated, it is a *cliché*, they say. Instead, the writer is encouraged to be constant in invention, he must say the same thing in a novel way and he has responded out of all proportion to the advice given to him.

So it has come about that the reader has been subjected to the second-rate in ever increasing variety and quantity and so much so that his appetite for the sensational, the clever and intriguing has been whetted, tempting him to call for more and more, with the consequence that he has lost sight altogether of the fundamentally true, and no longer takes any interest in it.

Perhaps this is a little strong, and I must not be over-serious. At any rate one feels that something might be done by roasting the old 'chestnuts' more often, to bring out their flavour, and that writers might with advantage try this for a time instead of applying themselves so constantly and ardently to the invention of new expressions for the same thing.

Be this as it may, I have this to say. It is not the wickedness, not the cruelty, not the selfishness of human nature, however terrifying these are, which strike one most as its distinguishing mark, but its stupidity.

And this brings me back at once to Carl Fabergé. As sharp as a needle, there was nothing stupid about him. Instead of placing difficulties in the way of his fellow men he made everything as easy as possible and benefited accordingly. That is the whole gospel of Fabergé. Take one facet of him. None of us exactly delights in legal documents, but there can hardly be one of us who has not made use of them sometime or another to protect what we call our 'legal rights', to make it as difficult as possible for our neighbour to take away anything from us. And that is only one example of the hundred and one ways in which each one of us makes a contribution to our much vaunted civilization. To Fabergé the whole business was anathema, and woebetide you if you suggested entering into a legal agreement with him.

At one time it was my business to represent him in an action at law and when he visited London in 1908 I asked him for a Power of Attorney. 'We've been together now for some time and got on very well without one. Why won't the judge believe what you say, just as I do?' was the way he received the request. When after much discussion he agreed and the lawyers sent along a document of a few lines empowering me to do what I liked, even to selling up his business, he signed it without reading it. When I remonstrated with him he replied: 'If you are a dishonest man this document will not make of you an honest one'.

That was Carl Fabergé to a T, and if in these pages I appear as a pedagogue and pedant for ever spoon-feeding my readers with doses of wisdom on matters which have come to be only of trifling present concern, then they must forgive me, for I have no other way out if the Craftsman and his ways are to be made a reality to them.

And so we can return to the workmasters, knowing very largely where we are and how we stand. We will expect little, if anything, from heaven, but much from earth; nothing startling, nothing mysterious, but above all, nothing stupid.

There is no doubt that Fabergé could have carried on his business without the designers; it would have been much less extensive of course, and he would have missed his destiny, but still he could have done something. Without the workmasters and workmen he could have done nothing. What he conceived they carried into effect. If therefore they were to give of their best not only was it necessary that they should be near to him so that their work might be examined at every stage of its production, but it was vital that they should be properly and comfortably housed and not only care but intense care given to their welfare.

And so at 24 Morskaya we not only find the workmasters and workmen properly housed, but everything done to keep their minds free to accomplish their work with ease, without worry of any kind. The workshops were free to the workmasters; all the precious metals of silver, gold and platinum, all the precious stones, diamonds, emeralds, rubies and all the rest, all the designs and models to work from, were supplied to them. The only thing the workmaster was responsible for was the workmanship. He engaged the workmen and paid their wages.

When one remembers that commissions came to Fabergé not only from Russia but from all over the world, in ever constant flow, and that objects were always in the making for stock, it needs no further words of mine to impress the fact that the workmasters and workmen of Fabergé were always in clover, and four-leaved clover at that, for every object in the making was an assurance that as soon as it was finished there would be another to take its place.

As I write there flashes across my mind a democracy, practising all the freedoms we dream of, at work within the greatest autocracy the world has ever known. Something to think about.

Some long way back in this record I stressed the point that if we would know Fabergé we must know Russia first, and what I have to say now is that in the fathering of those working for him Fabergé was practising something very Russian indeed. Instead of 'fathering', a better word is 'mothering'. Countries no doubt have gender and that of Russia is essentially feminine, but a femininity not effeminate but very virile in quality.

It is this strong femininity of hers which accounts for Russia's peculiar fertility. Give her the start, the seed, for she has always been a borrower, and she mothers it in her own peculiar way to quite astonishing results. It is this same femininity which accounts for her sensitiveness, richness, voluptuousness,

PLATE 109

Fig. 1
CARPENTER (*plotnik*).
Height: 4¾ inches.

Fig. 2
PEASANT from the Ukraine (*hohol*).
Height: 5 inches.
(*Collection of Sir William Seeds, K.C.M.G.*)

Fig. 3
HOUSEMAN (*dwornik*).
Height: 5 inches.

PLATE 110

Fig. 1
PEASANT (*mujik*).
Height: 6½ inches.

Fig. 2
LABOURER (*zemlekop*).
Height: 4½ inches.
(*Collection of Sir William Seeds, K.C.M.G.*)

Fig. 3
NOBLEMAN (*boyarin*).
Height: 5¾ inches.

PLATE 111

CIGARETTE CASE
In red and yellow gold, ribbed. Cabochon sapphire thumb-piece. Measurements: $3\frac{5}{16}$ in. $\times$ $2\frac{3}{4}$ in.
(*Collection of Mr. Michael Pugh.*)

PLATE 112

(*Top*) CIGARETTE CASE. With place for matches and tinder, in red and yellow gold, sunray design. Thumb-piece, cabochon ruby. Measurements: $3\frac{3}{4}$ in. $\times$ $2\frac{7}{16}$ in. $\times$ $\frac{9}{16}$ in.
(*Below*) CIGARETTE CASE. In rhodonite (often called orletz), mounted in rose-diamonds, hinges in gold. Measurements: $3\frac{5}{16}$ in. $\times$ 2 in. $\times$ $\frac{9}{16}$ in.
(*From King George VI's Collection.*)

capriciousness and imagination. Certainly no other country has such a store of folk-lore, folkiness and fairy stories, not thin and emaciated, but round and fat and full of life.

Look through the history of Russia and you will find women very much to the fore and feminine rule no exception in all walks of life. The degree of liberty in women was such that the presence of an Empress on the throne instead of an Emperor was considered perfectly natural. It was this same degree of liberty which gave women the control of their own fortunes, and made them quite independent of their husbands in such matters.

In view of all this there is nothing astonishing in the fact that Russia has produced a type of womanhood peculiarly her own. Motherly, simple and full of practical wisdom, the very antipodes of prudish, and above all not stupid, and these qualities not the monopoly of any one class, but common to all. If Englishmen and women have kept their eyes open they will have seen all these qualities expressed to a remarkable degree in the examples of Russian women of high degree who have found a domicile in England since the Revolution. They do not scream.

It may appear strange to say, but it is in the time of the serfs in the Eighteenth Century that one finds the virile femininity of Russia showing up in most convincing manner. And I cannot do better than cite the case of Agathoclea Alexandrovna Poltaratsky who lived in the middle of that century. Mr. Alexander Polovtsoff gives an account of this extraordinary woman in his book *Russian Exhibition Gossip* when drawing attention to her portrait by Levitsky.

The daughter of a humble squire called Shishkov, she married at the age of fifteen and by her husband Poltaratsky brought into the world twenty-two children.

At an early age having decided to become rich, and having succeeded in bringing together a pretty considerable fortune, 'She lived', says Polovtsoff,

'in her country seat, Grusino, near Torjok, in a beautiful house built by Rastrelli with all the additions: theatre, riding school, etc., which were the usual complements of the sumptuous life led in those days. . . . An insignificant husband and twenty-two children were a sufficient incentive for developing her constructive powers; these in their turn followed a path marked out by ancient traditions and untrammelled by personal culture. The independence of Russian women in money matters at a time when money matters were scored in serfs, the peasants being attached to the land and the land being of no value if desert, turned business women into administrators, *for their affairs were only prosperous when the peasants on their land were rich and healthy; this made them attend to the welfare of the people they owned. The common saying of the peasants was "We belong to you but the land belongs to us".'*

The italics are mine. Madame Poltaratsky's existence was a caricature, she exaggerated her type, of which there are many examples in Russian history, that of a shrewd and energetic old lady firmly resolved to build her nest according to her instincts, and she was not stupid. She recognized the fact that if she were to be prosperous, those surrounding her and dependent upon her must be prosperous too.

But this idea of 'mothering' sprang from other causes as well as the acquisitiveness of the owner of the land. Russia was then split up into vast estates far removed from one another, each one self-contained and existing by developing its own resources.* Each man was dependent on his brother and the owner of the land father or mother to them all. But however far from one another during the warm periods of the year, in the winter, and this was long, they were entirely cut off, with the snow as their constant companion and there is no other fertiliser like this for warming the hearts of men just as much as the earth they tread. It was at this time more than ever that the Great House of the estate came into its own as universal provider and protector. A peasant lost a cow, then up to the House for a new one; a child was ill, then it was the House again which came to the rescue and provided the doctoring.

Above all, that reptile 'centralization', cold-blooded, sly and venomous, had not yet raised its head to devour the sanctity, the individuality and the morality of men. It may well be that in some future century a tribunal will sit which will condemn to death 'by hanging' all those who have been responsible for centralization of control as having committed the greatest of all 'crimes against humanity'.

It is in this way that I account for Russia's great capability. But it matters little how I account for it; the 'mothering' is there and has been ever since she pressed Rurik to her bosom 1,085 years ago. It is inherent in her and such a sensitive soul as Carl Fabergé could not fail to be influenced by this vitality of hers, and to no less a degree than his artistic gifts were developed by living and working within her bounds.

It remains now to enumerate the workmasters and give those particulars about them which are available. I am indebted to Eugène and Agathon Fabergé for this information, and the pity is that we did not list them forty years ago when the facts were to be obtained in so much more detail. However, we have the satisfaction at least of saving some of the names from oblivion.

It will be noted that against each workmaster's name only a few particulars are given of the special characteristics of his work. The reason by now I hope will be obvious; throughout the work of the House of Fabergé, there is only one characteristic to note, namely that it is 'Fabergé' and what that means I hope I have made clear in Chapter III. This does not mean of course that each workmaster succeeded to the same degree in carrying into effect the 'Fabergé' idiom. Again, some were engaged upon work which was more important and intricate than others; for instance, to produce an Imperial Easter Egg was a much more complicated matter than to make a pencil case. Therefore against the names of workmasters who were first rate in every respect I have put a star. I have listed

* In his book, *Russian Art*, Mr. Cyril Bunt has very happily envisaged for us the rural life and activities of old Russia, with an interesting account of peasant arts and crafts—house building, making of sledges, implements, furniture, kitchen utensils, salt boxes, looms, gingerbread moulds, toys of wood and dolls of straw, moss and pine cones, candlesticks and picture frames, musical instruments and clothes.

the whole of them under two headings: Objects of Fantasy, that is impersonal objects for the vitrine, writing table, etc., and Objects of Jewellery, that is personal objects for the adornment of the body.

OBJECTS OF FANTASY

*EDWARD KOLLIN, a Swedish Finn[1] was a native of Ekenäs, born in 1836. He died in 1901. Except for August Holmström, chief jewellery workmaster, he worked exclusively for the firm of Fabergé longer than any of the other workmasters. He learnt his trade first in Ekenäs and then in St. Petersburg where he opened his own workshop. When he started working exclusively for Fabergé I cannot say, but it must have been before 1870 when Carl Fabergé took over the control of the firm. It was Kollin who made the reproductions of the ancient Greek gold ornaments (400 B.C.) found in the Crimea, the originals of which were housed in the Hermitage Museum in the Winter Palace, St. Petersburg (Leningrad), and no doubt are still there. After the International Exhibition in Nürnberg in 1885, where these reproductions were exhibited with great success, they created quite a vogue; to-day they are never seen and one wonders where they have all gone.

Essentially a goldsmith, Kollin's work is of the highest order. He limited himself largely to working in gold alone, and rarely are his pieces enamelled; where he did not employ gold alone he seems to have been attracted to ornamenting objects made in nephrite, rock-crystal, etc., with finely worked gold pedestals and borders. As less of his work is seen to-day than that of any of the workmasters of Fabergé I illustrate some of his pieces in Plate 102. His mark is E.K.

*MICHAEL EVANPIEVICH PERCHIN, a Russian, born in 1860, a native of Petrozavodsk. Of all the workmasters of Fabergé perhaps the most remarkable. He started life as a peasant and by applying himself assiduously to the art and craft of goldsmithery in various unknown workshops, he learned enough to open his own workshop in 1886 when he worked exclusively for Fabergé. He continued in this service for seventeen years up to the year of his death in 1903. If the year 1883 is correct as being the year when Carl Fabergé first approached the Emperor Alexander III about the Imperial Easter Eggs, it follows that Perchin did not make the very early ones. As there is some doubt about this year, and as Perchin did not begin working for Fabergé until 1886 it is far more likely that the first egg was not made until 1886. It is almost certain that all the Imperial Eggs from 1886 up to the time of his death in 1903 were made in Perchin's workshop, unless some came from the workshop of August Holmström.

[1] It is interesting to note that some 75 per cent of Fabergé's workmen were either Finns or Swedish Finns.

The fact that in seventeen years some twenty-six Imperial Easter Eggs were made under the supervision of this workmaster is enough to establish his fame, but this was not a tithe of his output. Cigarette cases, writing sets, bibelots of all kinds for the table, and to carry about, poured from his workshop. One has only to examine the Fabergé collections of to-day, and note the number of the pieces on which his mark appears, to be assured not only of the enormous output of Perchin but of the rich quality of his work. There is nothing 'quasi' about any of it. Every piece is the real thing.

There was nothing 'gigantic' about Perchin, he made no altars of gold or silver. His claim to a high place in the annals of goldsmithery rests on his ability to turn out innumerable small objects, perfectly executed, capable of impregnating the imagination of hundreds of people the world over who delighted in seeing, handling, and enjoying nice things.

Perchin's mark is M.Π.

*HENRIK WIGSTRÖM, a Swedish Finn, was a native of Ekenäs, born in 1862. When Perchin started his workshop in 1886 he employed Wigström as his assistant and chief workman. In 1903 on the death of Perchin, Wigström took over the workshop and continued working for Fabergé until the dissolution of the firm in 1918. He maintained the high standard of his predecessor in every thing which continued to come from the workshop—in the Imperial Easter Eggs, flowers, cigarette cases and bibelots of all kinds. Indeed to-day his name, among collectors and art dealers, is as much a household one as that of Fabergé himself. His mark is H.W.

Perchin was before my time, but Wigström I saw every year on my visits to St. Petersburg. A big, fat, jolly man, I have a particular reason for never forgetting him, for it was he who first introduced me to the Imperial Easter Eggs; in fact but for him it is more than likely that I should never have heard of them until years after the firm of Fabergé had come to an end. Coming through the offices one morning he was carrying something the like of which I had never seen before; when I enquired what it was I heard the story of the Imperial Eggs for the first time.

This brings out a striking fact about the House of Fabergé, namely its ability for not allowing its left hand to know what its right was doing. There was I, admitted to every intimacy by the Head of the House and his family, with *carte blanche* to roam where I liked and do what I liked on the business premises, ask questions of anybody, and open any drawers that took my fancy, and yet but for this chance happening I should have remained ignorant of the finest objects the House was all the time producing.

It shows for one thing the degree to which the House respected the confidence of its customers, and no firm can ever have possessed more secrets; for another, nothing brings out more clearly the multiplicity of its undertakings.

*AUGUST HOLLMING, a Finn from Tavasthus, was a specialist in work in gold. He made many cigarette-cases, and objects of fantasy in gold and Siberian stones such as nephrite, and in enamel, but not Imperial Easter Eggs or flowers. He made jewellery too, such as brooches in enamel with precious stones. (See also as for Thielemann.) His mark is A*H. The star should be noted as this differentiates him from Holmström the chief jeweller. After Hollming's death his son Väinö took over control of the workshop, assisted by Hanhinen, a Finn.

I cannot pass over these three craftsmen, Perchin, Wigström and Hollming without cigarette cases coming to mind, for between them they were responsible for the greater number of those made in the Petersburg workshops. If I have said something about them before, they merit another mention. Of all the productions of Fabergé, even counting the Imperial Easter Eggs, flowers, animals and all the other objects of fantasy, and if the lapse of time is finally to give Fabergé a place which can never be assailed, the same which the comparatively few who know him give to him now and that on a par with the makers of the Eighteenth Century French snuff boxes (and do not let us forget the English), I say of all the productions of Fabergé, it is, in my opinion, his cigarette cases which should finally bring about this happy consummation.

Not only should the extraordinary large number of them contribute towards this but the main reason is that in them is the whole, not a portion, of the art of Fabergé. In the range of them every material made use of by Fabergé is employed; platinum, gold, silver, enamel, stone, wood (those in Karelian birch and other woods attract many people on account of their light weight and the simplicity of ornamentation in gold), precious stones, and they give an opportunity not only to the goldsmith but the lapidary and stone setter to display their separate crafts. They serve a useful purpose, and as constant companions endear themselves to the possessor, they are pleasing to look at and pleasant to feel, and above all have in them that quality I have called 'substance' which creates that sense of well-being which I believe to be the main reason for the attraction of all Fabergé objects.

To give a really representative display of these cigarette cases would call for a volume solely devoted to them because each one is different. Ironically enough, of all Fabergé objects a reasonably representative number of them has been most difficult to find and although those I illustrate are fine specimens they are by no means sufficiently representative of the whole. (See Plates 103-108, 113-115.) In Plates 112 and 120-125 are shown some cigarette cases in the collection of H.M. King George VI, to which reference is made in Chapter V, pages 108-109.

*VICTOR AARNE, a Finn, whose mark is B.A., was a specialist in very fine goldsmith's work with enamel.

*HJALMAR AV ARMFELT, a Swedish Finn. He succeeded Aarne. His mark is Я.A.

*JOSEPH RAPPOPORT was a native of Germany, born in 1854. He studied in Berlin at Scheffs. In 1883 he went to St. Petersburg and started his own workshop, working for Fabergé up to the dissolution of the firm in 1918. He was a maker of large important silver pieces, such as *surtouts de table*, bowls and large animals and birds. From time to time his silver birds are offered for sale in London. His mark is I.P.

S. WÄKÄWÄ, a Finn. He was a maker of table silver and large silver objects. His mark is S.W.

AFANASSIEFF, a Russian, was a maker of smaller enamelled objects of fantasy. His mark is Ф.А.

NAVALAINEN, a Finn, was a maker of the smaller silver and gold objects. His mark is A.N.

NUIKKANEN, a Finn, was a maker of cigarette cases and the smaller silver and gold objects. His mark is uncertain.

RUTSCH, a German from Heidelberg, was a chain maker. His mark is uncertain.

*EPIFANOFF, a Russian, was an engraver on metals. He had no mark.

*ZAHUDALIN, a Russian, was also an engraver on metals. No mark.

G. PESTOU, a German of French extraction, also an engraver, more especially on stones. No mark.

*KREMLEFF, a young Russian, executed the finest and most delicate work in different stones; animals, flowers and other objects, but especially flowers, the very delicate stalks of which he was capable of executing in stone. A superb craftsman. Working in stone, he had no mark.

*DERBYSHEFF, a Russian, was also a fine lapidary, engaged on much the same class of work as Kremleff. He too had no mark.

*KARL WOERFFEL, a German from St. Petersburg, controlled the large workshops for the execution of the majority of the animals in stone. As well as these a large number of objects, both very large and small, were made in Siberian stones, nephrite, rhodonite, etc., such as bowls, vases, etc., many of which were left unadorned with any work in gold or silver. Of the number of workmen employed in these workshops there is no information available though it must have been large, but of the quality of the work there is no doubt whatever and that can be seen in every animal illustrated and the other stone objects reproduced. On the death of Woerffel, Alexander Meier took control, neither of these workmasters had a mark.

*ALEXANDER PETROFF, a Russian, was the chief enameller for all Fabergé objects. A great craftsman. After his death he was succeeded by his son Nicholas. The Petroffs' work being in enamel, they had no mark.

*W. BOITZOFF, a Russian, and also an enameller for all Fabergé objects. He had no mark.

But I cannot dismiss these two workshops with these perfunctory lines. Everything concerning Fabergé in the last resort comes back very largely to them, for every piece that was enamelled in the Head Establishment in St. Petersburg

---

¹ The workshops for the execution of the very large objects such as bowls, vases, etc., were situated in Karavannya Street.

was enamelled by the Petroffs or Boitzoff, and that means something which certainly I for one did not appreciate when I watched these men at their furnaces. Petroff the elder and Boitzoff I cannot call to mind, but Petroff the younger I remember as of a somewhat rough character and completely impersonal, fully absorbed by his work.

Fabergé was happy in having craftsmen who could keep pace with his fast moving inventiveness, originality and fantasy, and if he were alive to-day he would be the first to sing a pæan in praise of his enamellers. As I have said before in Chapter III, it was the work of Fabergé to make flatness come alive and that he accomplished this by large flat surfaces of brilliant translucent enamels on guilloché backgrounds of gold or silver, sometimes described as the *en plein* method.

In taking into account what the Petroffs and Boitzoff did for Fabergé we must remind ourselves again that the goldsmith and silversmith works in great measure in miniature and that in the last resort his work must be judged in all respects by delicacy of finish.* And there must be severity of judgment and no sentiment or particular feeling for this century or that just because the work we happen to be judging was the product of any particular period. We must have the honesty to realise that every art and craft has its Chamber of Horrors and into it we must be prepared to put any object which in execution falls short of the most recently established standard. In other words we must not worship idols.

In the craft of the goldsmith and silversmith the standard is simple enough. Perfection. And one of the main features of this perfection is the perfect fitting of parts. In a box you can have all the glory of gold and enamel but if the lid does not fit then you must away with it. It is the straight and narrow way and the only way.

Now, however one may glorify *cloisonné*, *champlevé* and painted enamelled objects, as produced in Russia, and to whatever century one looks, delicacy of execution is lacking and the fitting of parts in particular. Well adapted, no doubt, to massive pieces for ecclesiastical service, such as caskets, nimbi, pectoral crosses, pastoral staffs, and the like, these techniques were much in evidence in objects made for the worship of the Almighty. But it must be remembered that they were displayed for the most part in dark and sombre places where delicacy of finish had no part to play and before masses of people for whom this same perfection was of no consequence whatever.

In the case of the execution of objects in which large surfaces of translucent enamels are the main feature, you have to come right out into the open and in more ways than one. The work has to pass the very close examination of cultured men and women who delight in the fit and finish of the things they enjoy. In the

* This deserves a footnote. Collectors are not given to the use of the magnifying glass, they rely on a general impression. The satisfaction they enjoy is, of course, due to the cumulative effect of the minute attention to detail which Fabergé gave to all his objects as they were built up. Collectors should examine this detail under the magnifying glass—the sharpness of the chiselling of gold borders; the finish of the thin opaque white enamel borders about which there is nothing ragged or uneven and finished generally flat, not bombé; and the delicacy of applied ornaments and monograms to cigarette cases, etc., set with precious stones. There is no excess or heaviness of metal setting to give an impression of precious stones where there are no precious stones.

execution of such objects defects in enamelling are glaringly apparent which in the case of the *cloisonné* and *champlevé* techniques so easily elude scrutiny. The whole surface of the enamel must be a particularly clean job free from any unevenness and blemish of any kind, and you must have all this and at the same time produce an object which in all its fittings is as nearly perfect as possible.

Now any one with any knowledge of large surface enamelling is well aware that all these perfections are impossible of attainment without the most painstaking care on the part of the enameller. All sorts of difficulties beset him and not the least, the buckling in the furnace of the precious metal base. And more. Every piece to be enamelled is an experiment, with perhaps many trials before anything like perfection is obtained. There is no royal road.

Combating all the difficulties, and turning out thousands of pieces as nearly perfect as humanly possible, it can be said without the slightest exaggeration that the Petroffs and Boitzoff did a stupendous job. There is no wonder I found the younger Petroff a little irritable at times.

For all that I have said about the *cloisonné* and *champlevé* and painted enamel techniques there is one use of them by which the goldsmith and silversmith is enabled to turn out gems, i.e., when he keeps strictly to the niceties of his trade and works in miniature. I give an example of Fabergé's work in this direction in the ikon which forms the centre of a panagia shown in Plate 116. This ikon measures $1\frac{3}{4}$ inches by $1\frac{1}{2}$ inches, and is in opaque blue, purple, white, black and green enamels against a golden background. It is a reproduction after one of the nine medallions which formed part of a set which once decorated the ikon (now destroyed) of the Archangel Gabriel in the Monastery of Djumati in Georgia (see the famous work by N. Kondakov on the Collection of A. Swenigorodski, published in Frankfurt in 1892).

This brings to mind one important fact about Fabergé, whenever he made a reproduction (and from time to time he made these at the request of his customers who possessed original pieces and who wished to give away a reproduction) of any work of a period previous to his own he always stamped these with the mark of his firm and/or that of one of his workmasters. In the case of the panagia it is stamped H.W., the mark of Wigström, and the chain К.Ф. The enamelling is by one of the Petersburg enamellers, Petroff or Boitzoff.

In concluding these few remarks on large surface enamelling it is only right that I should draw attention to the fact that while so much has been written about the *cloisonné, champlevé*, and painted enamel techniques as being characteristically Russian, very little, *if anything at all*, has been said about that of the *en plein*. It would appear that this method has played no part whatever in the development of Russian art and craft and to give this impression is not only to be neglectful of the truth but to treat with contempt the great contribution to the art and craft of enamelling on gold and silver which the enamellers of Russia (and the enamellers of Fabergé were not the only ones engaged in this work) made in the Nineteenth and the beginning of the Twentieth Centuries. Of course, it is all on a par with the idea that all things characteristically Russian came to a dead, but glorious, end in Moscow in the early Eighteenth Century.

I have listed the names of the Petroffs and Boitzoff under the classification 'Objects of Fantasy' because the major part of their work was concerned with these objects, but of course it was their task also to enamel all the objects of jewellery which required to be enamelled.

OBJECTS OF JEWELLERY

*AUGUST HOLMSTRÖM, a Swedish Finn, was born in Helsingfors in 1829. He received his training in St. Petersburg where in 1857 he bought a workshop belonging to Hammerstrem, since which time he worked exclusively for Fabergé, becoming chief jewellery workmaster of the firm.

In describing the work of Fabergé and those associated with him I have had, of necessity, to confine myself so much to the superlative I feel almost afraid to proceed further in this vein, but I cannot place Holmström except on the very top rung of the Fabergé ladder. No jeweller in Europe could beat him, but he was much more than a setter of precious stones.

It is right to say of a jeweller, in general terms, that he 'rides home' in the last resort on the back of the precious stones he sets and that the goldsmith rides home on his ingenuity, but so many jewellers are equally goldsmiths. At least this was true of nearly all the workmasters and very many of the workmen of Fabergé, and remarkably so of Holmström. Not only did he succeed in turning out objects of jewellery for personal adornment and jewelled objects in the way of Imperial Easter Eggs and their 'surprises', and of the finest quality,[1] but he was equally successful in goldsmithery, pure and simple. For example it was he who made the tiny gold model of the cruiser 'Pamiat Azova', exact in every detail of guns, chains, anchor and rigging, in which Nicholas II, when heir to the throne, made his voyage round the world. This model is the 'surprise' in the Imperial Easter Egg, made in jasper and ornamented with chased gold and diamonds in Louis XV style, which the Emperor presented to his mother, the Dowager Empress Marie Feodorovna.

August Holmström died in 1903 and his workshop then came under the control of his son, Albert Holmström, who continued in the fine tradition of his father. Their mark is A.H. I never saw Holmström the elder, but the younger I remember very well, having the appearance of a man about town, particular about his clothes.

A. THIELEMANN, a German, born in St. Petersburg, was the second jeweller of Fabergé. After his death Nikolaef his assistant took over the control of his workshop. Thielemann's mark is A.T. He was a maker of many of the

[1] Look at Queen Mary's egg, Plates 51 and 55, and the double-headed eagle, the 'surprise' in the 1912 egg given to the Empress Alexandra Feodorovna and now part of the Lillian Thomas Pratt Collection of the Virginia Museum of Fine Arts, Plate 49.

small brooches and pendants (one calls to mind those with surfaces of enamel, round and oval up to the size of a penny, on a guilloché background of gold or silver and with one precious stone, not in the centre but approaching the edge, as though it had just dropped there by accident, simple enough and to be bought forty years ago for £7 to £20, but most convincing), cuff links, and those small eggs to hang on chains, in enamel, different Siberian stones, and precious stones and which travellers to Russia brought home as presents. One wonders to-day where all these have gone, so rarely are they seen, especially brooches and pendants in 'Mecca-stones' (chalcedony) with a simple surround of diamonds. Ladies might very well search their jewel boxes; I am sure many would then come to light.

But one thing Thielemann had no hand in, in a general way, and that was the making of objects of fantasy. It is well to note this and for this reason. Hahn, a contemporary jeweller and goldsmith in St. Petersburg, employed a workman called A. Tillander and he made objects of fantasy and marked them A.T. If an object of fantasy should turn up to-day marked A.T. and it falls to someone to assess it who is unacquainted with the workmanship of Fabergé, unless the mark is supported by the mark of Fabergé[1] it should not be accepted as a Fabergé object.

T. RINGE, a German from St. Petersburg, was a maker of jewellery much after that described under Thielemann. He also made some silver fantasy objects and cigarette cases. His mark is T.R. After his death he was succeeded by V. SOLOVIEFF, a Russian, mark B.C., and MICHELSON, a Swedish Finn.

W. REIMER, a native of the Baltic, was, like Ringe, a maker of jewellery and also of gold fantasy objects. His mark is W.R. He was succeeded by Goorianoff, a Russian.

E. SCHRAMM, a German from St. Petersburg, was a jeweller for small objects. Mark uncertain, possibly E.S.

*KÄKI and his successor KÄMÄRÄ, both Finns, were makers of the holly-wood boxes for both jewellery and fantasy objects. In early days birch wood, polished, was used in many cases.

SAIKKONEN, a Finn, and his successor MARIPOU, an Estonian, made the oak boxes for silver articles, such as bowls, animals, etc.

All these men merit remembrance here, especially the makers of the white holly-wood boxes. So far as my knowledge goes, Fabergé was the only jeweller and goldsmith who ever used such a simple material for boxing such valuable objects, and in their mint condition of ivory white, close fitting lid, hinges and clasps always in the right proportion, these boxes were most striking. They in themselves 'hall-mark' every object they contain, and can be quite a help, to those who are not fully acquainted with Fabergé objects, in identifying them. Note that the box is pleasingly proportionate to the object it contains and that this

[1] See Chapter VIII which deals with the marks used by Fabergé.

130

latter fits closely into the white or cream coloured velvet at bottom, and if this is soiled where it touches the edges of the object, so much the better, it is as good a proof as you can have that the box is the original one made to fit the particular object. I give two illustrations of the markings on the satin on the inside of the lid of two of the boxes (Plate 117). Below the double-headed eagle in one is St. Petersburg and Moscow in Russian characters; in the other is St. Petersburg, Moscow, then London, also in Russian characters. In some cases Odessa takes the place of London; in some both are there. In a general way, whether St. Petersburg or Moscow comes first indicates where the object was made, but this is not always so. Sometimes the double-headed eagle and the letters are in gilt, sometimes black. The Imperial Easter Eggs were contained in egg-shaped boxes covered with velvet, the colours varying.

Such were the men controlling the workshops they owned in the Head Establishment of Fabergé in St. Petersburg. The system under which they worked was peculiar to it. It was designed to give the maximum of personal interest and incentive to enterprise to every one employed, and to the employer it brought great satisfaction in that the objects he conceived were materialised by a craftsmanship rarely if ever exceeded. The total results make it difficult to imagine a more convincing proof that private enterprise and ownership, if it is not the cure for all ills, is the spur which drives men on to great achievement.

We now come to the workshops of the House in Moscow. The system of working here was different, the workshops being owned and staffed by the firm and controlled by managers. They possessed no mark of their own, but used in common those of the firm, the name in full, K. FABERGÉ, superimposed by a double-headed eagle. There were three departments, one for silver articles, one for jewellery, and one for objects of fantasy.

The silver department was the largest, making silver and cutlery for the table, *surtouts de table*, *jardinières*, bowls, tea sets, large animals and birds, and ornaments of all kinds.

*MICHEL TCHEPOURNOFF, a Russian, was the manager of this silver department and a craftsman of the first order.

The jewellery workshops were under the management of *OSCAR PIHL, a Swedish Finn, and later, after his death, of MITKEVITCH, a Pole. Both fine craftsmen.

The workshops devoted to the making of objects of fantasy, and goldsmithery in general, were under the management of *G. JAHR, a native of the Baltic. He, too, was a craftsman of the first order. Very many cigarette cases were made in Moscow, in gold, silver, and enamel, and what I have said about those under the names of the Petersburg workmasters Perchin, Wigström and Hollming, applies largely also to those of Moscow.

I come now to a task I should have preferred to leave alone, because it is tedious; that of stating the differences between the productions of St. Petersburg and Moscow. In a record of this kind there is a choice between three courses, first to say as little as possible and whet no appetite, second, to say a little more but

131

not enough, third, to go into every detail. The first is useless and the second is exasperating, which leaves the third, the only course to take.

The difference very largely, if not wholly so, is the difference between the cities of Moscow and Petersburg themselves; between St. Basil's and the Cathedral of St. Peter and St. Paul; between the 'strong wind', the 'earthquake', and the 'fire', on the one hand, and the 'still small voice' on the other. Either Peter the Great lived and this is true or he is a myth. If one may be permitted to bring anything to the notice of those who rule in high places it is this, that the present rulers of Russia elected to return to Moscow rather than remain in Petersburg. If ever a banner was unfurled here it is. The catastrophic significance of this backward act takes precedence over all else to-day, or should do so. Having said this we can confine ourselves to the less tragic significance of Moscow.

Established as it was in this city it was natural that the Moscow Branch of Fabergé should in all its works give a preference to the more popularly accepted outward characteristics of Russia and of Old Russia in particular—*Monumental conception and imposing splendour*. It was the façade not the inner meaning of Russia to which it was attracted. You see 'the big idea' displayed on every piece coming from the Fabergé Moscow workshops. There is a swing about them, a freedom from restraint typical of Russia as generally conceived.

There is nothing surprising, therefore, that the Moscow House should have been attracted to those styles of ornamentation which can be developed with the least restriction. Thus it is that 'the naturalistic' spreads itself very largely over everything which Moscow produced from table silver to cigarette cases.

Then, of course, there were the objects in *cloisonné*, *champlevé* and painted enamels in the way of ikons, kovshi, tea sets, salt cellars, spoons, cigarette cases, etc. The number of them coming from the Moscow workshops must have been legion. I have said something of this work before, and now need only say that these objects added in no way to the international fame of Fabergé. They were nothing more than the stock-in-trade of every Russian silversmith and had been so for generations. Outside Russia they created no interest whatever and the only thing that can be said for the Fabergé productions of this kind is that they were rescued from a too extravagant flamboyance by a discreet choice of colours.

With that we come to objects in Old Russian Style which Moscow cherished as a mother her ewe lamb and again naturally so. This particular style, as developed by Fabergé, was the result of the Craftsman's study of the mural decorations, documents, pieces of pottery and gold and silversmith's work of the time of Ivan the Terrible. This invention is an outstanding contribution to Russian Art. The Moscow House made use of this style almost *ad infinitum* in silver work of every kind such as tankards, bratini, ikons, bowls, cigarette cases, etc., and in silver work associated with Siberian stones. These objects were made much use of as presentation gifts to Emirs and Khans, visiting foreign potentates, statesmen, etc.

If I may state my own opinion nothing brought the work of Petersburg and Moscow together more than this art. It made possible the production of objects which had in them all the easily recognizable outer characteristics of Russia but deprived of that flamboyance so distasteful and distressing both to the cultured people of Russia and to those abroad. I have already shown examples of this work in Chapter III, Plates 13-16.

The geometric, too, was a style much in evidence in Moscow's work.

Over all, it was in her work in the silver workshops that Moscow made its chief contribution to the fame of Fabergé, but this was localised in great measure to Russia.

But there was something else at work in Moscow which in a general way affected all its productions. Allan Bowe, Fabergé's partner in the Moscow business, was an astute business man, the very antipodes of the Craftsman. A clever business man is always a showman, wherever he may be, but in Moscow he becomes a super-showman; he cannot help it for this present capital of Russia is the very hot-bed of showmanship. It is the façade all the time. Showmanship being twin brother to commercialism there will be no surprise when I say that the way the Moscow Branch was run was an attempt to exploit the genius of Fabergé on a commercial basis. That it came through the operation so successfully with the objects retaining their 'Fabergé' individuality is only proof of the far-reaching influence of the Head of the House and the loyalty to craftsmanship of Tcherpournoff, Pihl and Jahr.

But one must be fair to Allan Bowe and not forget that there are many mansions. No one possesses all the gifts which an all-beneficent Providence has strewn here and there with such largesse. But for him it is more than likely that London would never have possessed a Branch of the House of Fabergé, and that would have been more than a pity.

And now for Petersburg. She applied herself more especially to the classical mode, but just as Moscow made use of these styles in some of her work, so Petersburg with an understanding that the classical by no means satisfies all the yearnings of mankind, worked too in the naturalistic and realistic styles, for example in her animals, flowers and from time to time in the Imperial Easter Eggs and other objects. Taking the whole of the work of the two places that of Moscow is on the showy side, Petersburg on the restrained. But this is not to bring out the difference quite clearly, for that we must go to the Head of the House himself.

Fabergé made none of the Imperial Easter Eggs in Moscow. Now you can call these by any name you like, you can be all for them or all against, but of one thing there can be no two opinions. As examples of the goldsmith's, jeweller's, enameller's and lapidary's combined crafts they are perfect or as near so as is humanly possible. If in the opinion of Fabergé himself Moscow could have reached this perfection, then as the making of them was endless both as to the skill they required and the time they took to produce, there can be no doubt he would have called in Moscow's help, but he did not.

On the Craftsman's own showing, therefore, the palm must go to Petersburg for all things, whether Imperial Easter Eggs or other objects which called for the very acme of skill and restraint.

The reason for the perfection of craftsmanship reached by Petersburg, if I may again state my own view, is to be found in what I have already said, the nearness of Fabergé to his workmasters and workmen, and, whatever the novices may say, to that now much maligned goose which lays the golden egg, the personal private ownership of the workshops by the workmasters themselves. By the time the influence of Fabergé had spread to Moscow and through his partner Allan Bowe to the managers of departments and through them to the workmen, something of the vital spark had gone out of it; it was bound to be so, for whoever yet heard of a workman giving his last ounce to a salaried official and not to his immediate employer always at hand and working with him.

Having read over what I have written I wonder whether I have said too much. 'Why all this toil and trouble?' Will collectors and art dealers, having read in the next chapter how to distinguish Petersburg productions from those of Moscow, shun the latter? That would be a disaster. And then are there not so many exceptions to what I have said that the general statement I have made becomes largely redundant? Let me give just one or two of these exceptions.

In Plate 111 I have reproduced in colour a small ribbed cigarette case in two coloured golds. It is quite an unpretentious little thing. It is not ornamented in any of the styles we have discussed, it belongs to no period so far generally acknowledged. Yet it has in it the very acme of 'style'. It will appeal to men of taste of the future just as much as it has fascinated those of the past and present, for it looks 'good', and feels 'good', having in it just the right weight of precious metal to measurements, viz, just over 4 ounces troy of gold to measurements $3\frac{5}{16}''$ x $2\frac{3}{8}''$ or $8\frac{3}{4}$ dwts. of gold of 14 carat to every 1 sq. inch of area, and it serves the best of purposes. It has been reproduced in colour to accentuate its simplicity and as being typical of hundreds of others which have come from the House of Fabergé, and without paying any attention to the workshop which made it. It was only after I had made my choice that I found out that I had chosen an object made in the city of bulbous domes.[1] In the same way, having extolled the cigarette case in blue enamel on gold (Plate 70) on account of its fine enamelling, I looked to the marking and found that of Moscow.

Another object which for me has always had attraction is the clock in Old Russian style, reproduced in Plate 16. I have never paid any attention to its markings and it was only while preparing for the chapter on the marks of Fabergé that I discovered that it also had been made in Moscow.[2]

Two things therefore emerge from the cases I have brought to notice. First, they are only further proof of the all-searching and all-powerful influence of Fabergé himself against which neither distance nor methods of business with which he had not the slightest sympathy, were of any avail. Second, that just as both the cities of Petersburg and Moscow must come into an estimate if we are

---

[1] In Plate 118 I reproduce a ribbed gold cigarette case, equally simple and fascinating. This was made in Petersburg by Hollming. It measures $3\frac{1}{2}$ inches long by $2\frac{7}{16}$ inches wide and weighs 4.1 oz. troy. The proportion of gold of 14 carat to area is very close to that made in Moscow, viz, $9\frac{1}{2}$ dwts. to 1 sq. inch. In the same Plate is another cigarette case of exceptional finish and fitting, so fine is the hinge that it is nearly invisible. The proportion of gold of 14 carat to area is $11\frac{1}{4}$ dwts. to 1 sq. inch. This case was made in Moscow.

[2] The same remarks apply to the triptych shown in Plate 31.

to see Russia as a whole, so to leave out the Moscow Branch when estimating the worth of Fabergé is to know only half the story.

Conclusion. Let all men and women of culture have the courage of their taste. Regardless of marks and styles, and of whatever they have been told, let them be guided by their own good sense of sight and touch. They will find that the House of Fabergé has provided something for all the best occasions, whether male or female, and that it used not only its Head Establishment but also its Branch in Moscow to bring about this happy state of things.

Having exhausted the reader's patience on a matter which nevertheless is very necessary in a record of this kind, we can turn to the enumeration of those responsible for the designing and modelling of Fabergé objects. And first PETERSBURG. Those working in the Head Establishment were:

FRANÇOIS BIRBAUM, a Swiss. He was the chief designer of the finest objects, whether articles of fantasy, of jewellery, of gold and of silver of every description. Qualifying words are but a poor way to give an idea of his work, you must look around, for every Fabergé collection is a monument to his worth.

ALEXANDER IVASHOFF, a Russian, was a designer of fantasy and silver objects.

EUGÈNE JACOBSON, a native of the Baltic, designed silver objects of every description.

OSCAR MAY, a German from St. Petersburg, designed objects of fantasy and jewellery.

HUGO OEBURG, a Swede from Moscow, designed jewellery and objects of fantasy.

ZOSIM KRITZKY, a Russian, designed objects of fantasy and silver.

VASSILY ZUIEFF, a Russian, a miniature painter of the first order.

BORIS FROEDMAN-CLUZEL, a Swede from St. Petersburg; KURTZ and TIMUS, both natives of the Baltic; GRATCHOFF, a Russian; GRUNBERG-SALKALN, a Lettonian; GEORG MALYCHEFF, a Russian; and STRICH, a Jew; were all modellers. It was they who made the majority of the models for the stone animals. Of all the productions of Fabergé these perhaps have given the greatest delight, at any rate to ladies. Of those who came to model the Sandringham animals in the time of King Edward VII, I only now remember Froedman-Cluzel. Malycheff modelled tiny monuments for the Imperial Easter Eggs including those of Peter I and Alexander III.

The designers and modellers working at the MOSCOW Branch were as follows: MICHEL IVANOFF, NAVOZOFF, KOZLOFF, KOSTRIOUKOFF, all Russians; BARON de KLODT, a native of the Baltic; and JAN LIEBERG-NYBERG, a Lettonian; were all designers. The modellers were

135

SOKOLOFF, SOKOLOVSKY, HELENA SHISHKINA, all Russians; BARON de KLODT, brother of the before-mentioned and a descendant of the famous sculptor of the *Horse-tamers* on the Anitchkoff bridge in St. Petersburg; and LUIGI BUZZI, an Italian.

In the KIEFF Branch was a designer, BALACHOFF, evidently Russian. As to the ODESSA Branch there is no information available.

In the London Branch there was one designer, R. A. PINKS, of Irish descent, and two modellers, FRANK LUTIGER, a Swiss, and ALFRED POCOCK, an Englishman. Lutiger joined the artists sent from Petersburg to model, on the spot, the Sandringham animals to which a chapter has been devoted. He did the same at Ascott where Mr. Leopold de Rothschild's animals were modelled.

Pocock is interesting for one or two reasons. He was not merely the sole Englishman who modelled for Fabergé but eventually he cut his own models in stone. His association with Fabergé, like my own, came about by pure chance, and his beginning was a very small one. It was in 1905 or 1906 that Queen Alexandra called for one or two animals of which she wished to see the wax models before they were cut in stone, and to meet her wishes at short notice it became necessary to get these made in London. Application was made to the Royal Academy Schools and they recommended a scholarship pupil, Alfred Pocock, then in his twenties. He succeeded in pleasing the Queen and the models were cut in stone in St. Petersburg.

This would probably have been the end, had it not been that Pocock shortly afterwards turned up with an elephant, which he had himself cut out of a pebble he found on Hampstead Heath, with tusks in chalcedony cut out of the inside of another pebble he found at Beer in S. Devon; and an owl cut in Labradorite. Fabergé or no Fabergé, such initiative could only be encouraged and the Queen informed. She presented the owl to Lady De Grey as a sample she said 'of what an Englishman can do', and this I illustrate in the back centre of the group in Plate 76, Chapter V.

Following the Queen's wishes, Pocock from time to time executed a number of animals, a cow from a Budleigh Salterton pebble with red and white patches; a giraffe, seated, from a Devonshire fossil coralquartzite; a camel with Egyptian characters carved underneath; a large toad in bloodstone; a red squirrel from a red and white cornelian found at Felixstowe; a donkey in grey chalcedony (now in the Sandringham collection), and other birds, fishes, horses and 'Buster Brown'. It was Pocock, too, who made the models in wax representing Canada, Australia, South Africa, India, etc., to which I have previously referred and with which I plagued Fabergé so unmercifully.

Pocock's models are finely cut and mostly in caricature. In execution they follow a technique of the artist's own, with the finished surface polished in varying degrees following the natural characteristics of the animal, but leaning towards the mat. In comparing them with the animals modelled and cut by Fabergé in St. Petersburg, the following is to be noted. The Fabergé animals are

PLATE 113

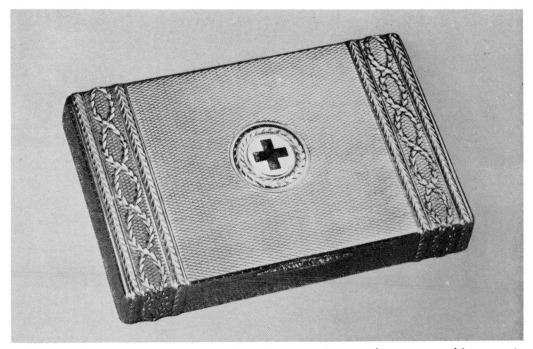

CIGARETTE CASE. In gold, guilloché surface. Red cross in enamel on opaque white enamel ground. Engraved on back: 'Plus qu'hier, moins que demain'. Rose-diamond thumb-piece. Measurements: $3\frac{1}{2}$ in. × $2\frac{1}{4}$ in. × $\frac{1}{2}$ in.
(*Collection of Sir Harold Wernher, Bt.*)

CIGARETTE CASE. Of translucent white jade, bordered with enamelled gold rim. Opal cameo of Tsarina Alexandra Feodorovna and two daughters, Olga and Tatiana, enclosed in a frame of diamond leaf design. Pearl thumb-piece. Approximate actual size.
(*By courtesy of Hammer Galleries.*)

PLATE 114

BOX. In translucent mauve enamel on silver, bordered in red and green gold, leaf pattern. Central miniature of Nicholas II, surrounded by diamonds, surmounted by Imperial Crown in diamonds. Four double-headed eagles in rose-diamonds.
(*From H.M. Queen Elizabeth, the Queen Mother's Collection.*)

CIGARETTE CASE. With place for matches. In red gold guilloché, with decoration in yellow gold.
Measurements: $4\frac{1}{16}$ in. $\times$ $2\frac{3}{8}$ in. $\times$ $\frac{5}{8}$ in.
(*By courtesy of Messrs. S. J. Phillips.*)

PLATE 115

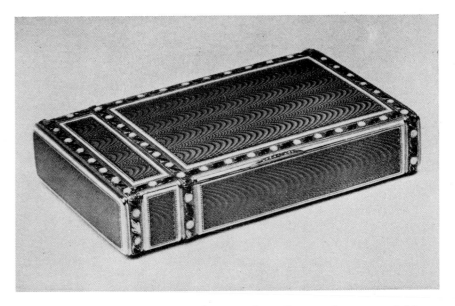

CIGARETTE CASE. With place for matches. In translucent steel-blue enamel on gold, bordered with opaque white enamel, translucent green enamel leaves and white opal enamel dots. Rose-diamond thumb-piece. Measurements: 4 in. × 2½ in. × ¾ in.
(*Privately owned.*)

CIGARETTE BOX. Gold, translucent pinkish-mauve and cream enamels mounted in green and red gold and diamonds. Monogram of Tsar Nicholas II in an oval border of diamonds surmounted by Imperial Crown in diamonds. Outside border in mat gold.
(*By courtesy of Messrs. Wartski.*)

PLATE 116

PANAGIA
In gold, set with cabochon sapphires and rubies, rose-diamonds (one large one surmounting crown)
and whole pearls. Gold chain. Actual size.
(*By courtesy of Messrs. Berry-Hill.*)

PLATE 117

Markings on the inside silk lining of lid of holly-wood boxes, approximately double size.
Fabergé—St. Petersburg, Moscow, London.

Markings on the inside silk lining of lid of holly-wood boxes, approximately double size.
Fabergé—St. Petersburg, Moscow.

PLATE 118

CIGARETTE CASE. In red gold, ribbed; cabochon sapphire thumb-piece. Measurements: $3\frac{1}{2}$ in. $\times$ $2\frac{7}{16}$ in.
(*Collection of Mr. Geoffrey Hutchinson, Q.C.*)

CIGARETTE CASE. With pencil and place for matches in polished red gold. Monogram of Nicholas II, the Empress Alexandra Feodorovna and Crown in mat yellow gold. Pencil top, cabochon sapphire and diamonds. Thumb-piece cabochon sapphire. Note superb fitting of hinge lid.
(*Collection of Dr. James Hasson.*)

PLATE 119

CIGARETTE CASE. In silver niello-work. Made in Moscow. Measurements: $3\frac{1}{4}$ in. × $2\frac{1}{2}$ in. × $\frac{3}{4}$ in. This is the only example of niello-work by Fabergé which the author has come across.
(By courtesy of Mr. Kenneth Snowman.)

Reverse of the cigarette case shown above.

PLATE 120

CIGARETTE CASE. In red gold, with tinder and place for matches. Sunray design, with one brilliant. Thumb-piece, cabochon sapphire. Measurements: $3\frac{5}{8}$ in. $\times$ $2\frac{7}{16}$ in. $\times$ $\frac{5}{8}$ in.
(From King George VI's Collection.)

CIGARETTE CASE. In nephrite, with tinder and place for matches. Mounted in gold, translucent red and opaque white enamels. Miniature of Tsar Nicholas II under table diamond with surround and crown in diamonds. Thumb-piece in diamonds. Measurements: $3\frac{9}{16}$ in. $\times$ $2\frac{7}{16}$ in. $\times$ $\frac{5}{8}$ in. A 'museum piece', perfect in every way. Bears English hall-mark as well as Russian.
(From King George VI's Collection.)

PLATE 121

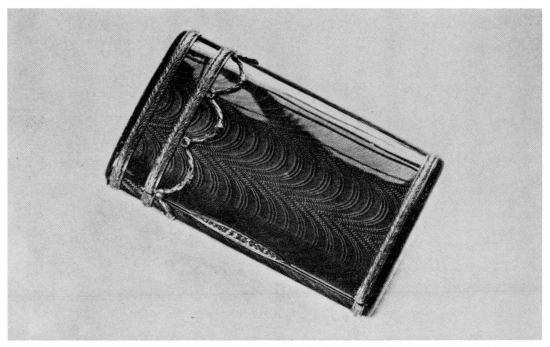

CIGARETTE CASE. In red enamel on silver, ornamented with gold and rose-diamonds. Thumb-piece in rose-diamonds. Measurements: $3\frac{13}{16}$ in. $\times$ $2\frac{1}{4}$ in. $\times$ $\frac{11}{16}$ in.
(*From King George VI's Collection.*)

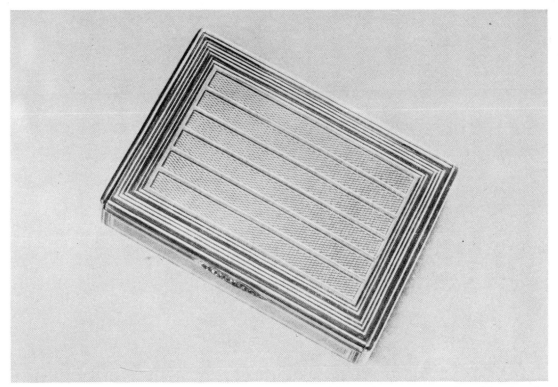

CIGARETTE CASE. In green gold. The six central guilloché panels are separated and bordered with opaque white enamel. Then come ribbed gold, border of opaque blue enamel, ribbed gold again and finally border of opaque blue enamel. Thumb-piece in rose-diamonds.
(*From King George VI's Collection.*)

PLATE 122

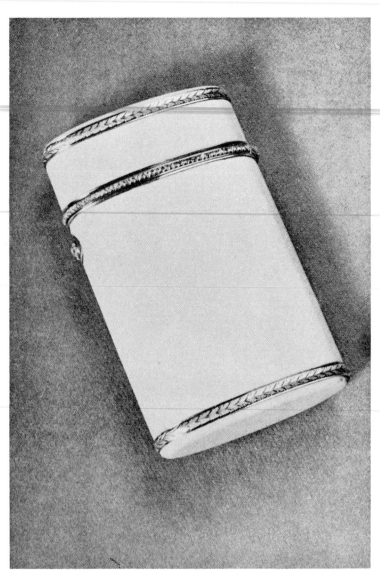

CIGARETTE CASE. In pink opaque enamel with mat surface, enamelled on silver. Mounted with gold leaf borders and set with rose-diamonds. Thumb-piece, rose-diamond. Measurements: $3\frac{3}{8}$ in. $\times$ 2 in. $\times \frac{7}{8}$ in. This case is representative of a number of Fabergé objects made in opaque enamel with mat surface as a change from those in translucent enamel. The opaque mat enamel gave them a distinguished appearance. This case is only the second of such objects seen by the author in the last thirty years.
(*From King George VI's Collection.*)

PLATE 123

CIGARETTE CASE. In green gold, 'ciselé', with place for matches. Thumb-piece, cabochon sapphire. A portion of place for matches is in red gold. Measurements: $3\frac{7}{8}$ in. × $2\frac{3}{4}$ in. × $\frac{5}{8}$ in.
(From King George VI's Collection.)

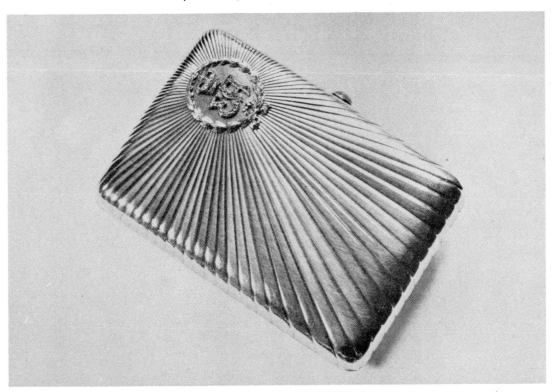

CIGARETTE CASE. In red and yellow gold. Sunray design. Monogram and crown in rose-diamonds, wreathed in green and red gold. On reverse is medallion with X.L. in rose-diamonds, dated March 10th, 1863–1903. Thumb-piece, cabochon ruby. Measurements: $3\frac{11}{16}$ in. × $2\frac{9}{16}$ in. × $\frac{9}{16}$ in.
(From King George VI's Collection.)

PLATE 124

CIGARETTE CASE. In red gold, ribbed. Double-headed eagle in gold. Thumb-piece, cabochon sapphire. Measurements: $3\frac{3}{4}$ in. $\times$ $2\frac{1}{2}$ in. $\times$ $\frac{9}{16}$ in.
(*From King George VI's Collection.*)

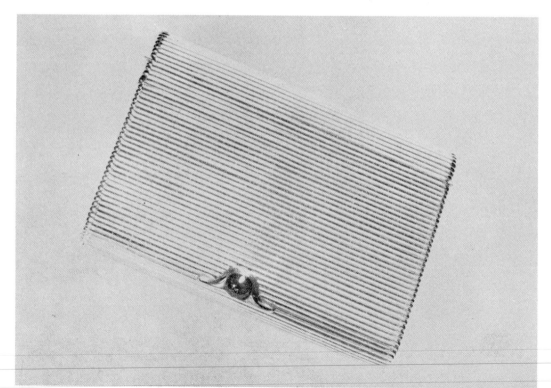

CIGARETTE CASE. In red gold, ribbed, with place for matches and tinder. Thumb-piece, cabochon sapphire. Measurements: $3\frac{5}{8}$ in. $\times$ $2\frac{7}{16}$ in. $\times$ $\frac{11}{16}$ in. Inside of lid is engraved: 'Formerly the property of H.R.H. The Duke of Clarence. To Lord Revelstoke from George R.I. 1926.'
(*From King George VI's Collection.*)

PLATE 125

CIGARETTE CASE. In red and yellow gold, ribbed. Thumb-piece, cabochon sapphire. Measurements: $3\frac{1}{2}$ in. $\times$ $2\frac{7}{16}$ in. $\times$ $\frac{5}{8}$ in.
(*From King George VI's Collection.*)

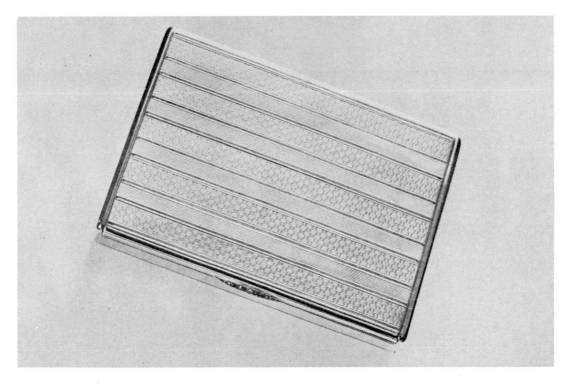

CIGARETTE CASE. The four finely ribbed portions are in green gold. The five guilloché portions are in gold of a beautiful light coppery hue. The case is edged with green gold. Thumb-piece in rose-diamonds. Measurements: $3\frac{5}{8}$ in. $\times$ $2\frac{7}{16}$ in. $\times$ $\frac{5}{8}$ in.
(*From King George VI's Collection.*)

PLATE 126

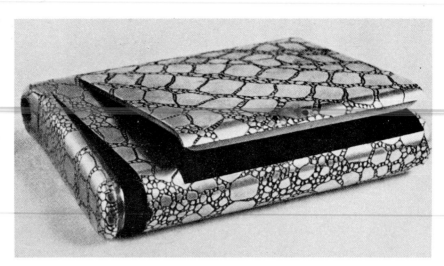

CIGARETTE CASE. In gold, with place for matches and tinder. Crocodile
skin design incised.
(*By courtesy of Messrs. Berry-Hill.*)

CIGARETTE CASE. In blackened steel with place for matches and tinder, hinge in gold, thumb-
piece gold and cabochon sapphire. Measurements: $3\frac{7}{10}$ in. $\times$ $2\frac{3}{8}$ in. $\times$ $\frac{11}{16}$ in.
(*By courtesy of Messrs. Berry-Hill.*)

PLATE 127

CIGARETTE BOX. In nephrite. Trellis-work and garland in rose-diamonds; miniature in colour of Tsar Nicholas II surrounded by rose-diamonds, surmounted by crown in brilliants and rose-diamonds; rim of lid bordered in gold, leaf pattern. An Imperial presentation piece of outstanding quality. Measurements: $3\frac{11}{16}$ in. $\times$ $2\frac{1}{2}$ in. $\times$ $1\frac{1}{4}$ in.
(*Privately owned.*)

PLATE 128

Fig. 1.

Fig. 2.

Fig. 2.

Fig. 3.

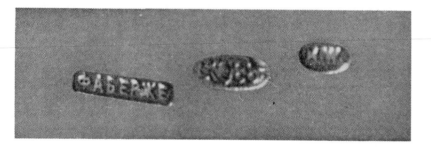

Fig. 4.

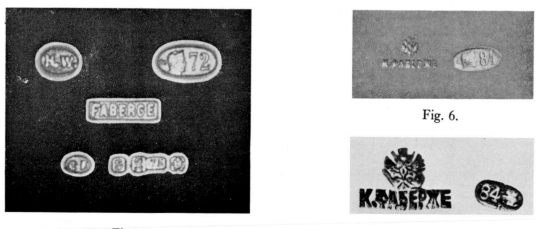

Fig. 5.

Fig. 6.

Fig. 7.

Figs. 1–7. MARKS OF FABERGÉ with Russian State Hall-marks.

invariably highly polished and they are modelled to give that fat, contented, well-fed appearance which brings out the one quality common to all Fabergé productions, that is, substance.

I go into all these details because the circumstances of the association of Mr. Pocock with Fabergé were quite extraordinary, in fact unique. Here was the Queen of England and the 'Last of the Great Craftsmen', owing to a small revealing chance, going out of their way to encourage the talents of a then quite unknown young artist. Nothing brings out more clearly the spontaneous nature of the Queen, which prompted her to give her patronage at once where she considered it was due (and especially is this to be noted in Pocock's case as Fabergé objects were everything to her), and the generous nature of Fabergé whose business was strictly limited to dealing in objects made in his own workshops.

CHAPTER VIII

THE MARKS OF FABERGÉ

JUST as no reputable painter is dependent on his signature to his pictures for the sale of them, so it is true that no goldsmith and silversmith of repute of any country, the maker of the wares which he sells, is dependent on his mark for the sale of them. His good name suffices.

This is not to say that makers' marks have no place. They have, but only when the wares are sold by a goldsmith who is not the maker and so become more and more of value as the years go by, when the original maker is dead and his house no longer exists. Even then such marks should be given only a confirmatory, never a primary, place as a certificate of authenticity.

But however all this may be in a general way, it applies to Fabergé with certainty. Never once did I hear the subject of marks mentioned in St. Petersburg by the Craftsman or his staff, never once did I myself look for them on pieces sent to me for sale. In saying this I do not include the time when Fabergé was bringing his test case against the Worshipful Company of Goldsmiths in London in consequence of which it became necessary to study both the Russian and English hall-marks for the purpose of carrying on the action.

With one solitary exception, never did customers interest themselves in the degree of fineness of the precious metals when making their purchases; hall-marks were never mentioned. If a gold cigarette case was wanted, it was asked for and accepted as such without comment, there never was any question whether it was 18-carat or otherwise. The degree of fineness was a question for the Craftsman alone, and it was understood that he would use the fineness of gold best suited to his purpose and charge accordingly.

The same with an enamelled case. Whether the enamelling was done on gold or silver was never enquired into. It was a matter of appearance entirely. Speaking generally, in one case the colour of the enamel would look softer, the finish of the borders would be sharper and the total appearance would be such as to give the greatest pleasure. Such a case would be both enamelled on, and bordered in, gold. In another the colour would have a harder look, the finish of the borders would not be so fine and the total appearance would be one not to give the same satisfaction as the other. Such a case would be both enamelled on, and bordered in, silver. The price of the gold one would be, say, £100, that of the other perhaps £25.

The customer did not quibble; each article would be clearly ticketed with its price, and in accordance with his taste and his pocket he would choose the one which suited his purpose best without further question.

I can remember only one exception to this general custom, and that was in the matter of the silver ikon of the Madonna and Child made to the order of the late Duchess of Norfolk, to which I have referred in a previous chapter (page 84), when the old Duke, in answer to a question put to him by a lady of his House who did not believe that silver with a mat surface could possibly be silver, even after the English hall-mark had been pointed out to her, replied, 'If Mr. Fabergé says it is silver then silver it must be'.

This dictum of the Duke's expresses far better than any testimony of mine the basis of understanding which existed between Fabergé and his customers.

To-day Fabergé is no longer here and his wares, owing to their own worth and to many circumstances and events as well as to the fact that they can never be made again, have reached a pinnacle of esteem which it is true to say has never before been approached by those of any goldsmith in the short period between his death and the present time, namely only twenty-seven years.

So much are they valued that no opportunity is lost to attribute to Fabergé any object of gold, silver and enamel of Russian origin, or of Siberian stones. And there is more, for instance French gold boxes of the Eighteenth Century have been submitted to me stamped with the forged mark of Fabergé, and one could not but be amused by the fact that in order to enhance the value of Eighteenth Century productions it had been thought necessary to stamp them with the mark of a Nineteenth Century craftsman. The mark of Fabergé punched on these objects was sharp and harsh with no attempt whatever to soften it by polishing down a little. The same harshness applied equally to the bulge immediately behind the mark and caused by the punching. The very crudity of the whole performance was sufficient to illuminate and at the same time disgust anyone called in to give an opinion. I have seen a similar forged mark on a small ikon in mosaic where the metal frame was stamped in a similar crude manner.

Still more, and this is much more disturbing because it concerns objects made with malice aforethought. I have seen a number of flower subjects not only attributed to Fabergé, but stamped on the gold stem most clearly with his forged mark, plus the hall-marks of the Russian State, which certainly had never been made by the Russian Craftsman. Here the maker's zeal had run away with him: much more convincing would it have been not to have marked them at all. Fabergé by no means marked all his flowers; some of the finest specimens have no mark at all. For example, the Japanese tree, illustrated in Plate 75, although entirely of gold, trunk and all, and something that one would expect to see fully marked owing to the amount of precious metal in it, is, as I have said before, not marked at all.

But that is enough. It all goes to show how necessary it is for collectors and dealers alike to give their first attention to the appearance of supposed Fabergé objects, to ascertain that all the characteristics are there and then only to turn to the maker's mark and hall-marks for confirmation. I know one collector who with remarkable acumen recognises at once Fabergé stone animals, and these have no marks. Characteristics are all he has to guide him. And yet when the maker's mark is indistinct on a gold or silver object which he recognises as Fabergé, he loses faith in his own judgment. He is of those who worship marks, and the more perfect they are the better he is satisfied.

Now to my mind the more indistinct the marks, provided they are clear enough to be recognised, the greater their value. Their indistinctness is almost certain proof of their authenticity and for this reason. They are almost invariably stamped on objects of gold and silver when they are in the rough, and before they are in a finished state, enamelled, chased, etc., a good deal of work has to be done, and in the course of this finishing the marks are subjected to wear and may quite easily in some cases be nearly polished out altogether.

Almost unrecognisable marks, although sufficiently recognisable to the expert, are of no use whatever to one who is intent on giving the impression that objects *not* made by the Russian Craftsman *have* been executed by him. To succeed in such pernicious practices it is vital that the maker's marks should be as nearly perfect as possible, as in the case of the flowers to which I have referred.

Such are some of the pitfalls. We will now turn to a consideration of the Fabergé marks themselves and we will take those of the St. Petersburg Head Establishment first.

PETERSBURG. In a general way, each object is stamped with the mark of the workmaster—E.K.; H.W., etc.—in whose workshop it was made, plus that of the firm, which consists of the name in Russian characters, ФАБЕРЖЕ (without the initial К.), or the initials К.Ф. On those objects made especially for the English market the name often appears in Latin characters, FABERGÉ. Sometimes only the mark of the workmaster appears; sometimes only that of the firm.

Moscow. As previously stated, the only mark is that of the firm, namely, К.ФАБЕРЖЕ super-imposed by a Russian double-headed eagle, and let it be noted that the initial К. always appears, whereas in the case of Petersburg the name is without the initial and without the double-headed eagle.* Occasionally Moscow used the initials of the firm К.Ф. In a general way it is wiser to accept the full name with eagle and leave those objects marked with initials to the judgment of experts.

And here I must call a halt, perhaps the last one, to say something. Throughout this record it will have been noted, I hope, that I have endeavoured to show that it was not the artistic gifts of Carl Fabergé, however great they were, which were the primary cause of his success in life, but his character. That topsy-turvy combination of idiosyncratic qualities which distinguished him from all other men, at any rate from all other men I myself have met.

In the course of this record I have from time to time gone off on similar rambling excursions, perhaps too many, to impress this fact, and I have to say that even now I am not satisfied that I have succeeded in producing just the picture I want. I feel I may not yet have convinced the reader that the Craftsman was successful beyond dreams because he consistently followed that way of life which we persistently dub 'the ideal', as though it were something to be avoided at all costs in practice.

In short, I feel that what readers would like is some glaring example far removed from my own personal experience of the Craftsman and so convincing that they would at once be impelled to stand up and repeat, 'Blessed are the

* Captain Harold Spink has brought to the writer's notice a curiosity, a light blue enamelled inkpot marked K. FABERGÉ in Russian characters, A.R., but no double-headed eagle. The K before the full name is evidence enough that it was made in Moscow. Why the eagle is omitted and who A.R. was is not known. The marking is a vagary and must not deflect anyone for a moment from the truth of the above general statement.

meek, for they shall inherit the earth', knowing that at last they had their finger on the solution of the enigma of Fabergé. I have always maintained that the Craftsman has much to say to this barren age of ours.

Such an example actually came my way on September 2nd, 1947, and it concerns the double-headed eagle. For years I have wondered why it was that Fabergé objects made by the Moscow Branch of the firm bear the double-headed eagle stamped upon them and objects made by the Head Establishment in St. Petersburg make no showing whatever of this rampant bird. Its appearance or non-appearance on Fabergé objects is the one sure way, by marks, to fix their origin as of Moscow or St. Petersburg. Was it that Moscow thinking herself more Russian than the Capital conceived the idea that the adoption of the eagle would give her a further Russian uplift? Or was it that Moscow by some special deed had won for herself the right to use the emblem denied to Petersburg?

These questions, as I have said, have bothered me for years, and being pernickety about my facts (because for some reason or another I have had the notion that if I escaped being caught napping over these there was all the more hope that the Fabergé philosophy would the more readily be accepted. A curious deduction to make, but there it is), and not having heard from Eugène Fabergé for some eight years, I sent off an emissary to Paris shortly after the end of the war, to try to find him in order that I might put my questions to him and so solve the puzzle. I thought it as important as that. But Eugène was not to be found.*

So I proceeded with my notes and later this record. But as I advanced all sorts of other questions cropped up. For instance: what was the exact weight of the Orloff diamond? Was it 193 carats exactly, or a fraction of a carat below or above this figure, a matter of some importance in a stone of such fabulous worth? I remembered Agathon Fabergé telling me that there had always been some disagreement as to its exact weight and that it was only fixed for certain when the stone was weighed after dropping out of its setting into the palm of his hand. Another question. Whose workshop was responsible for the making of the cage-like jewelled egg now in the possession of Queen Mary? Was it Holmström's for certain? And why the engraving of C. FABERGÉ on the egg and of G. FABERGÉ on the pedestal of the cameo. Was the 'G' an error? Another. What exactly was the behaviour of the Bolsheviks towards the firm of Fabergé in 1918 when Carl Fabergé fled from Petrograd (Leningrad by now, I suppose)?

Questions like these kept on cropping up which were quite outside my own knowledge and something had to be done about them, if the record were to be complete. But what? And then 'out of the blue', as usual, it all came. In the early summer of 1947, Mr. K. R. Hilton arrived from abroad with a message from Agathon Fabergé. 'Was there anything I wanted to know?' I had not heard anything from Agathon for nearly ten years and now here he was safe and sound. I tabulated all my queries and his answers are now incorporated in the text of this record, all with the exception of the matter of the double-headed eagle which Agathon explained as now follows.

---

* I have since heard (August 10th, 1948), that Eugène Fabergé is still in Paris carrying on his work.

As goldsmith and jeweller to the Court the firm of Fabergé had the right to the use of the Imperial emblem, the double-headed eagle, in all its trade activities, with the extended right to its use when showing the firm's wares at public exhibitions.

The Moscow Branch lost no opportunity to use the emblem on every possible occasion to advertise itself and its wares (refer to what has been said about the difference between the productions of Petersburg and Moscow in the last chapter). It is thus that the double-headed eagle is to be seen as marked on every piece coming from the workshops of the Moscow Branch.

On the other hand the Head Establishment in St. Petersburg, as ruled over completely by the Craftsman himself, made use of the emblem only as an acknowledgment of the honour which had been conferred upon the firm by the granting of it, and not for the purpose of gaining publicity and pushing the sale of its wares. Thus it is that on no piece emanating from the Petersburg workshops do you see the double-headed eagle. This conclusive demonstration of the meekness of Carl Fabergé, coming as it does from a source quite outside my own experience and *self-evident on every single piece coming from the workshops of St. Petersburg*, is in my opinion the greatest contribution that I as a biographer can make not only to show the greatness of the Craftsman, but to demonstrate the fact that by ruling his life in a way uncommon to mankind in general, by accepting wholeheartedly a dictum from Heaven with which all men are fully acquainted but which a mere handful of them follow, he made such a supreme success of his life. Men to-day cry famine over a heap of corn and they might with much advantage to themselves turn to Carl Fabergé to help them out of their difficulties. Anyone wishing to satisfy himself still further and possessing one of the Imperial Easter Eggs has only to examine it very closely to be assured. And if ever there was justification for a display of the emblem it was surely on such objects, in fact it would have been a pretty compliment on the part of the Craftsman to pay his Imperial Patron, who alone had the power to confer the privilege of the use of the emblem.

What I have said calls for no further comment from me. I can just add this, when I put the facts before my publishers, through the medium of their Director, my much esteemed and long-suffering friend, Mr. W. Hanneford-Smith, he said: 'What Fabergé refused for himself we should give him now, don't you think?' I did think, and so the Imperial Emblem appears on the cover of this book.

With that we can take leave of the marks of Fabergé and proceed to the hall-marks of the Russian State.

RUSSIAN STATE. Fabergé objects were made in the Petersburg and Moscow workshops only, therefore it is the marks of these two cities which alone interest us.

At the end of the Tsarist régime the mark adopted throughout Russia for objects of gold or silver of legal quality was the woman's head with head-dress (*kokoshnik*). When Petersburg and Moscow ceased to have separate marks of their own it is not now possible to say exactly. The authorities differ. What is known is that in the middle of the Eighteenth Century the hall-mark of Petersburg was two crossed anchors intersected by a sceptre, and that of Moscow, St. George and the Dragon. Beuque, in his *Dictionnaire des Poinçons* (1925), speaking of the woman's head, says this was the 'Poinçon utilisé depuis le 30 juin, 1861, par la Russie pour la marque des ouvrages en métal précieux aux titres légaux'; Markham, in his *Handbook to Foreign Hall-Marks*, speaking of the crossed anchors and sceptre, says, 'This mark within a circle is used at the present time', which would be a year or two previous to 1898 when his book was published.

This confusion as to the Petersburg hall-mark is very largely cleared up by hall-marks which appear on the Fabergé Imperial Easter Eggs made in Perchin's workshop. On four of the eggs, dated 1893 to 1896, the crossed anchors appear, then in 1897 the head appears, in 1898 the crossed anchors re-appear, but finally on four eggs dated from 1899 to 1903 inclusive, the head re-appears. As the Easter eggs took anything from one to four years to make, and as they would be marked in an early rough state, the year 1896 can, I think, be taken as a very close approximation to the time when the woman's head came to be adopted by Petersburg as the hall-mark for gold and silver plate.[1]

As for Moscow, there are no dated Easter eggs and no other dated pieces available, and I cannot find any information to throw light on the time when this city discarded the device of St. George and the Dragon and started to use the woman's head, but it is reasonable to conclude that Moscow, as well as all the other towns, did the same as Petersburg and adopted in the State hall-mark the woman's head about 1896.[2]

At the end of the Tsarist régime all objects of gold or silver had to comply with certain standards. How long these standards had been in force I do not know, perhaps from the beginning of the Nineteenth Century, perhaps before, but certainly during the whole lifetime of the firm of Fabergé.[3] Those for gold are represented by the numerals 56, 72 and 92, and the proportion of pure gold in each of the standards is represented by the numerals given. For instance, 56 means 56 *zolotniks*[4] of pure gold in 96 *zolotniks* of alloy, 72 means 72 *zolotniks* of pure gold in 96 *zolotniks* of alloy and so on.

The only Russian standards which interest us in regard to Fabergé objects are 56 and 72.

To turn Russian gold standards into their equivalents in English carats all one has to remember is that in 96 parts of alloy in Russia there are 56, 72, or 92 parts, as the case may be, of pure gold, and in England in 24 parts (carats) of alloy are 9, 12, 15, 18 or 22 parts, as the case may be, of pure gold. Therefore, by dividing the Russian standards by 4, the equivalent in English carats is obtained, 56 Russian=14 carats English, 72 Russian=18 carats English.

[1] The fan, Plate 44, Chapter III, bears the hall-mark of the woman's head and the year 1901. It was marked no doubt in 1900 and this is evidence that in that year the hall-mark of the woman's head was used by St. Petersburg.

[2] Since writing this I have ascertained that the triptych, shown in Plate 31, bears the hall-mark of St. George and the Dragon, and the year 1894. The time of marking was probably early 1894 or late 1893, and this is evidence that St. George and the Dragon was the hall-mark of Moscow at that time.

[3] According to Mr. Agathon Fabergé the time was the first half of the Nineteenth Century.

[4] 96 *zolotniks* equal 1 Russian pound.

The silver standards are represented by the numerals 84, 88, and 91, which in each case means the number of *zolotniks* of pure silver in 96 *zolotniks* of silver alloy. In 1,000 parts, therefore, of alloy in each case are 875, 916.6, 947.9 parts of pure silver, so the comparison with the English standard of 925 parts of pure silver in 1,000 parts of alloy is seen at once. The 88 Russian standard is below the English, and the 91 above.

All that has been said will I hope be made clear from the illustrations shown in the following figures and those on Plate 128 (figs. 1-7).

Fig. 1 shows the hall-mark of the St. Petersburg Assay Office for all objects whether in gold or silver up to legal standard, two crossed anchors intercepted by a sceptre, before its adoption of the device of a woman's head with head-dress (*kokoshnik*).

Fig. 2 shows the hall-mark of the Moscow Assay Office for all objects whether in gold or silver up to legal standard, St. George and the Dragon, before its adoption of the device of a woman's head with head-dress.

Fig. 3 shows the device of a woman's head with head-dress which was eventually adopted by all Russia as the hall-mark for all objects in gold or silver up to legal standard.

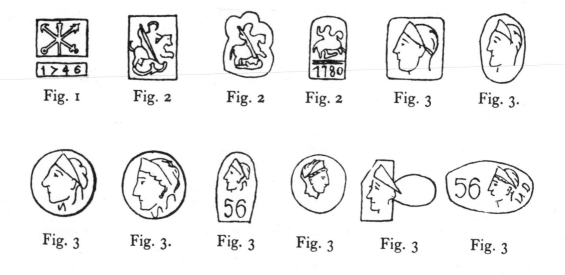

| Fig. 1 | Fig. 2 | Fig. 2 | Fig. 2 | Fig. 3 | Fig. 3. |

| Fig. 3 | Fig. 3. | Fig. 3 | Fig. 3 | Fig. 3 | Fig. 3 |

Figs. 1—3. RUSSIAN STATE HALL-MARKS

The varied forms here depicted are copied from Beuque's *Dictionnaire des Poinçons.*

Fig. 1 (Plate 128) shows a complete marking on an object in gold made in the Petersburg workshops of Fabergé when the Assay Office of this city used as hall-mark the device of the crossed anchors and sceptre. Note that the mark of work-master Michael Perchin is upside down. The markings are taken from one of the liqueur glasses illustrated in Plate 87.

144

Fig. 2 (Plate 128) shows a complete marking on an object enamelled on gold made in the Petersburg workshops of Fabergé when the Assay Office of this city had adopted the hall-mark of a woman's head with head-dress. Henrik Wigström is the workmaster, and the markings are taken from two different places on a translucent steel blue cigarette-case illustrated in Plate 115.

Fig. 3 (Plate 128) shows a complete marking on another gold object made in the St. Petersburg workshops. The workmaster is Hollming. The markings are on a gold cigarette-case in the possession of Mr. Michael Pugh.

Fig. 4 (Plate 128) shows a complete marking on a buckle enamelled on silver made in the St. Petersburg workshops. The hall-mark device here is the woman's head. The markings are taken from a buckle in translucent rose-coloured enamel in possession of Major W. H. Daubney. Note, the woman's head is upside down.

Fig. 5 (Plate 128) shows a complete very clear marking on an object made in the Petersburg workshops for the English market. The object is a clock in purpurine possessed by Major W. H. Daubney illustrated in Plate 42. The woman's head is particularly clear. Next to the English hall-marks is the English maker's mark of Fabergé, C.F., registered at Goldsmiths' Hall, London.

This purpurine clock is interesting as an example of what Fabergé did to comply with the demands of English law after his test action against the Worshipful Company of Goldsmiths, notice of which will presently be taken, but it is doubly interesting as showing the thoroughness, one might say the over-thoroughness, of Fabergé, or perhaps better, the vagaries of an artist.

I have already referred to the fact that the Craftsman often used silver when you would rather have expected him to use gold, and *vice versa*. In the case of an object in silver he sometimes flaunts the silver hall-mark, and in an object of gold sometimes no hall-mark appears.* And this is a good opportunity to take note of something else.

In the beginning of this chapter I referred in general terms to the difference in appearance between objects enamelled on and bordered with gold, and those enamelled on and bordered with silver, but this difference in general terms must not be allowed to prejudice a very large number of objects enamelled on silver— *but bordered with gold*, cigarette cases especially. (See green enamel case, Plate 91, and lower case on Plate 107.) In these cases, by giving much attention to the enamelling, and by choosing colours soft in themselves, such as rose pink, raspberry red and soft greens, and by bordering the objects with finely chiselled gold, an object was produced which gave much æsthetic satisfaction and at the same time met the pockets of many people who were prepared to go to £35/50 (I refer, of course, to fifty years ago) but for whom £100 and over (as it would have been in the case of gold) was too much for the purpose they had in view. The gold borders of such objects are almost invariably hall-marked 56 or 72, and the silver foundation for the enamel sometimes bears the silver hall-marks of 84, 88 or 91, and sometimes not. In the case of a cigarette-case, after the form of an *étui*, if you search long and deep enough you may find the silver mark on the very bottom of the inside.

* An outstanding example is the Pelican egg, here illustrated in Plate 67. It is entirely of gold, but no gold hall-mark appears.

But to return to the clock in purpurine. Here is an example, as I have said, of the meticulous thoroughness of Fabergé for not only are the small clock face and the leaf border in gold, but the plate covering the key box on the bottom, and there for a purely utilitarian purpose and never seen, is not only also of gold, but 18 carat at that, and marked.

Fig. 6 (Plate 128) shows a complete marking of a silver object made in the workshops of the Fabergé Branch Establishment in Moscow. Here is seen the name K. Fabergé in Russian, superimposed by the double-headed eagle together with the Moscow Assay Office hall-mark after it had adopted the woman's head, and the silver standard mark of 84. *Fig.* 7 (Plate 128) shows a complete marking on a silver Moscow object with St. George and the Dragon.

The complete markings on the gold objects made in the Moscow workshops are the same as for silver except, of course, that the gold standard hall-marks of 56 or 72 appear instead of the silver hall-marks of 84, 88 or 91. I have come across only three objects made in Moscow on which the device of St. George and the Dragon appears.[1] This Branch was not established until 1887, forty-five years after the foundation of the firm in St. Petersburg, and as the hall-mark of St. George and the Dragon was replaced by the woman's head about 1896, it is clear that it is the device of the woman's head which one would expect to see on the greater portion of Moscow's output.

The illustrations I have given show complete markings, but there are objects incompletely marked, as I have stated before, in fact all sorts of combinations occur down to no combination at all, when one mark alone appears and that either of initials of the firm or those of the workmaster (in the case of a Petersburg object) without any State hall-marks at all. Thus it is that К.Ф. can occur as the only mark and it is possible that this may apply to a Moscow article, owing to the vagaries of marking, even without the double-headed eagle, as well as to one made in Petersburg. In the same way in the case of a Petersburg article the initial of the workmaster may be the only mark to appear and especially is this so in the case of Kollin, initials E.K. He was the first of the workmasters (employed on objects of fantasy) to be established with Fabergé, and perhaps in his early days hall-marking was not so strictly regulated as afterwards. But this is only a guess.

Generally I would say this, that the further the markings on any object depart from those I have given as complete, the more necessity is there for care before being guided by them.[2]

I cannot close the subject without expressing my special thanks to Major W. H. Daubney, Dr. James Hasson and to Mr. and Mrs. Michael Pugh for the way they have responded to my many requests by supplying photographs of marks or loaning objects for examination, sometimes over prolonged periods.[3]

---

[1] The splendid triptych illustrated in Plate 31, as previously noted, bears the hall-mark of St. George and the Dragon and so do the gold cigarette case with Imperial monogram (Plate 118) and a piece of mounted pottery, in possession of Messrs. Wartski, from which the markings (*Fig.* 7, Plate 128) are taken.

[2] This does not mean that because an object is completely marked it is less likely to be a fake. Craftiness is just as capable of copying even a State hall-mark as it is of copying a maker's mark.

[3] The same acknowledgment is also due to Mr. Geoffrey Hutchinson, Q.C., and Mrs. Hasson.

No record of Fabergé would be complete without some mention of the test case he brought against the Worshipful Company of Goldsmiths, to which I have previously referred. It is now woven into the annals of the Goldsmithery of England.

For some five years the firm of Fabergé had been in the habit of sending articles from St. Petersburg and Moscow to its branch establishment in London by parcel post and registered letter when in July 1908 a packet was stopped by the customs authorities and handed to the Goldsmiths' Company which is a guild or corporation 'with divers privileges confirmed and enlarged from time to time by divers statutes and several charters, amongst other things, for the searching, assaying, marking and regulating wrought plate in order to ascertain the standard thereof for the good and safety of the public'.

The packet contained amongst other things nineteen match-boxes enamelled on silver, one cigarette-case enamelled on gold, seven cigarette-cases enamelled on silver, three gold or silver letter-clips with parts ornamented with enamel.

After inspection of these articles the Goldsmiths' Company claimed that they were all wares of gold and silver and gold and silver plate within the meaning of, and subject to the provisions of, the Customs Act, 1842 (5 and 6 Vict.C. 47), and other statutory provisions relating to or governing the assaying, stamping and marking of gold and silver plate imported into the United Kingdom from foreign parts, and that the articles were liable to be hall-marked before they could legally be sold in the United Kingdom. As the Goldsmiths' Company maintained that these articles could not be hall-marked without damaging them, this in effect meant that they would have to be returned to the country of origin or broken up.*

Fabergé was thus confronted with a very harassing situation. Only a few months before he had undertaken a special journey from St. Petersburg to London for the purpose of examining the premises which had been taken on the first floor at 48 Dover Street, Piccadilly. These, as I have said before, were his gesture to the then Queen Consort of England. For Fabergé everything centred round her, she was his great Patron of the West, therefore everything must be made easy for her to see his latest productions. But here was the authority in whom was vested the duty of protecting the public from 'frauds and abuses' in the sale of gold and silver wares under powers which had accumulated under statutes of Edward I, Henry VI, Elizabeth, William III, Anne, George II, George III, Queen Victoria, and Edward VII, making it as difficult as possible. That was the plain English of the situation so far as it concerned Fabergé.

The Goldsmiths' Company, of course, had no knowledge of all this. As an impersonal unprejudiced body its concern was the 'good and safety of the public'. As for the Craftsman he was quite unaware that he was in any way endangering this by his activities. There was no public exposure of his wares on the street, no invitation to come upstairs to buy; the name on either side of the entrance, simply 'FABERGÉ' in small letters, meant nothing at all to the passer-by. Often as I stood at that door watching King George V, then Prince of Wales, merging

* There was no question of Customs Duty, this further difficulty to the importation of such articles had not then been re-imposed.

into the crowd in Piccadilly, I wondered what would happen if H.R.H. stopped someone and said: 'I have just been to Fabergé's!' Would they have thought he was wandering in his mind? Queen Alexandra was quite unaware of what was going on and was, of course, quite outside the controversy.

Well, what was Fabergé to do? As a man to whom all legal contention was anathema, I feel sure he would have shut up shop had he not already been heavily involved in giving pleasure to the Queen and finding much satisfaction to himself in so doing.

So by counsel's advice the statutes were ransacked, with the result that it appeared just possible that amidst all the verbiage and the exceptions contained in the statutes, there might be a way out. It all depended on the interpretation of an Act then one hundred and seventy years old, 12 Geo. II, C.26, 1738.

So it was that Fabergé brought his test case against the Goldsmiths' Company and the same was tried on Nov. 7th, 8th and 9th, 1910. He pleaded:

(1) 'That the gold or silver in each article constituted a small part thereof, either in bulk or value; that the main ingredient therein was the enamel or precious stones, or both, the gold or silver being merely used as foundation or setting; that the design and workmanship of the enamel and the precious stones and the setting thereof gave each article its distinctive character and value; and that none of the articles were gold or silver plate.'

Alternatively he pleaded that if the articles or any one of them were gold or silver plate within the meaning of the statute, then:

(2) 'The enamel used in the enamelled articles was within the meaning of the expression "jewels or other stones" used in sections 2 and 6 of the Plate Offences Act, 1738 (12 Geo. II, C.26).'

(3) 'All the objects were "jewellers' works" within the meaning of section 2 of the same Act, and accordingly exempt from the statutory requirements as to assaying, stamping and marking.'

(4) 'The enamelled gold cigarette-case was exempt from the statutory requirements by virtue of section 6 of the Act of 1738 as being a manufacture of gold "so richly engraved, carved or chased, or set with jewels or other stones, as not to admit of an assay to be taken of, or a mark to be struck thereon, without damaging, prejudicing, or defacing the same".'

Such were the Fabergé pleadings. I have purposely not included two watch-bracelets in the packet because they were of little concern.

PLEADING No. 1. In his judgment the learned judge, Mr. Justice Parker, among other things, said this: 'The base or foundation of silver or gold on which the artist commences to enamel a picture or design may not be, in any true sense of the word, a manufacture of gold or silver, and, if this be so, it could not very well become a manufacture of gold or silver merely because it was used as the base or foundation of artistic work in enamel. But it seems to me a fallacy to argue from this that an undoubted manufacture of gold or silver, such as a match-box, cigarette case, or letter-clip, ceases to be such because it is used as the base or foundation of enamel work. . . .'

'In my opinion, therefore, no article which is once a manufacture of gold or silver within the statute, can cease to be such because it is used as the base or foundation of enamel work, however great may be the artistic merit of such enamel work compared with the value of the metal employed.'

PLEADING Nos. 2 and 3. Among other things the learned judge said this: 'It is suggested that enamels are jewels, but even assuming this, it is, in my opinion, impossible to hold that the gold or silver foundations on which enamels are worked is gold or silver in which they are "set" within the meaning of the statute.'

PLEADING No. 4. Section 6 of the Act of Geo. II, which prompted this pleading, is interesting as containing many curiosities; for instance, it exempts from hall-marking, among a number of smaller objects, gold chains, gold sliding pencils, gold pencil cases, wrought seals of gold or seals with cornelian or other stones, gold pipe lighters, gold thimbles, gold rims of snuff-boxes whereof tops or bottoms are made of shell or stone, gold mounts, screws or stoppers to stone or glass bottles or phials, as to which there is no limit stated to weight of precious metal.

These exemptions covered many objects which Fabergé made and no question was raised during the proceedings that all of them were exempt from hall-marking.

But the last exemption was the most important of all namely any manufacture of gold 'so richly engraved, carved or chased or set with jewels or other stones as not to admit of an assay being taken of, or a mark to be struck thereon, without damaging, prejudicing, or defacing the same'. Here was something with great hope in it. If this could be upheld in regard to the enamelled gold cigarette case in question then a very large number of Fabergé productions would be admissible without assaying or stamping.

Would the judge be hard and fast, taking the exemption as stated word for word? Or would he say: 'Here is an outlook sane and far-seeing, which acknowledges that at the time there were finished objects and still more likely in the future to be finished objects of all kinds, impossible in 1738 to define particularly, to which obstacles of admission into England must never be placed if her people were to rise above the self-sufficiency of her own particular productions. We have advanced over 170 years since this exemption was drawn up. The wording carries with it an implication that at the time there was an intention to make a sweeping exception in favour of objects which were so worked and adorned, however effected, and that to stamp them would damage them.'

Apart altogether from the way of thinking of those advising Fabergé and whatever may have been the loopholes they had in mind by which Fabergé might escape, that was my way of thinking. I had not to wait very long to be completely disillusioned and to know that no English Court of Law is concerned with 'intention' unless there is ambiguity, and there was no ambiguity whatever in the wording of the clause under review. It said 'richly engraved, carved or chased, or set with jewels or other stones', that and nothing more, nothing less. If the word 'enamelled' had appeared, what a difference!

So it was the learned judge gave this ruling: 'I do not think the enamelled gold cigarette case in question can be properly described as engraved, carved or chased at all; nor (if an enamel can be called a jewel) can it be properly described as a gold cigarette case richly set with jewels.'

This brought the action to an end, the judge concluding, 'I have come to the conclusion, therefore, that all the enamelled articles in question are within the provisions of the Customs Act, 1842, section 10 of the Revenue Act, 1883, and the Hall-marking of Foreign Plate Act, 1904, and ought to be assayed, and, if up to standard, marked by the Goldsmiths' Company before they are admitted into this country.'*

Before giving this final judgment the judge referred to a practice followed by the Goldsmiths' Company for over 150 years of assaying and hall-marking articles in the rough and to the habit of the enamellers of the United Kingdom of submitting their objects to the Goldsmiths' Hall for assaying and hall-marking before enamelling and thus avoiding any risk attendant on marking after the enamel work had been completed. 'There seems no reason', he said, 'why importers of gold and silver articles should not proceed in the same way. They are in this respect in no worse position than the manufacturers in the United Kingdom, *except, possibly, that the cost of sending their articles in the rough to the Goldsmiths' Company may be slightly greater.*'

The italics are mine. What the learned judge forgot was the great loss of time and the added irritation to a craft which already had irritations enough. No goldsmith needs to be reminded that in every respect there is a very substantial difference between taking an article just round the corner and sending it some thousands of miles, three times the distance between St. Petersburg and London. Nevertheless as soon as the action was over this is what Fabergé did, and he continued to send articles in the rough to London until it was not possible to carry on owing to the First Great War. A most encouraging example of the height to which individual private enterprise can rise even under the most harassing bureaucratic conditions. It is for this reason that to-day many Fabergé objects are seen with the hall-marks of England as well as those of Russia. I have already given an example of such marking.

Not for a moment must it be imagined that it was to prove an easy matter for Fabergé to comply with the English regulations as established by the test case. The sending in the rough for assaying and hall-marking, although causing tribulation no end by way of delay, expense and irritation, was to be the least of the difficulties encountered. It was the technical difficulties which were to prove the stumbling block. And not as regards enamelling on gold, it was the enamelling on silver of the required fineness to meet the English standard which was to cause the trouble.

Up to the time of the action Fabergé used silver bases of 84 and 88, mostly 88. As we already know, silver of this fineness is below the English standard, therefore it became necessary for Fabergé to experiment with silver of the next Russian fineness, namely 91, which was above the English standard. And this for

---

* See *The Law and Practice of Hall-Marking Gold and Silver Wares*, by J. Paul de Castro.

the reason that it was felt at the time not to be an all-round practicable proposition to make Fabergé objects, in a general way, for the English market alone.

Turning up the correspondence with St. Petersburg after the action, I am reminded that the difficulties became so great it was impossible entirely to surmount them, especially in the case of objects requiring a large surface of enamel like cigarette cases, and upon which the fame of Fabergé largely rested. In the end Fabergé had to abandon the idea of enamelling on silver 91 except for those objects destined specially for England, and these never attained the full excellence of those enamelled on a base of 88.

Thus it came about that owing to a fixed determination to stick firmly to her Sovereign Rights, England for the future had to be satisfied with the second best so far as concerned those objects enamelled on a foundation of silver.

Now it must not be concluded from what has been said that the Worshipful Company of Goldsmiths is the black sheep of Europe in regard to the stringency of its regulations for hall-marking gold and silver plate. All countries are strict and Russia no less than the others; at least this was so before the Revolution. What it is now I do not know. France was the most enlightened, at any rate in my experience. Time and again, forty years ago I submitted the most highly finished enamelled objects to the assay office in Paris and with infinite care it managed to assay them and stamp them without damaging them in any way. Quite a number of such Fabergé objects will be found with the three hall-marks of Russia, England and France, and that of France the merest, gentlest touch. I am speaking without the book but I never remember it being even suggested by the Paris office that articles should be submitted in the rough.

And so we come to the end of the record of Fabergé. Looking back over forty years of the most intimate personal experience of him and his wares I ask myself what, out of his total performance, was his greatest achievement? Was it his decision with his brother Agathon to switch over from the making of jewellery to that of objects of fantasy and thereby bring out the fact that however wonderful are the works of nature it is man's business to turn them to effect, not to worship them just for what they are? Was it the making of the Imperial Easter Eggs whereby he brought his total art and craft to bear on the alleviation of the ever-constant anxieties of the Empress Marie Feodorovna? Was it the joy he brought to Queen Alexandra on her birthday mornings? Was it the delight he brought to many, many hundreds of cultured people all over the world which prompted them to make his wares the vehicle whereby good will was spread world-wide, regardless of race and creed? Was it the materialisation of the spirit of Russia in all his works of gold, silver, enamel and rare stones, an achievement which places him in the great tradition and of the band of supreme artists, whom Russia captured never to let go, and whom she so worked upon with her magic that everything they touched turned to solid gold or in another word, 'substance'? Was it the intensely humanitarian way of working which brought such satisfaction to himself and to all those working for him? Was it the resuscitation of the art of enamelling on large surfaces of gold and silver, *en plein* as they say?

To each one of these in turn I have given first place as I have dealt with it, so all-important has each one appeared at the time, and now I have just come out of the clash between Fabergé and the Goldsmiths' Company which for the time being over-shadows all. I cannot help saying to myself, 'Here is the really big thing, a foolish thing may be, but then what really great thing is not foolish!'

Why was Fabergé, once his mind was made up, so determined to persist in his action? Was he out to sweep away all obstacles, smash all competition and open up business on a scale which was to stagger the English goldsmiths? Or did he see in the action of the Goldsmiths' Company a type of silliness which was widespread over Europe, and as the silliness had come his way that it was not only his business but his bounden duty to combat it without more to say or more ado?

You, reader, now know as much as I do. I have given you the facts. Fabergé was not the type of man to try to stagger anyone, let alone by the impossible method of making the kind of objects of fantasy for which he was so famed. The high-road to financial fortune is not by way of such things, not even with the assistance of all the cultured people in the world. It is a sheer impossibility to make objects enough. As for competition, it made no difference where you looked, whether in Russia, Germany, France, the United States of America, Italy or England, it was all the same, he had none; and to-day, thirty-seven years after the action was fought, the only competition his objects ever meet with is in the auction rooms, where would-be purchasers wrangle to possess them.

Never was nick-name more justified: 'The Last of the Great Craftsmen'. And well said, Leopold Davis!

No, reader, in this matter you cannot read Fabergé aright by labelling him with the ambitions of ordinary men, you must give him the altitude which his altruistic idiosyncracies demand, and you must be prepared to climb up to his height and take a look with him.

Will you see the nations of Europe as purists, completely carried away with the idea of the sacredness of the precious metals, and each one determined to keep gold and silver free from contamination at all costs? Or will you see in all the charters, rules and regulations in regard to the hall-marking of gold and silver plate nothing more than the protection of home industry?

And at once it must be said that to answer these questions separately would only be misleading, they must be taken together. Chaffers, on page xxv of his introduction to *Hall-Marks on Gold and Silver Plate* (tenth edition), referring to the first charter granted to the Goldsmiths' Company in 1327, says this: 'This charter especially provided for protection of the home industry' and, quoting the charter, he proceeds to say why it had been necessary to make this provision, because 'private merchants and strangers from foreign lands counterfeited sterling, kept shops in obscure streets, made jewellery in which they set glass of divers colours, covered tin with silver so subtilely and with such sleight that the same could not be separated, and otherwise misbehaved themselves.'

When you come to the Charter of 1462 you find much the same reasons for the granting of it, 'for the preventing and taking away the subtilties and deceits practised in the said trade.'

Again the Charter of 1504 says the same thing, 'that divers persons in divers parts of this Kingdom do work and expose to sale gold and silver wrought worse than standard, and neither fear nor doubt to be punished.'

Again the great statute of 1738, 12 George II, c.26, headed 'An Act for the better preventing frauds and abuses in gold and silver wares', and adding further to the powers of the Goldsmiths' Company, hammers away at the 'deceits' and 'subtilities', ' . . . great frauds', it says 'are daily committed in the manufacturing of gold and silver wares. . . .'

Then in 1842 came the Customs Act, in 1883 the Revenue Act, and in 1904 the Hall-marking of Foreign Plate Act, all with their provisions as to the marking of gold and silver plate imported from abroad.

At long last, after the law of the land had done its utmost to prevent all the frauds and abuses (and it must be said that the home manufacturers were equally responsible with those of foreign lands, if not more so, for all the abuses), a buyer was able to enter a shop with the assurance that when he asked for gold and silver objects he would get those of standard quality.

So far so good. But you can have too much of a good thing. The rules and regulations as to hall-marking in England can be complied with by the English makers of gold and silver objects with very much greater ease than by the foreign maker. This I can vouch for from intimate personal experience. In fact it would appear that the English makers of to-day far from finding the regulations irksome actually welcome them, for you have only to walk into a shop to find things hall-marked which the law specifically exempts. And the reason is not far to seek. It is good for business.

Now it stands to reason if you put difficulties in the way of importers bringing their goods to this country you will find less of them for sale than if there were a freer entry. It also stands to reason that the fewer foreign goods there are for sale the better it is for the English maker. The buyer, willy-nilly, has to content himself very largely with wares of English make even when he would have preferred something from abroad. And this is not to say that this fair land of ours is not pre-eminent in many arts, she is, but by no means is she the home of all of them.

And that brings us back to Chaffers, and it must be agreed that what he says is true: 'This Charter especially provided for protection of the home industry. . . .' And every other statute since, while searching to keep gold and silver wares free from contamination, and quite rightly, has in the ultimate strengthened that protection. And, believe me, reader, this is the answer universally applicable to all countries.

Now no reasonable person can see any possible objection to any nation in its infancy protecting its citizens in their early efforts, just as a mother protects her child. But for any nation century after century, to tie its citizens to the apron-strings of age-old statutes and regulations, is not only to stultify their growth but to give them a totally false opinion of the importance of their own achievements.

Yet this is just what all the European nations have done in making as difficult as possible the entry within their bounds of the fine workmanship in gold and silver of other nations. And far worse. So enamoured of the idea have they become, they now exercise their hall-marking rules and regulations under the title of 'sovereign rights'.

And it is at this point that I finally commend Carl Gustavovitch Fabergé as a man of courage. I need not remind you, reader, that for any man to assail the sovereign rights of nations is akin to bashing his head against walls of granite; it is a futile, fatuous undertaking, laying him open to the ridicule of his fellows, and there were many titters in court on those three days in November 1910. It needed much courage on the part of the Craftsman to proceed as the cables arrived day by day in St. Petersburg reporting the citation of the statutes and clauses, which relentlessly, like machine-guns, continued to mow down the innocents of harmony and understanding in the shape of his wares in gold and silver, enamel and rare stones.

At times, so devastating was the blast, I hourly awaited instructions to haul down the flag, but those instructions never came.

Now although Fabergé had gone into action in the first instance to serve a most sympathetic Queen and one to whom he was for ever indebted, there is no doubt that as the preparations for the fight developed something else took shape within his mind. Every terse comment, every sarcastic aside, and he was never known to explain himself except in this way, led to only one belief, that for him the battle had become a crusade and that he was determined to see it through to its sweet or bitter end. The attitude of his mind can be expressed like this. If I had said to him 'Art has no frontiers, Carl Gustavovitch', he most certainly would have replied 'Hasn't it. You try!'

Since those harassing days one has seen the world rocked by two great convulsions such as have never been witnessed by mortal man before, enough one would think to open wide all eyes and bring about such changes that the world might be thought to be reasonably on the way to Paradise. But there is no justification whatever for such thinking. It is saner by far to see in all that has happened that Man has once again made the Great Refusal. And saner still to say not 'Man' but those who have been placed in authority over him. Regardless of race and creed the widespread blindness is terrifying.

One would have thought after such a display of wrath that authorities everywhere would be tumbling over themselves to set their houses in order. They are busy enough, heaven knows, but it is the direction of their activities which fills one with such foreboding. Their actions are all of them centrifugal, they fly outwards at bewildering speed to build an astonishing new world, and the scientists are among the worst offenders however they may excuse themselves. They load us with new inventions in the possession of which even the archangels themselves might fall. Is there any one of them whose actions can be called centripetal, those which continually seek the centre, which alone is able to hold in check all the high, fast-flying schemes? Is there any one of them which sees the crying need for first of all removing all the accumulated lumber of the past?

'Great issues', says Mr. W. J. Brown, M.P., 'are illustrated by little things. The test of a whole philosophy may lie in the experience of one man'. I therefore take the liberty to draw on personal experience again and well within the limits allowable in this record of Fabergé.

I can still, in this year of grace 1947, order an 'Albert' watch-chain up to any weight in gold I like, and the goldsmith supported by statute 12 Geo. II, C.26, 1738, can sell it to me without any hall-marks upon it whatever, but if I ask him to make me a match-box in gold or silver, or enamelled on these bases, and small enough to put into my waistcoat pocket, then the same age-old statute proclaims that it is a manufacture of gold or silver and must be hall-marked at Goldsmiths' Hall before he can sell it to me. The foreign goldsmith equally enjoys the inconsistencies of the law when introducing his wares to this country.

Now I am not concerned with the anomaly of these two cases; in fact, I would have gold watch-chains brought under the same regulations as to hall-marking as match-boxes. I like hall-marks; they are interesting, fascinating, very necessary things, and no one, I hope, would ever dream of doing away with them. What does concern me, however, is the foreigner who wishes to have his wares of gold and silver admitted to this country.

I ask, therefore, is there any valid reason why the English authorities should not acknowledge the hall-marks of other countries, provided the standards which the foreign marks represent are up to those required by English Law? In asking this I address myself in the same way to the authorities abroad.

In not having made this mutual acknowledgment long ago one asks 'are the nations suspicious of each other even in this very simple matter?' Is each one of them so impressed with the accuracy of its own methods of assaying and stamping that it is blind to the same accuracy in others? One could understand their diffidence to march forward boldly if the assaying of gold and silver were intricate processes demanding a skill possessed only by the most accomplished assayers and chemists. In point of fact the operations are of the simplest character and soon learned by the laboratory boy who washes the retorts, test tubes and dishes.

The fact that there is quite a number of Fabergé objects bearing the hall-marks of England, Russia and France, and representing the same standards of purity, is evidence enough that there is a firm basis already in existence for establishing mutual respect among the nations for each other's methods.

Of course, differences would be bound to occur from time to time and these not always concerned with methods of assaying. There would be times when it would be necessary for each nation to decide how far it should be adamant in the application of its own special point of view without appearing childish to other nations.

Looking back over forty years I call to mind only one serious difference of this kind with the Goldsmiths' Hall (excepting, of course, on the question of hall-marking in general of enamelled objects) and that concerned the silver ikon of Madonna and Child (illustrated in Plate 71). When this was examined at the Goldsmiths' Hall on January 21st, 1908, it was laid down by the then Deputy Warden, Mr. Robinson, that it should be taken to pieces in order that each part of it might be assayed separately.

The ikon itself, in all its parts, passed this examination as being of silver up to English standard, but the 300 small nuts which from behind held each part of the ikon proper in position were found to be of silver not fully up to English standard. By the strict letter of English law as interpreted by the Goldsmiths' Hall this was sufficient to condemn the whole of the ikon and call for its return to the country of origin. By the goodwill of the Deputy Warden I was allowed to replace the offending nuts by those of English standard quality made in England. When I enquired of Fabergé the reason for using nuts of lower quality I was told 'for the sake of hardness so that they might the more efficiently do their work'.

This is to recite something which took place forty years ago. With those forty years has come tolerance, that quality which time alone hammers into us as we age. Thus it is brought home to me, as I close this record, that the Worshipful Company of Goldsmiths[1] is bound by age-old statutes regulating its conduct and that however conscious it may be of the necessity for changes it can only act within the limit of its charters. It is on Parliament alone that the ultimate responsibility lies.

As I write these words I come to a standstill as I have come many times before in this record. It is then my Guardian Angel appears (Rudyard Kipling calls his, 'Daemon'). 'Stay a moment,' he says. 'I know what you want.'

And then it is by the merest chance that I meet the Prime Warden of the Worshipful Company of Goldsmiths and I am made aware of the fact that, far from resting content, this Worshipful Company is ever on the probe to make itself, more and more, a living influence. It is gratifying to me, therefore, to be given this opportunity to acknowledge the work that the Worshipful Company of Goldsmiths is doing at the present time to preserve a great craft, by giving all possible recognition to living craftsmen as well as to those who, like Fabergé, were leaders in their own generation.

With that I come back to Fabergé and final conclusion. 'Great issues are illustrated by little things.' It is a significant saying and I cannot do better than return to it. Indeed, every step we take, every bite we eat, is our contribution to the final outcome, the last consequence of universal happiness or misery, universal good or evil, of peace or war. There is, as ever, the eternal lesson still to be learned.

It fell to the lot of Peter Carl Fabergé to make a great contribution to the happiness of mankind and he accomplished this through the medium of craftsmanship; he showed what it is possible to do with the brain, the heart and the hands working in unison.

To-day that unison is lost. The brain is there, far too much of it. The heart is there, but not enough. Both of them, caught up in a confusion of many voices, are of no avail, are helpless, for they have no outlet. The world has lost the use of its hands.

[1] It is to be noted that the correct title is 'The Worshipful Company of Goldsmiths' and not 'The Worshipful Goldsmiths' Company'.

POSTSCRIPT

ON June 14th, 1949, the Worshipful Company of Goldsmiths called a meeting at Goldsmiths' Hall, graced by the presence of Her Majesty Queen Mary, to discuss the question 'How far will the traditional craft (of the enameller) be applicable to present-day conditions?'

It is a significant question, and no one man has all the answers. Of all the arts and crafts that of enamelling on bases of gold and silver is perhaps the most trying yet fruitful of results. Not only is the craftsman a scientist ever searching for new knowledge with unremitting care, but a saint of good heart at all times subjecting himself to discipline.

Such being the man (and, of course, the woman), it is the bounden duty of all those who can contribute anything to his well-being to do so.

Never would the writer presume to teach the present-day enameller his job, but having been privileged to take part in the discussion, and having been associated with one who did a great deal to resuscitate the art of enamelling at the end of the Nineteenth Century, he feels that a word or two from him will not be out of place. From these the craftsman and others (and it is to be noted that if the enameller is to find an outlet for his work he must have substantial encouragement to that end) may be able to pick out something to the advantage of all concerned.

That is the writer's apology for this postscript. In the first place he takes this opportunity to say that this record of Fabergé was not written solely to extol the work of a great Craftsman and his 700 assistants, the writer had in mind goldsmithery in general (with which the art of enamelling is bound up) and the purpose for which this craft exists. Working as it does quite outside the black side of life, the ills, suspicions, sorrows and dark depths of human nature, its purpose has always been and is, to keep happiness and goodwill alive.

And there is hope. It is quite a fallacy to think of the glorious past as a time of easy-going. The great patrons of the end of the Nineteenth Century and the beginning of the Twentieth were by no means easy buyers. They were easy in their trust when they found the right *fournisseur*, but discriminating to a degree in what they bought, and demanded craftsmanship of the highest order.

In his Foreword to this record of Fabergé, Mr. Sacheverell Sitwell says this: ' . . . it seems improbable that the world will see another great goldsmith', and the writer himself has said much the same thing on page 140: ' . . . they (Fabergé objects) can never be made again. . . .' As the House of Fabergé was constituted this no doubt is true. (And in parenthesis it must be noted that in this House the enameller *enamelled*; that was his sole occupation. He made no designs and he had nothing to do with the making of the object preparatory to enamelling; he neither chiselled gold borders nor engraved parts to be so adorned.)

Since the Goldsmiths' Hall meeting the writer is inclined to be more optimistic.

The craftsmen have a permanent patron in the Worshipful Company of Goldsmiths, who will not cease to be interested in their welfare. From the exhibits shown at that meeting it is evident that the craft is very much alive.

The enameller has always worked in a great tradition and whatever the changed circumstances and conditions he has always adapted himself to them. Granted, he has always been fortunate in his patrons and few of us are reliable prophets. But who can say that great patrons will not rise up; who can say that important firms of goldsmiths and jewellers will not see their way to bring the enameller more into their scheme of things by taking advantage of workshops already in existence; who can say that these workshops themselves will not work out their own salvation and, lastly, who can say that the Church, and why not the Ecclesiastical Commissioners, will not be inspired to make the Cathedrals and Churches of our towns and countryside the shrines of fine deeds and good lives lived, commemorated in pieces not only of brass and bronze but of exquisite enamel work on gold?

But amidst all the discord in which we are entangled, there is one theme upon which the goldsmith, enameller and jeweller can play *ad infinitum* and to his heart's delight and pocket's profit. We have so little left it is just as well to prize that which we possess. And no authority, at any rate in this country, can deprive us of our finest possession, our womankind.

It is a time for warmth and colour if ever there was one. So let us adorn our women. The range is without limit. Cloak-clasps (these, even in quite inexpensive materials like translucent chalcedony, enamel and small precious stones, can be extraordinarily rich), hat pins, brooches and pendants, flower brooches, buckles, vanity cases, chains, cigarette cases, bracelets and accessories of all kinds. Let the craftsman put all he knows into supplying this demand, for demand it is. 'Purchase Tax' need not deter him, for it is reasonably certain that objects in which the value of the workmanship exceeds that of the materials employed, will be exempt or at any rate subject to encouraging dispensation.

If the writer may be allowed to say a word or two more to those who took part in the discussion at Goldsmiths' Hall he would refer them to pages 48, 49, 56-58, 81, 127, 128, 150 and 151 of this record.

INDEX